EL LECTOR

MW00624733

LLILAS Translations from Latin America Series

EL LECTOR

A History of the Cigar Factory Reader

NO. 211 READER IN TOBACCO FACTORY

ARACELI TINAJERO

Translated by Judith E. Grasberg

UNIVERSITY OF TEXAS PRESS

TERESA LOZANO LONG INSTITUTE OF LATIN AMERICAN STUDIES

The author gratefully acknowledges the contribution of Patti Firth in providing the translations of José Martí and the poetry that appears in the book.

Originally published in 2007 as *El lector de tabaquería: Historia de una tradición Cubana*. Madrid: Editorial Verbum. Copyright © 2007 by Araceli Tinajero.

FRONTISPIECE: A hired reader reads to cigar makers hard at work in a Cuban cigar factory ca. 1900–1910. Copyright © Hulton-Deutsch Collection/ CORBIS.

TRANSLATION COPYRIGHT © 2010 BY THE UNIVERSITY OF TEXAS PRESS
All rights reserved
Printed in the United States of America
First University of Texas Press edition, 2010

Requests for permission to reproduce material from this work should be sent to:
Permissions
University of Texas Press
P.O. Box 7819
Austin, TX 78713-7819

www.utexas.edu/utpress/about/bpermission.html

♾ The paper used in this book meets the minimum requirements of ANSI/NISO Z39.48-1992 (R1997) (Permanence of Paper).

LIBRARY OF CONGRESS CATALOGING-IN-PUBLICATION DATA

Tinajero, Araceli, 1962–
  [Lector de tabaquería. English]
  El lector : a history of the cigar factory reader / by Araceli Tinajero ; translated by Judith E. Grasberg. — 1st ed.
    p. cm.
  Includes bibliographical references and index.
  ISBN 978-0-292-72576-8
  1. Oral reading.   2. Tobacco industry—Cuba—History.   3. Tobacco workers—Cuba—History.   4. Tobacco industry—Puerto Rico—History.   5. Tobacco workers—Puerto Rico—History.   6. Tobacco industry—United States—History.   7. Tobacco workers—United States—History.   I. Title.
    HD9144.C9T5613 2009
    306.4'88—dc22   2009045169

To Josefina Tinajero y López (1927–2009),

for her endless affection and compassion,

and who read aloud to me from the time I was born

CONTENTS

Photos follow page 154.

ACKNOWLEDGMENTS

I would like to express my gratitude to the *lectores* and *lectoras,* as well as to all those who granted me interviews, without which this book would have been incomplete. I also thank the cigar workers of Cuba, Mexico, and the Dominican Republic for their warm hospitality in cigar facilities during their long hours of hard work.

My meetings with historians Roger Chartier, Gilbert M. Joseph, and Gary R. Mormino, although brief, were extremely fruitful. Their sage advice lit my way when I was working on the Spanish edition.

I thank the librarians of the Biblioteca Nacional José Martí, the New York Public Library, and the University of South Florida Special Collections for their patience and professionalism. Jeffry Larson and especially César Rodríguez of the Sterling Memorial Library at Yale University assisted me in finding material of inestimable value. I will always be grateful to them for that, and for everything.

I am most fortunate to have friends with whom I maintain an ever-enriching intellectual dialogue. I sincerely thank Gerard Aching, Rolena Adorno, Sybil Alexandrov, Miguel Barnet, Mauricio A. Font, K. David Jackson, Martín Lienhard, William Luis, Aníbal González Pérez, Carlos Alberto González Sánchez, Floyd Merrell, Julio Ortega, Gustavo Pérez Firmat, Antonio José Ponte, Alfonso W. Quiroz, Julio Ramos, Rafael Rojas, Daniel Shapiro, Pío E. Serrano, Elzbieta Sklodowska, Noël Valis, and James Wojtaszek for their invaluable friendship and support. Most of all I thank Roberto González Echevarría for having explained to me in autumn 2000 what a cigar factory *lector* was.

Many thanks to Célida Álvarez, Julio Domínguez García, Araceli García Carranza, and Antonieta Fernández in Cuba for their ever-courteous attention in answering my queries about Cuban history and culture. For that, I will always be grateful.

I was enthusiastically received in Mexico by Álvaro Enrigue, Elsa Cross, Jesús D. Medina García, Marisol Schultz Manaut, and Jorge Ruedas de la Serna. Many thanks to them for their generosity and for having read the Spanish version of this book.

My colleagues and students at the City College of New York and the Graduate Center (City University of New York) encouraged me to complete the Spanish version and then to have it translated into English. I am especially grateful to Richard F. Calichman, Raquel Chang-Rodríguez, and Juan Carlos Mercado, who, as chair of my department, was very supportive. I also thank Geraldine Murphy, deputy dean of Humanities, for her judicious guidance. Many thanks as well to Isaías Lerner and Lía Schwartz of the Graduate Center for their confidence in my work.

I can always count on my loyal friends Maria Carlino, Sharon M. Eaton, Helene Hoedl, Lucy Levchuk, and Marcia Picallo. Words cannot express my gratitude for their devoted friendship.

The support of my relatives in the United States, Mexico, and Great Britain has given me the strength and courage to write what my intuition led me to write. Hugs and kisses to everyone in my family.

My most sincere thanks go out to Theresa May, assistant director and editor-in-chief of the University of Texas Press, and to Virginia Hagerty, managing editor of the Teresa Lozano Long Institute of Latin American Studies of the University of Texas at Austin, for their faith in my book. I thank copy editor Kathy Bork for her wonderfully precise contribution.

So many people offered me advice and information that I opted to thank them individually throughout the book, although, of course, that choice may not have prevented me from inadvertently having omitted someone.

PROLOGUE TO THE ENGLISH EDITION

―――――|━━━|―――――

Any scholar who has conducted research on Cuba knows how difficult it is to travel to the island and what a great challenge it is to do fieldwork once there, given the difficult economic and political conditions present in the country. Policies of both the U.S. and Cuban governments limit access to such basic means of communication as the telephone, the mail, and the electronic media. Under such circumstances, it was a major accomplishment to be able to write a book that deals in part with present-day Cuban culture.

This book belongs to the corpus of studies about the history of universal reading. I do not mention books banned by the Cuban government, since this study deals with actual public readings in state-controlled cigar factories; I have assumed that such books are never read to the workers. They should be part of a broader study about censorship, a topic that is beyond the scope of my book.

In June 2007, two months after the book was published in Spanish, I presented some of my findings in a number of places in Cuba, among them Casa de las Américas. I took the opportunity then to attend the Fifth International Conference on Culture and Development, where I delivered a talk about libraries and reading aloud in cigar factories. The audience was made up of librarians from all over the world—including many from the United States—and UNESCO's reading advocates. I noted that I felt it was necessary to study reading aloud in prisons and hospitals as it is practiced today. The idea was received very enthusiastically.

The Spanish-language version of the book has already served as an inspiration for some. In the Dominican Republic, for instance, a school for underprivileged children has opened in which reading aloud is practiced, and in Brazil and Nicaragua, consideration is being given to implementing reading aloud in some cigar factories. In Guadalajara, Mexico, cultural promoters began conducting seminars on reading aloud intended for both specialists and the general public, and in Cuba, this book is already part of the curriculum for cigar factory *lectores*. After a lecture I gave at Barnard College, a student decided to go to Bolivia to implement reading in some handicraft workshops in that country. When I began, I never imagined that this study would have such far-reaching implications.

Peaceful Lake Guadalupe is situated on the northern outskirts of Mexico City. The lake is an idyllic place for residents of the capital. Beautiful trees surround it and take people away from the noise of the city. My father lived for a time in a nursing home on the shores of the lake. On one of my visits to see him, I took him a copy of *El lector de tabaquería* in the hopes that one day he might read it. My father suffered from severe depression caused by the medications he took for a heart condition. He spent hours every day lying in bed or sitting in a chair, staring off into space, having neither the strength nor the will to do anything.

One day when I called him, he said that his doctor wanted to speak with me. My heart started pounding. The doctor told me that he had started reading my book to my father. "I've always read to my patients, because to them, time seems to pass very slowly," he added. To me, that was nothing short of a true revelation. Two months later, on October 23, 2007, my father died.

My book was the last one read to him.

ARACELI TINAJERO
New York, October 2008

INTRODUCTION

In Cuba, in the town of San Juan y Martínez in 2003, I had the good fortune of meeting Santos Segundo Domínguez Mena, an eighty-eight-year-old man. It was in this town that he shared with me his life's story. For sixty-five years, Mr. Domínguez Mena was a cigar factory *lector* (reader). In other words, his job was to read newspapers and works of literature aloud to cigar makers while they worked. His memory, withered by age, still brought back vague snippets of his past:

> I remember that as a child, in the early 1920s, my mother was a vendor at the doorway of La Caridad [Leaf-stripping Plant]. I had to be there to help her sell ice cream. And the first *lector* I ever heard from our spot outside the factory used to go there. And I liked it way back then; I really liked reading. Ever since elementary school, whenever parties were planned and something had to be read aloud, it was given to me. I soon grew accustomed to this. I had a better reading voice than other children. The others spoke too softly. I was the one who was chosen for parties. Besides that, I did recitations. When I became a cigar factory *lector* for the first time, it was because I already liked it.[1]

I asked him about the books he had read aloud, and he told me he could not recall their titles, which was no surprise, since his memory was already failing him. Then he said suddenly: "I liked a few universally renowned novels. After all, *Les Misérables* was a novel that I enjoyed along with everyone else. It was the best book I ever read. Everybody still likes that work. It's a masterpiece. I read all the novels by Victor Hugo and Alexandre Dumas that I could get my hands on."

Since he had stopped reading to others ten years earlier, I asked whether, when he read, he read aloud or silently. His answer has stayed with me as if it were written in bold red print: "When I have something important to read, I put on my eyeglasses. I read silently while I get my lips unstuck. I have to pay attention to it, just as others paid attention to me."

The sheer size of his cultural universe and his feeling for the written and spoken word were revealed in just a couple of sentences. Learned authors have expressed the same idea for centuries. Francisco de Quevedo, the seventeenth-century Spanish poet, states in the opening two quatrains of his sonnet "From the Tower of Juan Abad":

> Retiring to these deserts now in peace,
> with few but learned volumes to be read,
> I live in conversation with the dead,
> and listen with my eyes to those deceased.
> Though sometimes impenetrable they seem,
> they mend or they enrich all that I own;
> and they, in quiet counterpointed tones
> awake, address this life which is a dream.

And Mexican poet Sor Juana Inés de la Cruz writes:

> Hear me with your eyes,
> since now your ears are far away,
> and of former anger hear,
> in echoes of my pen, my plaint;
> since my rough voice cannot reach you,
> hear me deaf, since I am now mute.[2]

But what moved me most about Santos Segundo Domínguez Mena was that his natural loss of memory had condemned to oblivion the texts that he had read and heard throughout his life. This internal library was now erased for all time; its memory is not preserved anywhere.

I learned for the first time what a cigar factory *lector* was in the autumn of 2000. Curious to learn about the history, I went immediately to the library to research the subject. I started by rereading Fernando Ortiz's monumental *Cuban Counterpoint: Tobacco and Sugar* and painstakingly consulted his sources. I anxiously dusted off volumes and was increasingly surprised at how little had been written about the fascinating work of these *lectores*.

One day, much to my surprise, I learned that these cigar factory *lectores* still existed in Cuba. Without giving it a second thought, I took the first available opportunity to travel to Havana. I had spent so many months in the library stacks wondering about and intrigued by the history of the *lectores* that I truly was not prepared to meet any of them. The opportunity to go meet them in Cuba was too good to be true, and it was impossible for me to recognize its full impact at the time.

As soon as I arrived, I went to the Partagás Cigar Factory in Havana and asked if I could see the *lector*. It was 8:00 A.M., and the *lector* had not yet started to read, so he came out to meet me right away.

"Are you the *lector*?" I asked.

"Yes, I'm the *lector*. How may I help you?" he answered.

I wanted to ask him so many questions, but I began trembling and stuttering. I could not believe that *lectores* still existed, much less that I was standing in front of one of them. It was August 2001, and thus began my research about present-day *lectores*. Those who had already died could wait for me in the library archives. On that trip, I was able to meet and interview almost all the *lectores* in Havana. There are but a handful of factories in the capital, but they are huge.

That same summer I had the opportunity to go to Santa Clara, for I wanted to meet at least one *lector* from the provinces. It was my good fortune to meet one of Cuba's most dynamic *lectores*, Francisco Águila Medina, the *lector* at the LV-9 Factory.

During that trip, I also visited writer and ethnographer Miguel Barnet, who, with traditional Cuban hospitality, welcomed me into his home. I told him about my project and my "discovery": there were still *lectores*! He told me with much enthusiasm that my study sounded not only fascinating but also necessary, for very little had been written on the topic.

At that time, I also had the opportunity to work in the archives of the José Martí National Library under the guidance of renowned Cuban bibliographer Araceli García Carranza. I managed to ferret out a few (though very few) important essays and journalistic articles there.

Over the subsequent two years, I kept in touch with the *lectores* I had met and returned to Cuba in the summer of 2003 to interview others from the interior. I started by interviewing former *lectores* in Santa Clara. From there I went to Manicaragua, where I visited not only the factory that bears the town's name, but also a leaf-stripping plant. I was surprised to learn that reading aloud took place not just in cigar factories, that is, in large factories with a number of different departments, but also in specialized workshops in which the majority of the staff is female and whose job it is to strip the leaves (i.e., to remove the stem or center rib from tobacco leaves before they are rolled or cut).

This experience was completely transformational for me. I had never been inside such a dark workshop, where a hundred women were seated in rows at workbenches resembling classroom desks, all doing the same job. I sat quietly among them, and each minute that passed seemed an eternity. The *lectora* was not reading aloud; it was totally silent. And suddenly I realized that the smell of tobacco was stinging my eyes, skin, and throat. "How grateful these women must be every time someone reads to them," I thought. Then I recalled an article that José Martí had published in 1893 in his newspaper, *Patria*, which alludes to just such a leaf stripper, Carolina Rodríguez. The article states: "People speak ill of the cigar workers because they do not understand the value of the job these workers do, nor are they capable of doing with their own hands any sort of work; nor can these people understand at all the value of a life that is both free and respectable." With his customary brilliance, Martí was aware of oral reading in workshops and the enrichment it afforded the employees and thus adds: "This woman, who defied death for years on end, who is well versed and discerning with regard to the classics of history and literature, who fearlessly speaks her mind in a living language that naturalness and honor tend to endow with literary beauty, earns her daily bread . . . in her leather chair, before her leaf-stripping barrel."[3] There is no doubt that reading aloud—especially in the context of the overwhelming monotony to be found at a leaf-stripping workshop—not only educates, but also enriches the spirit.

I left my experience with the leaf strippers behind me and went to the town of Trinidad, where I interviewed two more *lectoras*. Next I went to Sancti Spíritus. I started at the Pedro Larrea Factory, which is located in the city proper, and from there went to Guayos and Cabaiguán. Since I was again so close to Las Villas, I decided to go to Placetas to interview that city's *lectora*. Afterward, not knowing what to expect up ahead, I headed east. When I reached Camagüey, I was lucky enough to spend a few days at El Surco Cigar Factory, where I spoke with cigar workers and the *lectora*, who had been reading in that same place for no fewer than thirty years.

The Day of the Cigar Worker, May 29, was drawing near; I thought it would be a good idea to go west to the province of Pinar del Río, the most fertile tobacco-producing region in Cuba. I began by visiting the Francisco Donatién Factory and the Niñita Valdés Leaf-stripping Plant. I also traveled to the remote location of El Corojo Tobacco Plantation near San Luis, where I met *lectores* who read without microphones to huge audiences. In Viñales, I was unable to meet the *lectora* at the VD-31 Leaf-stripping Plant, but I interviewed a charismatic former *lectora* who was much beloved in the cigar community. My travels ended with visits to workshops in San Juan y Martínez, source of the best tobacco in the world. Here I met Santos Segundo Domínguez Mena, the elderly gentleman who had spent his whole life reading aloud.

This book covers the history, culture, and literature of cigar factory *lectores* in Cuba, Spain, the United States (including Puerto Rico), Mexico, and the Dominican Republic. It is a story that must be told, because reading aloud to a group is a cultural practice that has gradually been lost over the centuries, and few people have taken on the task of making a record of who did the reading, what was read, and who the audience was. Reading aloud in cigar factories is a unique institution that traces its roots to nineteenth-century Cuba, and from there spread to several other parts of the world.

I knew I would have to do research in Florida, the Dominican Republic, and Mexico as well. Although reading aloud continues only in Cuba and the Dominican Republic, my research about other parts of the world has been quite fruitful, as it has brought into view again a cultural practice that had been relegated to oblivion.

As my background is in the field of literature, I am used to analyzing only written texts. Nevertheless, this research project required me to conduct interviews with real people in order to give structure to this history of the practice of reading aloud. To that end, as is often done in anthropological and ethnographic studies, I developed a questionnaire for use in each interview. In it I asked how the *lector* began to practice the profession, what material was read, who chose said material, which books had been read in the past, which books the *lector* enjoyed reading most, which books the audience liked best, which books had been read more than once, and so on.

In the case of Florida, where the practice of reading aloud was discontinued decades ago, I had to resort to consulting historical texts, mainly newspapers. This was an exhausting exercise, but necessary and worthwhile, for I recovered crucial facts about reading aloud in Spanish in Key West and Tampa. In the Dominican Republic, I conducted interviews and witnessed how reading aloud is still going on in that country. In the case of Mexico, I interviewed cigar workers in the state of Veracruz, who had only heard about the *lectores* of yesteryear. There remain only bits of information and literary texts about reading aloud in Spain and Puerto Rico, which nevertheless have contributed greatly to this study of the history of reading aloud.

The last two decades have seen important studies about the practice of reading aloud in a variety of time periods and contexts.[4] Still, there is a minimal number of projects that focus on the history of reading aloud, precisely because it is difficult and sometimes impossible to discover what was read during a certain time to a group of listeners. Therefore, this study attempts to recapture a cultural practice of critical importance.

I begin Part I with an overview of the tradition of reading aloud and later concentrate on the institution of reading in cigar factories in nineteenth-century Cuba. Afterward, I analyze reading aloud in Spain at the end of the same century. Part II centers on reading aloud in Key West, Tampa, New York, and Puerto Rico from 1868 to 1931. Part III deals with reading aloud in cigar factories in Cuba from 1902 to 2005. Because reading aloud has also played an important role in Mexico and the Dominican Republic, I cover in this section the tradition in those two countries as well.

PART ONE

READING ALOUD
IN CIGAR FACTORIES UNTIL 1900

PREVIOUS PAGE: José Martí—top center—with Tampa cigar workers on the steps of the Martínez Ybor Cigar Factory during a visit to Tampa, early 1890s (*Courtesy of the University of South Florida Libraries Special Collections*)

ONE

Cuba

——┤■-■┤——

THE TRADITION OF READING ALOUD

I would like to begin with the eighth stanza of the poem "To Cuba," which was written in 1924 by a relatively unknown poet, Alberto Castilla y del Busto:

I see the tobacco stretched out in the field
in Vueltabajo, a prodigious crop
the doting farmer irrigates his yield
and gives it to the workers in the shop,
this work was ne'er a sign of foolishness
because to it the humble flock has brought
a pulpit, *atalaya* of learnedness
where reading becomes a noble sermon taught.[1]

As we can see, the poetic voice alludes to the life cycle of tobacco, starting with the leaf sprouting in a field in Vueltabajo, a region in the western portion of the island and especially known for the excellence of its tobacco. We find ourselves in a geography that is verdant, dewy, pulsing, and aromatic, owing to the labors of the grower, who tends the leaf before delivering it to the workshop, the place where cigars are rolled. The allusion to the workshop not only transports us to a nostalgic place where a product is crafted by hand, but also connects us to the past.

Reading aloud in cigar factories occurred for the first time in Havana in 1865, during a period of radical change in the history of the cigar. At that time, a number of workshops began to call themselves factories, due to the increase in the number of workers they employed. Conversely, small workshops in which cigars were both made and sold started to be called *tabaquerías* (cigar shops).

A cigar factory *lector* is a person whose profession is that of reading newspapers, magazines, and works of fiction to the cigar workers while they do their jobs. Ironically, however, the *lectores* first began to read in factories, not in *tabaquerías*. Therefore, the practice of reading aloud was nothing short of a link to the past, to preindustrial times, when reading viva voce was the rule and not the exception.

The first *lectores* were cigar workers who took turns reading aloud every half hour, and their coworkers compensated them for the time lost from their jobs. Reading aloud was initiated by Saturnino Martínez, a man deserving a full-length biography. Saturnino was a cigar worker, *lector*, and editor of *La Aurora: Periódico Semanal Dedicado a los Artesanos*, which was essentially a literary newspaper.

Reading aloud was an unprecedented success, and it spread quickly to dozens of Havana factories and to every corner of Cuba. Thus, it is not surprising that the editorial section of the reformist newspaper *El Siglo* published an article about reading aloud in which the task of the *lector* was compared to that of Charles Dickens (January 25, 1866):

> Gathered silently in a room as if they were attending a performance, the audience bestows its attention on the *lector* or speaker, who, while expounding on any topic, which is usually announced in advance, frankly airs his opinions on the subject at hand, without the slightest hint of an interruption on the part of the listeners disturbing the semblance of assent they all project. ... [Charles Dickens], in reading his novels in cities throughout the United States, received much more from those sessions than he could have from publishers, who never failed to pay him as well as he deserved or to receive him well. Paying to hear someone speak, paying to listen to someone reading! Spending hours listening to someone reading speeches, essays, or the chapters of a novel! This is something better than that to which we are accustomed, and we find it irresistible.

However, as in all good stories, reading aloud had both its opponents and its enemies, who banned it repeatedly. These antagonists witnessed several *lectores* and cigar workers forced into exile in 1868, that is, at the beginning of what came to be known as the Ten Years' War (1868–1878). But let us return to Alberto Castilla's poem and reread the last five verses:

> and gives it to the workers in the shop,
> this work was ne'er a sign of foolishness
> because to it the humble flock has brought

a pulpit, *atalaya* of learnedness
where reading becomes a noble sermon taught.

We are back in the workshop, where, thanks to the reading, there is no room for nonsense or idleness, but, rather, the feeling of being part of the "flock," of the unity and fraternity of the workers. The allusion to the pulpit is another point of contact with the past, specifically, with the origins of reading aloud.

In the classical era, reading viva voce was the norm. Among the Greeks, works were published by way of being read aloud. First, the author read his work before a group of people, and later it would be given to professional readers so that his "voice" would be heard by much larger audiences. Likewise, readers who took turns one after another read the poetry of Homer at the Panathenaic Festival, and ancient Rome abounded with readers in the Athenaeum, in theaters, in any square, or on any corner of the city, as long as there was a listening audience.[2] Still, it was the Catholic Church that established the profession of the reader and gave him a fixed schedule, so the allusion to the pulpit is appropriate. In *The Holy Rule of Saint Benedict*, written toward the end of his life, Saint Benedict the Abbot devotes chapter XXXVIII to the "Weekly Reader":

> Reading must not be wanting at the table of the brethren when they are eating.
> Neither let anyone who may chance to take up the book venture to read there; but let him who is to read for the whole week enter upon that office on Sunday. . . . And let the following verse be said three times by all in the oratory, he beginning it: Lord, open my lips; my mouth will proclaim your praise (Ps 50 [51]:17), and thus having received the blessing let him enter upon the reading.
> Let the deepest silence be maintained that no whispering or voice be heard except that of the reader alone.[3]

The Rule was so strict with regard to reading aloud and the way it was to be undertaken that not only was anyone not paying attention punished, but the reader was as well. Chapter XLV focuses on "Those Who Commit a Fault in the Oratory" and reads as follows: "If anyone whilst he reciteth a psalm, a responsory, an antiphon, or a lesson, maketh a mistake, and doth not humble himself there before all by making satisfaction, let him undergo a greater punishment, because he would not correct by humility what he did amiss through negligence. But let children be beaten for such a fault."[4]

The Holy Rule of Saint Benedict has been the norm and spiritual guideline for an untold number of monastic communities for more than fifteen hundred years; therefore, the function of the reader, although the position is not financially compensated, has been in existence during refectory (at mealtime), and occasionally the task is carried out while some type of handicraft is being done. The practice of reading aloud and its strict schedule has always been tied to handiwork. Between the eighth and fourteenth centuries, craftwork in Benedictine convents was always done by the nuns. They devoted themselves to weaving, painting, embroidery, copying, bookbinding, sewing pages of books together, and book illustration.[5] These tasks were accompanied by reading aloud. Therefore, it is not surprising that the practice was welcomed into cigar facilities, specifically, where artisanal, preindustrial work was being done, and even more important, where the absence of noise permitted. During the Middle Ages, reading aloud not only took place within the milieu of monasteries and convents, but also continued to be the norm both in public and private spaces.

Following the invention of the printing press in the fifteenth century, reading aloud to a group of listeners did not decrease, despite the fact that the production and distribution of books constituted a radical cultural transformation. The custom of listening to a text read aloud was so deeply ingrained in people that reading silently to oneself did not become commonplace until centuries later. On one hand, in nearly all religions, the spoken word is of such great importance that, "for example, the Bible is read aloud at liturgical services. For God is thought of always as 'speaking' to human beings, not as writing to them." And, "In Western classical antiquity, it was taken for granted that a written text of any worth was meant to be and deserved to be read aloud, and the practice of reading texts aloud continued, quite commonly with many variations, through the nineteenth century."[6]

On the other hand, not only were texts intended for ritual or devout purposes "spoken," but all others as well. For example, in *Estoria de San Millán* (1221), Berceo writes: "Gentlemen and friends, all who gather here / You shall understand, if you will but hear," and *The Book of True Love* (1343) says: "That I, with little songs, may rhyme a book of poetry / So that those who can hear can find delight and modest glee" (29).[7]

When *Celestina* was published (1499), there was a proliferation of publications as a result of the printing press, but, nevertheless, most of the public still read aloud. There are several references to reading aloud in *Celestina*; an especially concrete example appears in the prologue: "So that, when 10 men shall meete togeather to reade [*above the line:* heere] this *Comedie*, in whome, perhaps, shall happen this difference of conditions, as vsuallie it falleth out, who will denie but that there is a contention in that thinge which suffers the censures of so manie men's Iudgmentes, and all of them differinge one from another?" (114).[8] And in Alonso de Proaza's epilogue: "If Calisto you would *read* with art sublime, / so as to *move* the hearts of *those who hear,* / you must know how to mutter or *speak* clear, . . . in *reading* feign a thousand arts and manners, / *then through the mouths of all ask and give answers.*"[9] In short, references to a listening audience and a reader are abundant.

A classic example of a passage that shows the atmosphere in which texts were read aloud can be observed in chapter XXXII of Part I of *Don Quixote* (1605), when, at Juan Palomeque's inn, the innkeeper says to the Priest: "At harvest time, you see, lots of the reapers come in here on rest-days, and there are always some who can read, and one of them picks up one of these books, and more than thirty of us gather around him, and we enjoy listening so much that it takes all our worries away."[10] This section alludes to the reading aloud of the novels that are found inside a case that a traveler forgot at the inn. In the same chapter, the Priest takes from the case "eight folios . . . written in such a fine hand" of *The Tale of Inappropriate Curiosity*, which he reads aloud to those gathered there. The reading of this intertext takes place in the following two chapters (XXXIII and XXXIV), but it is interrupted in chapter XXXV by Sancho Panza, when he announces Don Quixote's battle with the wineskins. Finally, importuned by all, the Priest finishes reading the novel.

Cervantes's texts are based on the sources of the oral tradition when they adopt and reproduce the resources of a narrator whose strategy is to abbreviate and pause, that is, when doing so creates suspense and keeps the audience alert. That narrator interrupts and makes reference to the narrative process, and does so because the author (not just Cervantes) anticipates that his writings will be read aloud by a reader surrounded by a group of listeners.[11]

Needless to say, the way a text is presented to be read plays an important role in the construction of its signification. Versions of the same literal text "are not the 'same' when the physical support that transmits it to readers, listeners or spectators varies."[12] A factor that must be taken into consideration is that reading aloud is generally associated with illiteracy, not only in the Golden Age, as in the passage by Cervantes I have just cited, but until the beginning of the twentieth century. Any study of the history of reading aloud must not be limited to researching postmortem inventories, printed catalogues of libraries, or the presence or absence of groups of literati, because to do so would fail to take into account the "the reading of books not owned by readers, but borrowed by them, or read at someone else's house, or listened to being read aloud."[13] But who was read to, and under what circumstances?

During the Renaissance, it was customary to read aloud to princes. During the sixteenth century in France, there was an official whose specific task was to be the "lecteur ordinaire du roi," and likewise, at the beginning of the seventeenth century in England, there was a "Reader to his/her Majesty."[14] In both instances, the position was desirable and highly sought after. However, the practice was not limited to monarchs, but also included aristocrats, such as ministers of government, and even writers such as Chaucer recruited professional readers to read them history, literature, and any other sort of text imaginable. Those readers were charged with the task of suggesting and selecting texts and commenting on them after having read them. Some servants were also readers, and although they were not paid to read to their masters during or after the evening meal, reading aloud was part of their daily duties. Hannah Wolley, author of *Gentlewoman's Companion* (1675), a guide intended to educate future maidservants, said that one of her most enriching tasks was reading aloud to her mistress. According to her, those readings of poetry and dramatic works not only taught her to read, but strengthened her diction as well.[15]

Now, if we return to the final verses of the stanza with which I started—"a pulpit, *atalaya* of learnedness / where reading becomes a noble sermon taught"—it seems to me symbolic to allude to an *atalaya*, a word of Arabic origin that literally means "sentinels" or "tower usually built in a high place, for the purpose of surveying from it the countryside or the ocean and announcing what is there discovered. . . . State or position from which the truth can be well observed."[16] In the general sense, the word *atalaya* denotes "to see" or "to realize something," to study, to have perspective. What I would like to propose here is that, symbolically, an *atalaya* reflects the task and profession of a cigar factory *lector*.

As I have indicated, the reference to the pulpit represents the origins of the profession of reader in the Christian tradition. And monasteries were the primary model for disciplinary rules in prisons, schools, hospitals, and, by extension, factories, since the strict schedule, the system of what one must and must not do, the constant supervision, the admonitions, and the mandatory readings were implemented according to an ecclesiastical standard. In prisons, Bible readings were mandatory and were supervised with the hope that they would be a positive spiritual influence on the inmates. Since many prisoners were often neither artisans nor workers, prison became a type of practical school in which the confinees were forced to learn how to work and to listen to religious readings.[17]

Likewise, in Havana, convicts who occupied the prison wards of the Arsenal del Apostadero during the nineteenth century listened to half an hour of reading from books with moralistic leanings after they finished working. Most of the prisoners were made to roll cigars and were paid a set amount for their work, which they received when they were released. Part of the prisoners' "wages" went toward compensating the *lector* and toward acquiring texts to be read in the future.[18] This took place under the strict supervision of a sentinel [*centinela*] and was a practice that began shortly before reading commenced in cigar factories. In a hierarchical structure such as that of a workshop, prison, or convent, the sentinels, foremen, or chaperones had the duty of studying and monitoring the behavior of subordinates or inmates. In other words, in a prison or on a battlefield, a sentinel was a soldier who was constantly observing the enemy or prisoner. Curiously, a chaperone [*escucha*] "in nunneries and girls' schools, [was] the one charged with the task of being in the parlor to accompany those who receive visitors in order to hear what is said"; a chaperone was also a sentinel "who advances at night near the location of the enemies in order to observe their movements."[19] In this sense, both chaperones and sentinels were agents who were always both observed and monitored by a force greater than themselves.

The profession of the *lector* is similar to that of a sentinel in an *atalaya*, since, while he is studying, discovering, and disseminating the truth, the *lector* is at the same time being monitored and controlled. Since the seventeenth century, artisanal workshops have had a sort of religious semblance because rules and discipline similar to those of convents have been in effect. Workshops modeled themselves after convents when they devised a code of conduct that spelled out starting times, quitting times, regularly scheduled activities, silence, respect, proper manners, and so forth. For example, craftspeople had to wash their hands in the morning, make the sign of the cross, offer their work to God by way of a prayer, and then begin to work.[20] It is interesting to note that, when reading aloud was instituted in Havana, workshops also had the atmosphere of convents, and reading reinforced the sense of a religious milieu when a set reading schedule was established. Although religious texts were not read, workshops became spaces with monastic atmospheres, that is, "a pulpit, *atalaya* of learnedness / where reading becomes a noble sermon taught." Later we shall see how reading, a sort of watchtower from which culture was studied and disseminated, transformed cigar workers.

READING ALOUD IN HAVANA IN 1865

Why, how, and for what purpose was reading aloud established in factories? As mentioned previously, in general, reading aloud is associated with illiteracy. Nevertheless, it is important to emphasize that both in Cuba and in other countries during the nineteenth century there were also numerous literary centers within the educated community where writers enjoyed what their peers had written; in addition, there were many literary circles, cultural associations, lyceums, theaters, and other public spaces where people could attend these oral presentations.

The cigar industry had a higher rate of literacy compared with other craft industries. A large number of workers, nevertheless, could not read; this does not mean they had no access to historical and literary texts, especially newspapers, magazines, or newspaper serials. To cite a few contemporaneous examples, after reading aloud was started in cigar factories, Mexico enjoyed an abundance of newspapers written for workers, for example, *El Amigo del Pueblo*, *La Reconstrucción*, and *Las Clases Productoras*; however, in spite of the high number of people who did not know how to read, the press exercised a decisive influence on the progress of the country.[21]

In 1860 in Madrid, 75 percent of the adult population was illiterate, and artisans' private libraries were famous for their absence of books other than *Don Quixote* and the odd Spanish novel. Nevertheless, workers had their own press and literary circles, they wrote their own pamphlets, they founded their own patriotic organizations, and they participated in public demonstrations.[22] In France, England, and Germany, what was called "mass literacy" had already come into existence. There, between the middle and the end of the nineteenth century, the working class also began to read and, therefore, to listen much more.[23]

Indubitably, the serialization of fiction in newspapers grew to vast proportions, and, thanks to this, European (as well as Cuban) workers found themselves nourished by the literature of the day. Newspapers represented a kind of mobile library replacing string literature, which had played such an important role in reading (especially reading aloud) among the working classes since the seventeenth century in Spain, England, and France.[24]

Still, in the nineteenth century, despite "mass literacy" among the working classes, reading aloud was preferred. Or, rather, the press was the only means by which, for example, Thomas Wood, an English worker, could get access to the written word from a stale newspaper he rented for one cent per week and which he read beside the fireplace, for he could not afford the cost of a candle.[25] Others who never learned to read took the opportunity to listen to a coworker reading before or after working hours. One moving story is that of a French worker, Norbert Truquin, who could not read, but who was enlightened through the reading aloud of his fellow workers from 1846 through 1870; this is the same period during which reading aloud started in the cigar factories in Cuba. Truquin's cultural landscape was so vast that, when he was arrested in 1870 and put in jail, he asked other prisoners to read him the *History of Mexico* by Hernán Cortés.

Truquin did not enjoy the same good fortune as his compatriot Jean

Valjean, the hero of *Les Misérables* (1862), by Victor Hugo. Valjean, while in prison in Toulon, "went [to school] when he was forty and learned to read, write, and calculate."[26] In 1872, Norbert Truquin set off for South America, and in Paraguay, at age forty, he learned to read and write. There he wrote his autobiography, *Mémoires et aventures d'un prolétaire*, which was published in France in 1888.

Therefore, all that was necessary for a group of people to enjoy reading, whether strictly literary or political topics, was that someone know how to read. Thanks to Truquin's autobiography, we know the texts people heard. In most cases, however, it is difficult to come by inventories of "libraries" that were read aloud.

The onset of reading aloud in cigar factories is contemporaneous with the debut of a weekly publication written for workers. To understand how reading viva voce was established in cigar factories, it is important to examine newspapers of the day, especially *El Siglo*, whose efforts were decisive, as well as inspirational, in the establishment of the practice.

In nineteenth-century Latin America, newspapers were the only publications that reached all social classes and stimulated progress in reading and education. As insightful studies about the nineteenth century have shown, newspapers introduced political profiles of society and transmitted world news. These papers disseminated both popular and national literature as well.[27] *El Siglo*, a preeminent reformist daily, began publication in 1861; in Cuba the Reformist Party took over its management in 1863, defended the rights of the working class, and promoted free education for workers. As far as the paper's editors were concerned, the newspaper was a textbook for the education of the less-privileged segments of society. But how to communicate their objectives to those who could not read or to those who had neither the time nor the habit of reading to themselves? The only way to achieve this was through reading aloud.

The newspaper's manager, Francisco Frías, Count of Pozos Dulces, a writer and economist, was the party's spokesman. The party was granted full legal recognition by a royal decree from Madrid in 1865; thereafter, it strove peacefully for its rights in Cuba from the Spanish government. There were 1.4 million people living in Cuba: approximately 70 percent of the white population and an astonishing 95 percent of the nonwhite population were illiterate.[28] Starting in 1842, there were free public elementary schools, although poor administration by the municipal governments running them failed to increase the number of schools.

The reformists soon realized that a good strategy for promoting education was through publications; thus, the voices of the underprivileged classes began to be heard and to serve as examples. In the newspaper section titled "Mesa revuelta," the paper published on July 12, 1865, the following poem, which had been written by a slave:

TO MY LORD
On his Departure.
Depart, my lord, to Almendares gladly,
Which spreads out golden sands
Beneath the highest ceiba and palm trees,
And, powerful and grand,
Modulates the songs its bards sing freely:
Go, take with you my tenderest farewell,
And your guardian angel to keep you well.
Arrive glad finally in Varela's land,
In Luz and in Zambrana,
And read these humble lines from my own hand;
From me, give greetings to Havana,
Since its press reveals to me all the land:
While I make plea to God Omnipotent
That you return ere long safe and content.

According to the newspaper's editor, the poem first appeared in the Cienfuegos daily *El Telégrafo* and was written by Máximo Hero de Neiva.

To a great extent, the newspaper was a sort of battlefield of ideological and social struggles going on in colonial Cuba. At the same time that the editors published a poem written by the slave Hero de Neiva, announcements like the following appeared in the pages of the daily: "SALES—SLAVES:" "FOR SALE—A mulatto, twenty years of age, strong, good appearance, excellent coachman, fair cook and buggy driver, accustomed to constant work, to let or for sale, for the owner has no need of him: see the doorman at house No. 40 for further information" (*El Siglo*, June 24, 1865).

What is surprising is not only the fact that slavery was still legal, but also that at the very same time texts written by the slaves themselves were being published.[29] Therefore, on one hand, the publication of the poem in the newspaper praised the fact that a slave could write and address not only "his Lord," that is, his master, who had likely granted him the privilege of learning to read and write, but, on the other hand, also allowed him to have his voice heard publicly: "And read these humble lines from my own hand; / From me, give greetings to Havana." Both the title and the tone function as a type of prayer or supplication invoking the "Lord" (not only his lord and master but also a divine being) by means of a chant: an oral intonement with repetitions. The text likewise shows the importance of the newspaper as a means of communication, since it is the vehicle by which the slave kept himself informed about the events that had taken place around him: "Since its press reveals to me all the land."

The slave-poet Máximo Hero de Neiva had the good fortune to have learned to read and write during a period in which the majority of the population—enslaved or not—was still illiterate. Nevertheless, those who had no access to the written word were accustomed to listening, repeating, and memorizing sermons and chants at church. Therefore, one may infer that the reading aloud of the newspaper was not necessarily anything new for listeners doubtless accustomed to having the Bible or the odd pamphlet read aloud to them.

El Siglo also addressed its voice to farmers as they advocated for "itinerant teachers" and for wider circulation of the newspaper (June 26, 1865):

> In other countries we have seen itinerant teachers who travel on horseback with saddlebags in which they keep paper and other writing implements, books, an atlas, and so forth; they are welcomed and well respected everywhere, especially by the parents of the children they teach. . . . The municipal government pays the teachers' salaries and provides them with horses and the necessities. . . . Agricultural training is achieved through special newspapers that are available to people of all stations, and this means of communication becomes even more beneficial when the humble abodes of the poorest among us receive it free. . . . For years we have published detailed articles about these rural schools, as such schools are not a new idea, although we did not permit slaves or emancipated blacks to attend them.

Publications such as these were in nearly daily circulation on the pages of newspapers, and, as in any project, they were not published by mere chance; the newspaper management insisted that there were ways in which slavery could be diminished or abolished, along with the concentration of wealth in rural areas. Therefore, the newspaper in essence functioned as a textbook; from the paper the rural citizenry everywhere could learn about science, history, and literature. Likewise, the newspaper addressed communities of readers in urban areas; it never failed to cover the openings of recreation centers and mutual aid society activities, as well as the recitals and cultural efforts of the theaters and lyceums.

El Siglo prided itself on presenting the educational activities of established organizations such as La Sociedad Económica de Amigos del País [the Economic Society of Friends of the Country], founded in 1793, and the more recent Sociedad del Pilar and the Liceo Artístico y Literario de la Habana [Havana Artistic and Literary Lyceum], both created in 1848.[30] The period's lack of labor unions, because factory owners did not permit them, did not stymie the cigar sector's creation of La Sociedad de Socorros Mutuos de Honrados Artesanos y Jornaleros [the Workers' and Day Laborers' Mutual Aid Society] in 1857, symbolically founded in the Parish of Jesus, Mary, and Joseph and dedicated to the Good Shepherdess.

The labor *sociedad* was under the protection, therefore, of the Virgin Mary and Joseph the Carpenter. Those societies were devoted to promoting charitable and mutual aid projects while also functioning in part as a type of social club and an organization providing financial assistance when necessary. It is important to emphasize that one of the societies' most important projects was the development and maintenance of education. For example, on June 15, 1865, La Sociedad del Pilar announced in *El Siglo* that it was offering free grammar and arithmetic classes to anyone wishing to attend, whether they were adults or youngsters. La Sociedad also offered classes in recitation and literature and provided lecture halls.

Many organizations and lyceums announced their programs in *El Siglo*. Calls to meetings were published as well, such as those at the Liceo Artístico y Literario de la Habana, which organized the Juegos Florales contest, in which poems and historical novels were submitted and judged. On July 11, 1865, the new Liceo de la Habana [Havana Lyceum] announced the production of a play—*El preceptor y su mujer*—and the Liceo de Matanzas [Matanzas Lyceum], founded April 11, 1866, publicized its free English classes. In short, as we shall see later, the period witnessed the emergence of numerous societies and lecture halls in which recitations and oral readings of different artistic productions were all the rage.

The newspaper included a section devoted to literature, in which works by poets such as Luis Victoriano Betancourt, Isaac Carrillo y O'Farril, Alfredo Torroella, Fernando Urzais, José Socorro de León, Pantaleón Tovar, Francisco Sellén, Carlos Navarrete y Romay, and Antonio Sellén were published. The section called "Mesa revuelta" featured countless poems that the readership dedicated to their loved ones, for example, Máximo Hero de Neiva's poem or the one written by "Amalia Gutiérrez, the young black slave girl," who had just learned to read and write and whose poem was dedicated to a physician (*El Siglo*, April 6, 1866).

Thrilling inserts in which the fusion of history and fiction was worthy of comparison to the style and form of the novels of Victor Hugo were published in installments. An anonymous collection of essays—"Causa sobre el asesinato de Lincoln"—appeared in *El Siglo* from April through August 1865, for example. The paper also published Jules de Saint-Félix's "Mujeres de negocios," Paul Feval's "El mendigo negro," Alexandre Dumas' *El clavel* and *Dramas marítimos*, Ponson du Terrail's *Los caballeros de la noche*, Arabic tales (e.g., "Hesdin-Norredin"), and Eugène Pelletan's excerpts of books that had been translated into Spanish (e.g., *El que pierde gana* and *La madre*). In addition, Faustina Sáez de Melgar's lengthy novels *La loca del encinar* and *La pastora de guadiela* as well as Luis Victoriano Betancourt's short story "Jente [*sic*] ordinaria" were published.

In large measure, what was published was intended to be didactic. Thus, readers and listeners were instructed by such hapless cases as Doña Escarrabaldada, the famously rude woman in Betancourt's "Jente ordinaria." At the end of the text, the narrator expresses prophetically: "She was like her mother, and her children and her children's children will be like her, as long as women remain in the place they now hold in society. . . . Education, dear philosophers, is for not only this person, or that one; freedom is not only for this person alone, and not for another; education is for all, and just as the sun is for all, so is freedom" (*El Siglo*, March 7, 1866).

In short, the literature that appeared in *El Siglo* had a didactic and moralizing tone, and its goal was to educate a number of different segments of society by promoting education among those who already knew how to read and to encourage those who did not. Thus, it is obvious that newspapers were as much for the educated as for the illiterate.

THE ESTABLISHMENT OF *LA AURORA:*
PERIÓDICO SEMANAL DEDICADO A LOS ARTESANOS

In 1865, in Havana alone, there were over five hundred cigar factories where more than fifteen thousand workers were employed.[31] With the advice and support of the Reformists, cigar workers such as Saturnino Martínez, who also worked in the public library of La Sociedad Económica de Amigos del País, saw the need to establish a newspaper devoted to workers.[32] Thus, along with Manuel Sellén, who was its first editor-in-chief, Martínez launched the weekly *La Aurora: Periódico Semanal Dedicado a los Artesanos*, on October 22, 1865. The weekly consisted of eight two-column pages and was published in the Viuda de Barcina y Compañía print shop. Its "Statement of Purpose," which appeared on page 1, reads (October 22, 1865):

> When a people begin to feel the development of the ideas of civilization and progress in their hearts, no power exists capable of impeding their

momentum. . . . Thus, we have come to add our grain of sand to the great edifice humanity is constructing. We are cosmopolitan by nature, and we come now to make manifest our ideas with whatever freedom is permitted to us, within the confines of a publication such as ours. We seek to establish fraternity with that group of enlightened workers who are zealous for the progress made in the sciences and in literature, and our goal will be to illuminate the masses.

It is obvious that the newspaper sought to carry out an educational task. The weekly was, on a large scale, first literary and then scientific; the exception was page 1, which generally focused on topics related to the education of the workers or to the promotion of association meetings organized by the workers themselves.

THE ESTABLISHMENT OF READING ALOUD
IN THE FACTORIES OF HAVANA

The founders of *La Aurora*, along with a council of political reformists such as Nicolás Azcárate, felt the need to educate the workers by reading aloud to them while they made cigars. Azcárate was the director of the Liceo de Guanabacoa [Guanabacoa Lyceum], where the educated community met; huge audiences attended cultural events held there.

The first reading in Havana took place in El Fígaro Cigar Factory on December 21, 1865. More than three hundred cigar rollers worked in that factory, and they chose the *lector* from among their own ranks. *La Aurora* immediately publicized the establishment of oral reading in "La lectura en los talleres" (January 7, 1866):

> Today, even in the heart of the workshops, and during the hours most suited to manual labor, imaginations are busily questioning scientific and philosophical truths meant to keep the workers abreast of the age to which they belong. They are talking and discussing; they are reading the works of good modern authors and consulting with each other about any point outside their intellectual grasp; in short, they are doing what they can to learn and to continue along the path of civilization. . . . We are not here to read works of little value, because no significant advantage can be derived therein. In all workers' gatherings or associations, be they recreational or of any other type, in which one attempts to improve one's habits, any work not subject to the domain of the intellect should be rejected. . . . The workers employed by *El Fígaro* will be well served, for they themselves pay the *lector* to have works worthy of study

read to them, and not works whose messages would permeate their hearts with the poisonous sorrows of vice.

As we can see, the publication of this article was a type of manifesto that promoted not only the reading of newspapers and intellectual works, but also reading viva voce as an integral institution within the workshops.

From the very beginning, the listeners paid for the reading themselves. In his groundbreaking study "La lectura en las tabaquerías," José Rivero Muñiz points out that the idea of reading aloud in the workplace originated with the Spanish traveler and writer Jacinto de Salas y Quiroga, whom Azcárate had read, when the former visited Cuba in 1839. Salas y Quiroga went on an excursion to a coffee plantation, and when he saw the slaves selecting the different coffee beans, it occurred to him that "there was nothing easier than occupying those hours for the good of the moral education of those unfortunate souls."[33] Rivero Muñiz adds that, at the beginning of the 1860s, the idea was first put into practice in Havana's jails, where prisoners listened to a person reading aloud after they had finished their daily tasks. Since a number of the inmates were cigar workers who were constantly visited by their coworkers, the news of the reading spread rapidly to the cigar factories; this inspired the workers to start it there.

I would like to add that reading in workshops, such as tailor shops, where the work permitted those employed there to hear the voice of a *lector* (because there was no loud machinery), also took place in Great Britain circa 1835. Each workshop bought a local newspaper and another one from somewhere else, such as London, Edinburgh, or Glasgow, and workers read the texts to their fellow workers. They took turns doing the reading, and compensation for the reading came from the workers themselves. Later, they resold the newspapers to other workers at a reduced price.[34] Although I am not insinuating that the Cuban cigar workers borrowed the idea of reading from British workshops, nor am I attempting to compare them, these examples illustrate that reading aloud within the work setting had already taken place in other contexts.

THE ESTABLISHMENT OF READING ALOUD
IN THE PARTAGÁS FACTORY

The establishment of reading aloud at El Fígaro inspired cigar workers in other factories. On January 9, 1866, reading aloud commenced in one of the largest and most important factories in Havana, the Partagás Factory. A grand ceremony celebrated the initiation.

Most large factories were of similar design. The ground floor housed offices and warehouses where tobacco leaves were stored in large bundles called *tercios* (bales). The second level held the main workshop where the workers rolled the cigars. When reading aloud began, those who opposed it began to call the main workshop the "*galera*" (prison ward), a pejorative name, because, according to them, the cigar workers were read to in similar fashion as to inmates in the jails. This space, that is, the *galera* (the name stuck and continues to be used today), is set up like a classroom with rows of workbenches resembling student desks. The cigar workers call these rows "*vapores*" (steamships). They sit shoulder to shoulder, each at his respective workbench. The main workshop has ventilation and lighting but is not very well lit so as not to damage the tobacco. The ceilings were—and still are— extremely high, often reaching thirty feet.

If the main workshop was large enough, the wrapper selectors, pickers, leaf strippers, and casers sat in the part that faced north. The wrapper selectors select the leaves according to their size, quality, and color, while the pickers, once the cigar has been rolled, pick it, bundle it, or wrap it. The leaf strippers, most of whom are women, remove the central vein or stem from the tobacco leaf. The casers line with paper and prepare the boxes in which the finished product is packaged.[35] There may be hundreds of workers in the *galera*. The team of workers in the different departments are called collectively "*tabaqueros*."

What sets the cigar worker apart from other workers is the way in which he carries out his tasks and how he receives his compensation. The work has always been piecework; that is, remuneration depends on the number of cigars rolled. Each cigar worker has always been in control of individual production as long as he is given enough raw materials for his job.

Cigar making is strictly skilled labor, because everything is done by hand; therefore, the cigar worker concentrates on his product by relying intensely on his eyes and hands. In fact, the only tool he uses is a type of knife called a "*chaveta*." However, because of the way the workshop is designed, and because cigar makers work alongside their colleagues, it is very common for seemingly never-ending conversations to be struck up. In fact, conversation has never kept them from doing their jobs. In an anonymous nineteenth-century popular poem, we can appreciate the harmony within the workplace just described:

Once you own a *chaveta*
that can cut very neat
no other tool is needed

this work to complete.
In fashioning the cigar cap
no one can do it as well
for me it's child's play
and for others . . . hell.
Tell those no-good fools
who are interested in me
that I make three hundred cigars
between nine and three.
So come, dear mulatto girl
my fortune to enjoy
and we will spend our life
in delicious joy.[36]

Learning to roll cigars is not easy. It is usually learned over the course of nine months of intensive training. Once the skill has been learned, however, to a certain extent, it becomes both monotonous and repetitive.

Obviously, the same occurs in the different departments. The absence of noise in the various departments allows for dialogue and the exchange of ideas among the cigar workers; as a result, the workers have always enjoyed a rather high degree of culture. Since there was no machinery, and the only noise to be heard was that of the *chavetas*, reading aloud in cigar factories was possible thanks to the silence and design of the workshop.

As I indicated earlier, workshops and schools were inspired by a monastic model that resembled the refectory, where monks sat on only one side of a rectangular or horseshoe-shaped table with their backs to the wall and facing the center of the room. They listened to the voice of the "weekly reader," who read standing before them with his book on a lectern. Reading aloud was one of the monks' most carefully tended and respected activities. They listened without interrupting, and if they had to communicate with one another, they did it by means of gestures.

The weekly reader was to read with the utmost care, and over time, he was allowed to use a dictionary left on the lectern in case he wanted to consult it before starting to read. If the reader read too rapidly, his superior tapped on the table so that he could adjust the tone and flow of the reading.[37]

Both the design and the atmosphere of the cigar factories resembled that of a monastery or convent, as well as its workshops where sacred art, ceramics, engraving design, book binding, and the restoration of antique icons took place.[38] *La* Aurora described the inaugural reading at the Partagás Factory as follows (January 14, 1866):

One of the young workers of the workshop, who sits among the multitude of laborers, who number close to two hundred, announced in a clear, resonant voice that he would begin to read a work, the lessons of which tended toward showing people the way to a destination worthy of the noble aspirations of the working classes of all civilized nations. And opening the volume to its title page, he began to read *Las luchas del siglo.* It is impossible to praise sufficiently the rapt attention the other workers lent him during the half hour he read; then another youth of identical circumstances took up the same book and continued to read for another half hour, and so on, until six o'clock in the evening; at that time, the laborers left the workshop.

The atmosphere in which reading took place was that of a monastic or academic milieu, with total silence and discipline. The *lector* read to a seated group of people, most of whom could see and hear him. The work that was read was first subject to the scrutiny of Jaime Partagás, the owner of the factory, who enthusiastically supported the reading, provided he approved the texts in advance. This superior authority thus controlled the reading program and its curriculum. Soon a need arose to negotiate what should and should not be read, because it was the cigar workers themselves who paid the *lector.*

But who made up the listening audience? The cigar workers were always racially and ethnically diverse: in one row of workbenches, blacks, whites, mixed-race individuals, Spaniards, and Chinese worked side by side. Although in most cases, factory owners and the highest-ranking, and consequently, the highest-paid employees were Spaniards or white Cubans, there was diversity. As I indicated earlier, by this time (1866) there were female cigar workers, who, although they worked mainly as leaf strippers, also worked as casers. Even though the audience was diverse, reading brought them together as part of the same community of listeners.

THE ESTABLISHMENT OF THE FIRST PLATFORM FOR THE *LECTOR*

One month after reading aloud was established in the Partagás Factory, the owner donated a platform so that the *lector* could do his job from it. A ceremony marked the delivery of this pulpit, though it certainly had neither a railing nor a canopy. The platform was placed in the middle of the workshop. The owner, Jaime Partagás, climbed up on the platform and from there, as might a priest, leader, or teacher, said a short prayer, to which the *lector* responded. The *lector* then went up and read a speech he had written for the occasion (*La Aurora*, February 11, 1866):

> I feel the flame of enthusiasm stir in my brain when I see such great unselfishness. Ladies and gentlemen: Whilst you are kneading the dough of your family's daily bread by the sweat of your brow, you listen to the evangelical voice of reading. With the foundation of reading, we have taken a giant step forward on the tortuous path of civilization. . . . May we be proud then, and, with each day that passes, may we grow more focused in our enthusiasm for the route upon which we have embarked; for otherwise it should not be possible for the workers of these regions to learn even slightly any of the various branches of knowledge; because, well and truly, we know nothing, we have not the slightest familiarity with the rudiments of the social sciences, which are the sciences of today; and we lack even the beginnings of an education, which is so necessary to mankind and so indispensable as we travel through life.

Once again, the workshop took on the ambiance of a convent. It resembled a religious space wherein a person ascends the pulpit or goes up to a lectern to read to a group of listeners. Note that the reading would be the "evangelical voice," as if a religious text were being read and the Word of the Lord was being heard.

Without a doubt, reading aloud is a practice with multiple differentiations, and the meaning of the text depends on the manner in which it is read: whether aloud, to oneself, individually, or to others. As we shall see, religious texts were not read in cigar factories, but, rather, those considered to have educational value.

As far as the artisans were concerned, and especially for those who fervently supported the reading, the installation of the platform was nothing short of a victory, because they knew that from there, from on high, an entire sector could be educated. The installation of the platform in the Partagás Factory was symbolic because it was an example to be followed by other factories both in the capital and the interior of Cuba.

In March of that year, 1866, an article entitled "Los talleres y los artesanos" stated (*La Aurora*, March 4, 1866): "Little by little, as was bound to happen, with admirable speed, magnificent platforms debut in the main rooms of the workshops, and the voice of science is sustained within the honorable sphere crafted by the noble sweat of the brow of an enthusiastic labor force." Just as quickly, reading aloud became an unprecedented success; by May of that year, dozens of factories had established their own programs.

TEXTS READ AND HEARD IN CIGAR FACTORIES
The "Uses" of Literature and Libraries

One of the most important questions to pose is what was read in the *galeras*? It is difficult, or impossible, to trace the inventories of what was read, but in terms of newspapers, there is no doubt that *El Siglo* and especially *La Aurora* were read. In an article entitled "Los periódicos," under the byline of J. de J. M. (José de Jesús Márquez was a cigar maker who regularly wrote for the weekly), it is noted that "we, young artisans, who follow the path down which our consciences guide us ... are such good friends of newspapers that we never tire of reading them; from their in-depth articles to the latest local news section, we always find the reading pleasant" (*La Aurora*, July 8, 1866).

Some newspapers were in continuous circulation, while others were short-lived. Two important newspapers read in cigar factories were the conservative and antireformist colossuses, *El Diario de la Marina* and *Prensa de la Habana*. Smaller newspapers circulated as well, such as *El Ajiaco, Don Junípero, La Sensitiva, La Estudiantina, El Recreo Social, El Amigo de las Mujeres*, as well as important newspapers from inland Cuba that reached Havana: *El Hórmigo*, from Las Tunas; *Progreso*, from Colón; *Fénix*, from Sancti Spíritus; *Regeneración*, from Bayamo; *La Atalaya*, from Remedios; *El Telégrafo*, from Cienfuegos; *El Comercio*, from Manzanillo; *La Colmena*, from Sagua la Grande; *Alba*, from Villa Clara; *La Noche, El Papalote, El Gavilán*, and *El Liceo*, from Matanzas; and so forth. Few registries of titles of literary, historical, or scientific texts read have been found, although there is no room for doubt that there were debates over what was to be read.

As I indicated previously, in "La lectura en los talleres," the writer suggests that "any work not subject to the domain of the intellect should be rejected," and since, after all, reading was paid for, he recommends that "works worthy of study [be] read to them and not works whose messages would permeate their hearts with the poisonous sorrows of vice" (*La Aurora*, January 7, 1866).

Others were of the opinion that all works had to pass scrutiny. In an article intended for artisans, "A los artesanos," the author says: "Much good and much bad can be provided us, honorable artisans, by the reading to which you listen in your workshops.... You must be extremely cautious in selecting works; do not begin reading anything without previously having submitted it to scholarly criticism" (*La Aurora*, March 4, 1866). Conversely, an article in *El Siglo* said that the best didactic works were treatises that were exclusively educational, but that in them law and scientific principles were expressed "dryly," and therefore one should "give preference to books in which [science] is set forth in pleasant language and in an enjoyable manner." With regard to books with moralistic leanings (*El Siglo*, January 25, 1866):

> no better literature than the biographies of useful, good men, of honorable artisans, especially those who set the example of Franklin, a printer, Palissy, a potter, Jacquard, a weaver, Lincoln, a woodsman, Hartzenbush, a carpenter, Watt, a mechanic, Moratín, a silversmith, Johnson, a tailor; adopting—as history texts—those in biographical form, true animated histories in which the specific details are tangible in captive imaginations and adding to the study of great personages, struggles, and feats, the interest at once of romance and the truth, which offer both solace and sustenance to the soul.

In spite of opinions about what should be read, reading aloud continued to be established quickly and officially in several Havana workshops, as well as in other parts of Cuba. As previously mentioned, there are few registries of the works heard, except when *La Aurora* published what was being read and what already had been read in the Partagás Factory (March 18, 1866): "*Las luchas del siglo*, one volume; *Economía política*, by Flores y Estrada, two quarto volumes; *El rey del mundo*, moral and philosophical novel by Fernández y González, one bound volume; *Historia de la revolución francesa*, two quarto volumes, Mayor; *Historia de España*, by Galeano, a three-volume set of six books; and *Misterios del juego* (which is currently being read)."

It is difficult to imagine that all these works were read aloud, especially if reading had just commenced in the Partagás Factory on January 9, 1866. Still, the allusion to these works and not others serves as a guide to what was read.

What set *La Aurora* apart was the fact that it was meant to be read aloud, as one of its priorities was a campaign for the standardization of reading in the workshops. *La Aurora* received regular submissions from Saturnino Martínez, Francisco and Manuel Sellén, Juan Pérez, Juan Francisco Anillo, J. J. de Márquez, Luis de Abrisqueta, Juan María Reyes, Francisco Montero, Santiago Pujol, Joaquín Lorenzo Luaces, J. J. Govantes, Alfredo Torroella, Luis Victoriano Betancourt, José Fornaris, Fernando Urzais, Ramona Pizarro, Ana María Cabrera, Rosa Marrero, and a number of cigar workers who published a poem here and there or wrote an opinion piece. Serialized novels such as *Laura* were written, as well as *La flor del azhar*, by Urzais; *Amor y pobreza: Drama en tres actos y en verso* and a short novel entitled *Los pobres*, by Torroella; *La hija del pueblo: Drama en tres actos y en verso*, by Fornaris; as well as essays titled "La artesana," by Ramona Pizarro, and "La educación de la mujer," "La educación de la niñez," "El niño enfermo," and "Los libros del siglo XIII." The weekly also had a section entitled "Cuentos de salón" in which works with moralizing tendencies were published. There was also space allotted for reviews of books or of works that were being edited, as the weekly announced: "We have had the pleasure of seeing, now that it has been finished, the first part of a three-act dramatic play that one of our friends is writing. It is entitled *El hombre de la panza,* or *Barriguilla el despalillador,* and we can assure you that it is a miracle of our Lord that we did not *split our sides* laughing. Let's have the remaining two acts at once, and let's set the ball rolling!" (*La Aurora,* June 24, 1866; original emphasis). Also heard were translations of poems and essays into Spanish from works written in French or German (e.g., by Chateaubriand, Hugo, and Schiller) and, in short, a panoply of literature which, had it not been read aloud, might never have reached such a large audience.

Victor Hugo was one of the very few writers who had the good fortune to learn that his novels had been heard by a crowd in a Havana factory: Partagás. For that reason, he wrote a letter to the cigar workers thanking them for their kind gesture. The letter was read aloud in the factory by the *lector,* hence establishing a link between the listeners and the French author.[39] In fact, *La Aurora* published and made possible the recitation of Hugo's magnificent essay "William Shakespeare."

The struggle for progress was not an easy one, since, as I will show later, those who contributed their work to *La Aurora* were surrounded by adversaries. Nevertheless, those who wrote for the weekly employed literature as a pedagogical tool. That is, it was thought that literature would help the workers improve themselves ethically and would further their education. Thus, the examples of men of letters were published; note below a sample from the editorial section from Sunday, April 22, 1866:

> The immortal Cervantes was as poor in fortune as he was rich and admirable in ingenuity; Moratín was a poor artisan, and became the first theorist of the theater and the Spanish language.[40] . . . Selgas y Carrasco was a clerk in an establishment in Murcia when he was called to Madrid by the Count of San Luis to fulfill a destiny that would allow him to cultivate his talent, and today he is one of the greatest men of letters in Madrid, and likewise, nearly all men of grand ideas have been sons of the working class.

Similarly, in many poetic compositions, the voice calls out in a lofty tone with the hope that the young will be transformed. The following poem, "To Youth," written by Saturnino Martínez (*La Aurora,* April 16, 1866), prays:

Oh! Dance not—Beyond the distant mountain
See how it appears
A fierce cloud which, blurring the horizon,
Announces a tempestuous storm is near.

The North Wind whips furiously
At the desert sand:
Alas for the boat which in the worldly sea
Spies no beacon to lead it to land!

What terror! The daylight and the dark
Battle in the West:
Oh young ones! from your crazed error depart
And before the altars bow your heads.

Bow them! and pray that at the battle's end
May reign the sacred light
And that the phantom of error may descend
In fragments into everlasting night.

The poem is a kind of prayer; the poetic voice evokes the desperation of someone who desires to change the world immediately. Note how, from the very beginning, it is apparent that dance—that is to say, leisure and pleasure—leaves no trace of itself. Conversely, the conclusion is reached that education, symbolized by the "altar" or "sacred light," will be victorious. A poem signed by A. S. is even more explicit (*La Aurora*, August 5, 1866):

"The Student and the Silkworm"
IMITATION
"How happy the butterfly
Who freely flies on high!"
Thus a miserable student
Exclaimed unhappily.
"To study both day and night
Without repose or rest,
Such is my terrible fate,
A prisoner distressed!"
Later to the silkworm
He asked in a low tone,
"How in your cursed prison
Can you work, little worm?"
And the insect answered him:

"My work goes gladly by
For soon you will see me changed
Into a butterfly!"

As we have observed, those writers (good or bad, famous or not) who contributed to the weekly made their voices—or the voices of those who would inspire the cigar makers to continue their education—heard. After all, as the above-quoted poem shows, the poet utilizes the time-honored method of using entertainment to teach.

The editors of *La Aurora* thought that the reading aloud of literature, more than of politics, would help the workers learn. For that reason, J. de J. Márquez wrote in an article entitled "El porvenir de la literatura" (*La Aurora*, May 6, 1866):

> We should all work for the good of this island, and seek peace through study. We should take an untiring interest in schools and libraries, in cultural associations and reading in workshops, so that our children might gather the fruit and praise the memories of their fathers and mothers before them, for they knew how to show them the way to enlightenment, of which the happiness of the people and the greatest guarantee of the security of governments are made. *La Aurora* has not addressed politics, much less the politics of this country, nor does it intend to, in order to do battle against its adversaries; it needs not be political to call for the abolition of bullfighting and cockfighting and monopolies and all that goes against the order of progress; without becoming involved in politics, it shall constantly defend the enlightenment of the workers, for the best defense one can provide his brother is the means by which he can educate himself.

Without exception, the rejection of bullfighting, cockfighting, billiards, and dancing becomes an obvious conclusion to be drawn from those who contributed to the weekly newspaper. In an article signed by "R," the writer says: "We wholeheartedly abhor cockfighting; that event where the worker leaves the daily wage he has earned so laboriously and which should be for his family's sustenance" (*La Aurora*, December 16, 1866).

Writers produced a number of poems, and what stands out is that through literature they took the opportunity to educate, to "illustrate." Consider the following poem by Torroella (*La Aurora*, December 17, 1865):

PROPRIETORS AND FARMERS
You are wrong to complain

Of your luck, Genaro,
For thorns you will harvest
When brambles you sow. . . .
So when each day you see
Your dark misfortunes grow,
With monte and cockfights
You would repair your woes.
And not succeeding there
With the sweat of your brow
Your tears bitterly flow
Into the fields you plow.

Monte bank, as we know, was a popular card game. This text is not unusual; frequently, people wrote about total repudiation of that sort of activity. It was thought that reading aloud in the workshops would eventually create in the workers the habit of studying. For that reason, Antonio López Prieto wrote: "Workers! Poetry, the precious daughter of sentiment, infuses us with the purest abundance of morality, honor, and virtue. Reading at home in the evening, or on holidays, which many waste on billiards, cockfights, and dances, would be much more beneficial, and one would acquire new knowledge of the nature of the works without even noticing" (*La Aurora*, July 22, 1866). In short, by literature's being read aloud, the weekly paper's writers not only instructed the workers, but also inspired them to continue their studies.

The positive impact generated by reading aloud in workshops not only began to transform the habits of the cigar workers with regard to studying, but also served as an impetus to open schools for them; in addition, libraries remained open in the evenings so that patrons could go there after their workday had ended. The writers in *La Aurora* were aware of their pedagogical task via reading aloud, and, bearing in mind that what they wrote would be heard by the masses, they wrote not only in exquisitely poetic prose, but also in a style that merited being read aloud (*La Aurora*, June 17, 1866; original emphasis):

> Indeed, when we, from the corner of a cigar workshop, rise to the pinnacle of publicity, we leave behind our horizons, which are overcast with the clouds of an unnamed darkness. . . . As poets of greater or lesser merit, we have taken up the trumpet of civilization and called our peers into the edifice of intelligence that they might bring forth and polish their ideas in the crucible of the new era: we have shown them the easiest way to reach the marketplace of great ideas. . . . As writers, *inexperienced in journalism*, we have always strived

to show them work as the only possible source of happiness here on earth, and as the only way to guarantee order and peace, by causing them to understand and appreciate the value of education along with the honor and virtue of the working man, and instilling in their minds the maxims of civic worth and morality that are so exalted by the human heart. In this regard, we believe we have also advanced somewhat, or at least we have endeavored to advance.

This optimistic view of the effects of education was not limited to the teaching of men, but, rather, also extended to women. Luis de Abrisqueta wrote that women were the victims of "terrible suffering," because they were "condemned to work without respite at a mindless, monotonous task." And he expanded on his thought by emphasizing that the only way for a woman to free herself was through education, "because locked as she is in the narrow, petty circle of worries, slave and most often plaything, subject to the whim of man," she could not advance. Later he added that for "the education and instruction of the poor woman, who has unfortunately been so behind the times until the present in Cuba, today the masters of education work without respite, to attain parity with that which exists in more civilized nations" (*La Aurora*, March 18, 1866). Reading aloud in cigar factories not only underscored the importance of education and encouraged cigar workers, both male and female, to go to school, but also served as their clarion; it kept the entire cigar sector up to date about what was taking place in the city or province.

Reading aloud enabled the listening audience to remain current about private or free classes given, and about the libraries' schedules. In fact, thanks to the support and efforts of the weekly newspaper, an *escuela para artesanos* [school for artisans] was opened in 1866. It is important to add here that, little by little, the weekly paper stimulated the organization of labor unions and convinced craftspeople to found a variety of *sociedades* for workers in the different fields. As a result, *La Aurora* was read aloud not only in cigar factories, but also in several associations established across the country, where the listening audiences were not exclusively from the cigar sector.

Using literature as a point of departure and as a way to pique the reader's interest, it was argued that education was a necessity. In an article titled "Instrucción," the author says (*La Aurora*, May 27, 1866):

We have come to the realm of publication with the sole notion of being useful to our peers in the area of literature. We cannot fail to advise them to abandon all spheres that do not tend toward morality, order, and study; they should attend during the early hours of the evening reading rooms, libraries, and night classes that are being established with such great success in several parts of this city . . . Let us open the books, let each of you plan your curriculum of study and continue, continue to move forward, fearing not whatever might befall you on your way.

But what was to be read in libraries or reading rooms? In the article "Huellas de progreso," signed by A. G. y C., the writer advises young people to study Newton, Archimedes, Pascal, and Galileo, because, thanks to science, the world had progressed. Likewise, he emphasizes the importance of studying literature (*La Aurora*, February 4, 1866):

> A course of study that is also very important and that should be attended with the utmost preference is that of literature: he who is not versed in this part of the language which he speaks, reads, and writes will not be able to enjoy the pleasure of those who excel in a text, will never be able to distinguish an elegant, correct sentence from one that is not. Literature is no doubt the continuation of grammar, and he who is ignorant of the latter can only poorly know the former; it is clear, then, that to be able to read well and to find pleasure in reading, one must know these two important branches of human knowledge.

Therefore, by way of reading with the voice of the *lector* as intermediary, the workers had the opportunity to work, be entertained, and learn at the same time. Without a doubt, reading successfully promoted the education of thousands of artisans and likewise convinced them or their families to attend the new schools that were "private" but free, as they had been founded by the cigar workers themselves. There was also an increase in the number of patrons of the various public libraries, which proves that reading aloud convinced the workers to read to themselves.

But that is not all. It is highly likely that the cigar workers went home and told their families about the texts they had heard during the day. Communication was much more intimate and pleasant in the sphere of the home, because people were accustomed to sitting around a table and listening to someone read the newspaper and then discussing the news or a serialized novel published in the newspaper.

But within circles that included the illiterate, people were used to listening to the voice of a *lector* from the neighborhood or town. With this in mind, we can virtually confirm that the reading that was heard in cigar factories spread to spaces beyond the workplace. In other words, reading aloud was limitless, as it served to educate, entertain, convince, and inform, a function that only many decades later would be performed by the radio.

At its beginnings, reading aloud in cigar factories was like an open book, like a novel whose plot was too good to be believed. In only six months, the practice became established in dozens of factories and encouraged the opening of schools and libraries; furthermore, it laid the groundwork for organized labor and increased cigar production. But as in all good stories, reading also had its antagonists, who not only spied on it and made threats against it, but who also organized a campaign of persecution against it.

THE STRUGGLE FOR READING ALOUD AND ITS BANNING

From its inception in 1865 through the end of the nineteenth century, reading aloud was threatened by antagonistic factions that objected to the practice for a variety of reasons. On one hand, it was believed that reading would distract the cigar workers from their work, or that it would create commotion in the workshop. On the other, there was great fear of educating the masses and awakening in them critical and civic awareness. From the beginning, *La Aurora* denounced factory owners who would not allow reading in their workshops (January 23, 1866):

> We cannot fathom, no matter how hard we try, what disadvantage there might be for an establishment that employs one hundred or more persons to have one of them read aloud while the others work, especially when those who reap the benefits are the very ones who compensate the *lector* for his labors, making it unnecessary for the shop's owner to have any involvement at all. . . . We shall conclude by asking, requesting, as you may wish, that those esteemed proprietors who deny permission to have reading in their factories emerge from the error in which they are engulfed and concede to those who have helped them to amass their wealth the authorization they ask of them, and they will certainly receive not only our gratitude but that, as well, of everyone.

In another article, the editors denounced the fact that owner of El Designio Cigar Factory had told his employees that "shops were for working and not for reading, and platforms were for lyceums and not for cigar factories" (February 11, 1866).

By publishing statements such as these, the newspaper put ever-increasing pressure on owners to incorporate reading aloud. On April 1, 1866, one journalist wrote: "There is no plan to establish reading pulpits in D. Julián Álvarez' factories. Can it be that those establishments are advancing at a snail's pace?"

Criticism of reading was fashionable, and it was in the press that these conflicts were especially evident. An article appeared on the editorial page in defense of reading to the workers (April 1, 1866): a right that had been criticized in the newspaper *El Ajiaco*. The editor of *La Aurora* responded: "[The writer] has not observed the good order that reigns in the workshops when it is time for reading. . . . What would *El Ajiaco* have the workers do? Are they by any chance attempting to direct them toward bullrings and cockfights as the only establishments worthy of their station? Well, they are deceiving themselves miserably if they think so, and they do wrong to mock a class that is so handy and beneficial and that is endeavoring to improve itself."

As we will see, however, criticism of reading in workshops was not limited to words. Spanish painter Víctor Patricio Landaluze drew for the newspaper *Don Junípero* a series of caricatures whose topics were based on the readings in the cigar factories. To cite a few examples, on May 6, 1866, two scenes appeared in that newspaper. At the top of the cartoon was the profile of a *lector* with unkempt hair, his clothing in tatters, and seated on a platform. In his left hand there is a book, *Los girondinos*. As he reads furiously, his right hand is made into a fist and pounds on the platform. Facing the platform is a group of cigar workers dressed much like the *lector*. They look riled up, or perhaps even scared, with their mouths open and their hands raised skyward. The title of the caricature is "Lecturas que entusiasman." It goes without saying that the goal of caricature is to ridicule, to parody, or to criticize. Therefore, the drawing is to be read on two basic levels: reading aloud in workshops was both scoffed at and accused of being a tool for distraction.

I must reiterate here that reading aloud, far from causing fights and uproar, encouraged discipline in the workshops. In fact, on April 8, 1866, a month before Landaluze published his caricatures, J. de J. M. made the following observation: "The order kept by the cigar workers in shops where platforms have been installed and where no sound is heard save that the voice of the *lector*, so as to take nothing away from their work, is the most obvious proof of how reading leads to enlightenment; these men, the greater part of whose day is occupied by their labors that deprive them even of the time needed to read a newspaper, have given us to understand that man can work without neglecting his studies."

Reading aloud encouraged discipline in workshops for the obvious reason that the workers had to remain silent while the reading was going on. From the inception of reading, the subject matter varied; serialized novels from newspapers, books on history and on other cultural topics, and news items from newspapers were read. The variety of reading material always assured a loyal and attentive audience. Therefore, Landaluze's criticism through his caricatures ultimately revealed any conservatives' apprehension about reading aloud. Fear of educating the masses and creating political awareness has always been deep-rooted in those who have wielded power and have opposed the social and educational advancement of workers. This fear, as we shall see, was justified.

Another caricature worthy of mention appeared the same day, that is, May 6, 1866. Its title was "Lectura que aprovecha" and featured a member of the Civil Guard sitting on the platform, reading "Bando de policía." This ostensible *lector* appears to be angry and very serious, having the customary look of a policeman giving orders to his subordinates. Before him is a row of five cigar makers at their workbenches rolling cigars, with their backs to the purported *lector*. The cigar workers look sad, resigned, and disillusioned.

Humiliated by Landaluze's criticism of reading in cigar factories, the editors of *La Aurora* hurried to publish the following in its defense (May 13, 1866; original emphasis):

> A number of cigar makers have approached us rightfully to register complaints against the issue of two Sundays ago of the newspaper *D. Junípero*, in which someone had the bright idea of caricaturing *Reading in Workshops*, expressing in the drawing titled *Lectura que aprovecha* things that are not true. What is all this, then! *D. Junípero* has jumped into the fray of those who wag their fingers at the good the cigar workers promote? And since we have mentioned *D. Junípero*, it occurs to us that, in its early days, this jocular weekly did not seem to us as much in favor of backwardness as it does at present. What was it that got into our colleague to cause him to have undergone such a fearsome change in his nature?

As these ideological conflicts became publicly known, reading aloud continued to generate awareness among the artisans, and the threat that the cigar sector would create groups antagonistic toward the colonial regime became more and more obvious. For example, *Diario de la Marina*, an extremely important newspaper and bitter foe of *La Aurora* and, by association, of *El Siglo*, made known its opposition to the practice of reading aloud. *La Aurora* published the following (March 18, 1866): "*Diario de la Marina* has openly declared its opposition to reading in workshops. We who have disseminated the idea are happy about this, for its opposition conclusively proves it to be a positive entity." Without a doubt, reading continued to gain popular momentum in spite of attacks and, at the same time, improved the educational, cultural, and political standards of the workers.

Reading aloud in cigar factories became a real threat to the colonial government and factory owners, who treated workers unfairly. *La Aurora* repeatedly denounced abuses by the owners, talked of the advancement of reading, and was a catalyst for labor unions or new artisans' associations, although not all of them were associated with the cigar sector. However, reading aloud was not officially banned until the captain general of Cuba wrote a document addressed to the police commander that forbade "distracting workers in cigar factories, workshops, and all other manner of establishments by the reading of books and newspapers, or discussions having no bearing on the tasks said workers undertake."[41] The captain general ordered police officers and factory foremen to monitor workshops so that reading aloud could not take place. The document indicated that the reason for the ban was that the selection of works to be read caused arguments among the workers, and that the workers were "feebleminded" and therefore unable to "judge" appropriately the works to which they listened. Strangely enough, although the document proscribed reading, one of its clauses advised cigar workers to devote themselves to Christian doctrine and "the lessons that taught one how to comport oneself with moderation and courtesy, as well as directing one to treatises written on the professions and the arts."[42] It is obvious that the ban on reading aloud had to do with the fear of some bosses and government officials when they saw that the working classes were achieving political awareness and a higher cultural standard.

Weeks after the practice of reading aloud had been stopped in cigar factories, those who had banned it became aware of its success, for it had not only spread to the farthest reaches of the island, but it had also been carried to farms and had been firmly established in leaf-stripping plants and selection facilities. On June 7, 1866, Francisco Lersundi, who was then a lieutenant general and captain general of Cuba, issued a bulletin to governors and lieutenant governors banning all gatherings that involved reading aloud. He emphasized in the bulletin that the reading aloud of books and newspapers in cigar factories and in the inland portions of Cuba led to "exaggerated notions," which resulted in disturbances to "public orderliness," arguments, "unruly scenes, and brawls."

As I have indicated, far from inciting unruly scenes, reading aloud was nothing less than an instrument of discipline; it encouraged silence among the workers, and thus production levels increased. The issue was purely political. The bulletin issued by Lersundi stemmed from the fear that large groups of workers might congregate and protest in favor of their labor, political, or social rights. The tone of the bulletin's language conveys a sense of concern and alarm:

But since the most harmful [readings] spread very quickly, and at times the watchfulness of the authorities is not sufficient to thwart their dissemination, they filter down to the simple folk on farms in the countryside, in workshops, and in all manner of establishments in a number of parts of the island. This produces, along with reading of political newspapers in the manner described herein, evils that I must need remedy. Thus, be forewarned that it is your solemn responsibility by all means at your disposal to endeavor, both in the countryside and in the towns, to eradicate such evils if they exist and not to consent in any case henceforth to any gathering whose goals and tendencies are well known.[43]

Although its opponents banned reading aloud in workshops in the country and in the cities, the "voice" of *La Aurora* stayed alive, because the weekly newspaper continued to be published. The editors showed how important reading was in the present and had been in the past, and how much they hoped it would be reestablished. The editorial page on Sunday, June 1, 1866, stated:

The order and good morals observed by our cigar makers in the work-shops, and the enthusiasm for learning, are these not obvious proof that we are advancing? . . . Just go into a workshop that employs two hundred and you will be astonished to observe the utmost order, you will see that all are encouraged by a common goal: to fulfill their obligations. . . . Study has become a habit among them; today they leave behind the cockfight in order to read a newspaper or book; now they scorn the bullring; today it is the the-ater, the library, and the centers of good association where they are seen in constant attendance.

As we can easily observe, *La Aurora* struggled against all sorts of odds to achieve its goals. On one hand, it defended reading aloud by extolling the transformation and progress it had brought about among the workers; on the other hand, it persuaded workers to continue to learn, in spite of the fact that they no longer heard the voice of the *lector* on the platform.

THE FIRST RESURRECTION OF READING
AND THE RUMBLINGS OF WAR

Reading was banned in 1866, and it was not until the beginning of 1868 that it began to be gradually reestablished in the more important factories in Cuba. At the same time, on Sunday, May 3, 1868, *La Aurora* changed its subtitle to *Semanario de Ciencias, Literatura y Crítica*. A sort of manifesto written by Saturnino Martínez appeared on page 1:

> [*La Aurora*], ever willing to listen and show respect, will welcome as many suggestions as are made, endeavoring never to skew the path of noble principles. And as the majority of its subscribers shall no doubt be of the working classes, as it is they who are most familiar with the editorial staff, who will make every effort to be of use to the workers and who will strive to the extent to which they are permitted, to bear in mind the workers' moral and material betterment, and help develop their intellectual faculties. . . . Thus it falls to us, as is well known by those who have made our acquaintance and who are familiar with our thoughts, from whence we came and where we are going: they also know very well that our newspaper covers science, literature, and criticism, and we shall do whatever we can to be of use to everyone, never allowing ourselves to be driven back by the storms that continually assault discussion arenas, and we shall be ever firm in the purpose of maintaining those moral principles endemic to us.

The report is nothing short of a protest gesture directed at the adversaries of reading aloud. Once again, and especially on this occasion, the editor, cigar maker, and leader took the point of departure that the "sciences, literature, and criticism" were a pedagogical tool for the working class. Note the subtle underscoring that reading aloud, far from turning workshops into "discussion arenas" of a political nature, instead favored the development of the "intellectual faculties" of the workers. Without a doubt, the reading of any text creates a critical awareness in the reader or listener, but what is interesting here is that, more than anything else, literature was the means by which thought was stimulated.

In the same issue of *La Aurora*, Saturnino Martínez published an eloquent dramatic poem intended this time not for the crafters of cigars but for the typesetters. The poem's publication is symbolic; it implies that reading aloud not only had taken place within the realm of the cigar factory, but also had spread to workers in other fields:

> To the Organization of Typesetters of Havana
> . . . Now opens the horizon of the idea,
> Error's domain by time is proven wrong
> Now light illumines spaces far and near
> And mortal eyes observe now in progress
> Each town, an oasis of happiness here,

Each nation a field of hopefulness,
Each man a foundation, and each arm strong
A sturdy column which, powerful, founds
For every noble act a monument,
A new platform in each and every town,
A temple in each home to sentiment
Its altar by enthusiasm fired,
And in each human heart by good inspired
A pedestal of love of thought's ascent.
There dawns for all the workers a new day
Oh, young typesetters!
You are the ones who soon will make your way
And from misfortune's grasp will steal away
The triumphant wreath of the conqueror.

The poem was certainly written to be read aloud first at the Sociedad de Cajistas [Typesetter's Organization]. As I noted elsewhere, the goal of the *sociedades* was to protect workers in case of illness, but most of all, they were educational and social centers. Therefore, by alluding to "the platform," the poetic voice is extolling the importance of reading as a pedagogical tool.

Likewise, from the tone of the poem there arises a call that is plaintive yet angry, that the young typesetters continue their labors, that they give order to letters so that words can be printed, then read aloud and heard. It is indubitable that this poetic voice knew that the written or spoken word would someday become the weapon and unique instrument of defense for the working classes. He implores: "You are the ones who soon will make your way / And from misfortune's grasp will steal away / The triumphant wreath of the conqueror." Symbolically, the typesetters are asked to fight and "soon make [their] way" through their work, so that the word may continue to be printed and eventually read and heard, starting from that golden "temple" called the workshop, or society itself.

In May of 1868, the month of publication of this poem, the rumblings of what came to be called the Ten Years' War could already be heard. Saturnino Martínez accurately foretold the catastrophes of the war and, once again, the interruption of reading aloud in workshops. The war left horrors in its wake, and reading aloud in cigar factories suffered as a consequence. The voice of the *lector* was not heard again for ten years.

As I have shown, with the exception of *La Aurora* and the other newspapers of the day, as well as the few texts we have been able to recover, it is difficult to make a comprehensive study of the "library" of what was read aloud, because no one catalogued the texts heard. It is important to note that in Cuba there was a wide circulation of books printed both domestically and abroad. In this rich cultural mix, there was also a proliferation of translations from English, French, Portuguese, Italian, and German. Cuban literary texts were disseminated, reviewed primarily in newspapers, and read aloud not only in the workplace but also in literary circles, lyceums, and cultural associations.

Cuban author Ambrosio Fornet points out that, in the political and social context of the colony, it was impossible for reading in cigar factories "to serve as a channel of distribution of national literary production or its cultural contribution."[44] His statement is correct only to a certain extent, because, as I have tried to show, since its inception, reading aloud has been marked by its diversity. Texts were not differentiated in terms of whether they were Cuban or from other countries, but, rather, they first passed owners' scrutiny based solely on content. As we have seen, *La Aurora* and *El Siglo* published Cuban literature more than that of other countries. To what extent Heredia, Milanés, Plácido, Avellaneda, Zenea, Suárez y Romero, or Villaverde (Cuba's foremost nineteenth-century writers) were heard is unknown. What is known is that until the Ten Years' War, reading aloud in cigar factories expanded the cultural horizon of a very wide sector that was nourished by both Cuban and foreign literatures via the spoken word.

READING BETWEEN THE WARS

The Ten Years' War was spearheaded by a great leader, attorney, and scholar, Carlos Manuel de Céspedes y Castillo. The war's essential goal was to free the island from the Spanish Empire, since, politically, there was oppression (slavery still existed); economically, there was dependence controlled by colonial exploitation; and, socially, there was stagnation caused by the homeland. Massacres, persecution, unjust incarceration, and fear of war caused poor and rich alike—professionals, workers, and country folk—to emigrate.[45] It is estimated that, before 1869, over 100,000 inhabitants had been cast out or had gone into exile.[46] These refugees from the war fled to the African island of Fernando Po, to Spain, Mexico, and, more than anywhere else, to the United States. But thanks to the cigar workers who had to leave Cuba, reading aloud in workshops was established abroad.

Once the Ten Years' War ended in 1878, great efforts were made to restore reading aloud in cigar factories. With the initiative of the Gremio de Obreros del Ramo de Tabaquerías [Cigar Workers' Guild], which was founded the same year, reading aloud resumed, although not immediately.

La Intimidad Factory heard once again two years later, in 1880, the voice of the *lector*.

As had occurred previously, other factories, too, longed for reading; its restoration this time was extremely difficult to bring about. Once more, certain manufacturers felt threatened by the makeup of the guild and also felt that elevating the cultural level of the workers would instill in them political awareness. Saturnino Martínez, who had given up his position as cigar maker for journalism, was still one of the cigar sector's most important labor leaders; he fought to have reading aloud restored in the Partagás Factory in 1882. By 1884, reading aloud had resumed in all the most important factories in Cuba.

The two newspapers that replaced *La Aurora* were *La Razón* and *Periódico de Literatura, Ciencia, Artes, Mercantil, Noticias y Anuncios*, the former published by Saturnino Martínez and the latter by J. de J. Márquez. Both newspapers were intended for workers. There are very few sources regarding what was read aloud from 1884 to 1895, until the beginning of the Spanish-American War. One of the first testimonies that exists of a cigar factory *lector* is found in the memoirs of the Spanish author and ideologue Ramiro de Maeztu. He devoted most of his life to journalism and lived in Spain, Cuba, England, and France until he was shot to death in 1936, at the beginning of the Spanish Civil War. In 1908, he published his experiences as a cigar factory *lector* in Cuba in *La correspondencia de España*:

> In 1893, this reporter was a *lector* in a cigar factory in Havana for a time. While the workers rolled cigars in a large workroom of suffocating atmosphere, the reporter read to them four hours each day, at times, books of social propaganda, at times, plays, at times, novels, at times, philosophical works, and scientific material written in the vernacular. In general, the books to be read were chosen by a Reading Committee, because the cigar workers, not the factory owners, paid for the reading directly, when they received their wages on Wednesdays and Saturdays. The *lector* received whatever they wished to contribute, some, five centavos, others, one peso. Sometimes the committee accepted suggestions from the *lector*. This reporter used to spend a few evenings translating books from foreign languages into Spanish and jotting down words he did not understand in the margins to look up in the dictionary. And thus he recalls having read works by Galdós, by D'Annunzio, by Kipling, by Schopenhauer, by Kropotkin, by Marx, and by Sudermann.[47]

This testimony is extremely important for several reasons. First, it underscores the sui generis specialization of the profession of *lector*. That is, before the Ten Years' War, *lectores* came from among the ranks of the cigar workers themselves and took turns reading to their coworkers, who compensated them for lost working time. But as we can see by way of this example, the *lector* evolved into a person from outside the factory who was recruited to practice his profession as a *lector*. Likewise, the reading schedule had changed, since it was no longer a matter of a half hour, but, rather, in this case, of four hours per day, although how the schedule was broken down is unknown. In other words, it is doubtful that the *lector* would have read four hours straight, because physical conditions would not have permitted him to do so. The workshops were huge, and reading before an audience of four hundred people without a microphone must have been an exhausting task. What is important to us here, however, is that, by 1893, the profession of *lector* had already come into existence, and the *lector* had a set work schedule. As in any profession, the person who devoted himself to reading aloud enjoyed a salary, but as we can see in the testimony, the salary depended on what the cigar workers wanted to contribute: "five centavos or one peso." Although the collection of the salary was determined by a fixed schedule, no doubt, compensation fluctuated each payday, since the *lector* worked in exchange for the cigar workers' contributions. In this sense, the listening audience was the "employer" of the *lector*, and exercised authority over him.

Another new feature of reading in workshops, as Maeztu shows, is the establishment of a Reading Committee. Documentary evidence suggests that the committee was constituted of cigar workers themselves. Therefore, what was to be read or not read was up to the workers. When reading aloud was established in 1865, there were no committees. It is important to recall that, from the beginning, texts were subject to the owners' scrutiny before they could be read aloud. It is quite possible that, even after the establishment of Reading Committees, the pieces selected still had to be reviewed by the owner or a foreman, but at least the *lector* had a voice and a vote, since he had the privilege of recommending works to the committee.

But if we stop for a moment to ponder the significance of being a cigar factory *lector* in this context, we can understand how difficult his profession was from its inception. The *lector* had to read what the committee told him to read, and there was no guarantee that the work to be read would be to the liking of the audience. It is also possible that the *lector* always felt he was being watched by the foreman or the owner, who no doubt listened intently to every word. The *lector* was always, as in the old saying, "between the devil and the deep blue sea," because he was being monitored while he was trying to please his audience.

The texts that were read had been selected by the committee, and we can see from Maeztu's piece that a bit of everything was read aloud. Note how the *lector* alludes to the manner in which he prepared his readings by "translating books from foreign languages," although it is difficult to ascertain whether he really translated entire books, or whether he is referring simply to translating foreign words. In any case, what we have here is a *lector* who prepared in advance before reading, who consulted the dictionary and wrote the meaning of words right in the text. This task had a dual purpose: first, he reviewed how the word was pronounced, and then he prepared himself in advance in case his audience had any questions.

If we continue to analyze Maeztu's story, it is symbolic that the writer alludes to his experience when he reads a literary work:

> One day, when I had only just begun to read, I observed that some listeners stopped working so that they might hear better, and in a few short minutes one could not hear even the clicking of the *chavetas* cutting the ends of the cigars. For the two hours' duration of the reading, there was nary a sound of coughing or rustling. The four hundred men in the room listened, holding their breath all the while. This was in Havana, in the midst of the tropics, and the audience comprised blacks, mulattos, *criollos*, Spaniards; many of them did not even know how to read; others were *ñáñigos*. What work could so intensely move those men? *Hedda Gabler*, Ibsen's wonderful drama. For two hours, those men lived the life of that woman who was too vivacious to suffer respectability and boredom, too much the coward to dare to live a bohemian, uncertain life. . . . Never, not even in Christiania, did Ibsen enjoy a more devoted, reserved audience.[48]

This story suggests that the reading of literary works took up two continuous hours, and if there was reading four hours per day, it is quite possible that literature was given first priority. The diversity of the audience in terms of race, color, and education was no obstacle, because all were members of a community of listeners sharing the enjoyment of reading within a common context. The fact that someone could not read was no barrier to understanding a drama translated from Norwegian into Spanish. It is critical to reiterate here that the cigar sector was the most literate in comparison with all other Cuban artisans at the turn of the century, as more than 90 percent of Havana cigar workers could read and write.[49]

It is no easy matter to listen to a play being read by a single *lector*, because the text would have been written to be acted out by several actors. Anyone who has read or seen an Ibsen play understands that his works deal with psychological problems and often are not easy to read, see, or listen to. Why, then, did this work so captivate the workers? Let us review the plot.

Hedda Gabler marries a history teacher who is writing a book and who aspires to be a university professor. Enter Ejlert Lövborg, historian and her husband's competition. He has just finished writing a manuscript and is interested in the position of history professor. Ejlert carelessly loses his manuscript. Hedda's husband finds it and gives it to her for safekeeping. She destroys the manuscript and advises Ejlert to commit suicide. He does so, with a gun belonging to Hedda's father, General Gabler. The judge learns what has happened and tries to blackmail her. When she finds herself trapped and deprived of her freedom, Hedda also commits suicide.

Ibsen's work is quite profound, and it is not easy to play the role of Hedda if the reader or actor is not willing to put himself in the place of a woman who is being suffocated by the reality surrounding her, or in the place of a prodigious writer (Ejlert) with an indecent past. Needless to say, a play is written to be performed. When one sees the play staged, the stance that the actors take toward Hedda, and the movements and expressions they make play a very important role. Hedda never leaves the stage, and thus we can see that she is completely overwhelmed until the day she takes her own life.

It is a challenge to listen to and visualize *Hedda Gabler* without seeing the play staged; thus, we can deduce that the *lector* was forced to read and dramatize at the same time, since, otherwise, the reading would have been very difficult to understand. Maeztu's testimony is one of the few that allude to reading and its processes in nineteenth-century Cuba, but we continue to wonder what else was read.

Starting in 1872, anarchist ideas began to take root in Cuba because of the efforts of Enrique Roig San Martín and Enrique Messonier, who established the Centro de Instrucción y Recreo [Education and Recreation Center] in Santiago de las Vegas and founded a newspaper, *El Obrero*. Their ideas made an impact in 1885, when the groundwork was laid for the Junta Central de Artesanos [Central Group of Artisans], and especially in 1887, when the newspaper *El Productor* was first published.[50]

In very general terms, it can be said that, owing to these new ideas, the cigar sector began to split into two factions: on one side were the reformists, led by Saturnino Martínez, and on the other, the anarchists, with Roig San Martín as their leader. With regard to reading in cigar factories, pamphlets written by José Llunas, a Catalán revolutionary, as well as works by Kropotkin, Proudhon, Bakunin, and the works Maeztu mentions in his testimony started to be read aloud.

It would be erroneous to think that reading aloud was oriented to strictly political texts. All kinds of works were read from the platform, but since the anarchist ideology was spreading in different parts of the world, especially in Spain, it was also disseminated in Cuba. Starting before the 1870s, Cuban anarchists had been active participants in the Ten Years' War. Anarchist ideology was in vogue in Spain, Russia, the United States, France, and Italy. The ideas of anarchist thinkers and organizers such as Mikhail Bakunin (1814–1876) had begun to filter into labor organizations in those countries. The establishment of the Alianza Revolucionaria Socialista [Revolutionary Socialist Alliance, 1864], the Alianza Democrática Internacional Socialista [International Democratic Socialist Alliance, 1868], and the Declaración de Principios del Anarquismo Europeo [European Anarchist Manifesto], all with the direct, active participation of Bakunin, influenced the development of Cuban anarchism.[51] This anarchism, which had already assimilated the ideas and concepts of organized labor elucidated by Pierre Joseph Proudhon (1809–1865), paved the way for the clearer and more precise ideas of Bakunin. With him, Cuban workers set out on a nearly irreversible path toward class consciousness. But although texts with anarchist leanings were read in cigar factories, they made up only part of a vast body of texts that were read aloud.

It would not be long until the Spanish-American War broke out, that is, Cuba's second and final war of independence (1895–1898); thus, cigar workers who favored the revolutionary cause saw this as their opportunity to use the platform of the *lector* as a space in which to reveal their separatist ideas. From the platform they also disseminated information about events unfolding in the United States, and, most of all, they listened intently to talk of the work being done by José Martí and the revolutionary clubs that were made up entirely of cigar workers who had fled the country. In theory, the reading of political texts was banned, especially any that opposed the colonial regime. Still, and even under the scrutiny of the factory foremen, the voice of the *lector* was heard reading uniquely subversive texts. Let us not forget that the cigar workers themselves were the ones who paid the *lector*, and the Reading Committee, on behalf of the cigar workers, chose the texts that were to be read. Therefore, the *lector* essentially read what his audience wanted to hear, whether that meant literary, political, or any other type of text. The audience had the last word.

Reading aloud again came under threat when the Spanish-American War broke out in 1895. The platform of the *lector* was once again viewed with suspicion, as from it revolutionary subject matter could quickly be disseminated to vast multitudes. On June 10, 1896, the *Diario de la Marina* published a memorandum signed by regional and civil governor José Porrúa:

In response to the various complaints received by this government about the difficulties occasioned by public readings that are being confirmed in places occupied by workers in factories and workshops.—In accordance with that which is set forth in Article 31 of Act 23, dated April 23, 1870, and in exercise of the powers therein vested in me, I have resolved to ban from this day forward the public reading of newspapers, books, and pamphlets in factories and workshops, with the owners being the primary parties responsible for ensuring prompt compliance with this order.

This time, the ban on reading was not taken lightly, as both cigar workers and *lectores* united to protest the governor's decision. Their displeasure was reported in newspapers, and they threatened owners with a strike until reading aloud was resumed. For the first time in history, the factory workers were united, thanks specifically to the establishment of organized labor. For example, the owners knew that a strike would do them severe damage, so they united to ask the governor to repeal the ban on reading aloud in order to ward off altercations. We must not forget that Cuba was in the middle of a war, and the last thing the concerned parties wanted was to start a new conflict.

At that time, well-known author Martín Morúa Delgado devoted part of his time to reading in the Villar y Villar Cigar Factory, and on behalf of the rest of Havana's *lectores*, he wrote an article he published in the newspaper *La Discusión*.[52] Under pressure from a multitude of cigar workers, the industrial sector, *lectores* and the press, Gov. José Porrúa cooperated and repealed the law on the condition that factory owners would not permit the reading of any revolutionary material. With that promise, reading aloud was reestablished gradually in several factories after having been banned for two weeks. Amid threats, cannon fire, and explosions, the *lector* remained steadfastly on his platform and thus survived the war.

THE TURN OF THE CENTURY: HOPE AND PROMISE

In spite of all the difficulties, by the turn of the century, reading aloud was an institution that made manifest its perseverance and success throughout the Spanish-American War. As we have seen, the practice of public reading aloud in Cuba took place both in cigar factories and aristocratic and scholarly circles. Newspapers as well as literary, historical, political, and scientific texts were heard in private and home settings as well as in public cultural and recreational spaces and the workplace. Although it is true that there were illiterate workers in the cigar sector, reading aloud was established in hopes of informing, educating, and continuing to broaden cultural horizons, even of those who were literate.

Likewise, reading aloud encouraged the workers to found labor associations. When the vast cigar sector was educated by way of reading aloud, a civic conscience was created, which was why the cigar workers fought for both their labor and their political rights. Reading was always under scrutiny because it represented a threat to the colonizing government.

But in spite of its having been banned several times, reading aloud rose like a phoenix reborn from its own ashes. The institution of reading aloud in workshops represented the resumption of a cultural practice that had been carried out for centuries in public squares and cultural associations, where reading aloud before a group of listeners was the rule and not the exception. Just when this type of reading had begun to disappear, the institution emerged in cigar factories and revived preindustrial, nostalgic times long past that prepared artisans to become educated for the future. Reading aloud among the artisan classes was a necessary practice and a key contribution to the cultural evolution of what was then colonial Cuba.

The nineteenth century was drawing to a close, and reading had survived two wars and a repressive government. A new century was dawning and Cuba was being reborn as an independent country. The platform of the *lector* promised nothing short of renewed hope.

TWO

From Cuba to Spain

Reading Aloud in Emilia Pardo Bazán's La Tribuna

———⊢▦▦⊣———

I

When Amparo, the protagonist of the novel *La Tribuna* (The Tribune of the People, 1882), by prolific Spanish writer Emilia Pardo Bazán, showed up for work for the first time at the cigar factory, there was little she was capable of producing.[1] But "it did no good to hurry," the narrator says, since, in order to make cigars,

> it was first necessary to stretch out the outer wrapping, the skin of the cigar, with the greatest of care on top of the rolling board; then to cut it with a semicircular knife, drawing a curve with an inclination of fifteen millimeters over the center of the leaf so that it would fit exactly around the cigar. This cigar wrapper required a wide, dry, fine leaf, the most select, just as the dermis of the cigar, the wrapper around the filler, allowed for a leaf of inferior quality; this was also true for the filling or the *inner filler*. But by far the most essential and difficult part was putting the finishing touches on the cigar, to form the tip with a skillful twist of the tip of the thumb and with a spatula dipped in liquid gum, and then clipping off the end with a swift snip of the scissors. A sharp tip, a somewhat oblong body, a wrapper rolled into an elegant spiral, the filler never pressed together so tight as to prevent the smoke from passing through, or so loosely packed that the cigar became wrinkled when it got dry: these are the characteristics of a quality cigar.[2]

Emilia Pardo Bazán's novel revolves around the life of Amparo, a *cigarrera*, or cigar maker, at La Granera Factory, in what had been the granary in the fictional town of Marineda. It portrays the political events that took place between the time of what was called the September Revolution of 1868 and the establishment of the first Republic, which took place in February of 1873.

Through Amparo's story, the text shows the political events, ideological context, and attitudes and clashes between moderates and those who supported the establishment of the Republic. Most of the cigar workers were on the side of the Republic, of advanced ideas and progress. But what is most intriguing is that Amparo was not only a cigar maker, but also a cigar factory *lectora*.

La Tribuna was published in 1882, when there were eleven cigar factories Spain. The tradition of cigar making in Spain began at the beginning of the eighteenth century, at the same time as in Cuba (prior to that time, the largest, most important tobacco factory, which was in Seville, produced only powdered tobacco).[3]

By the end of the eighteenth century, tobacco consumption had risen significantly; therefore, the way in which factories operated had to change. The making of tobacco powder was a mechanical task: heavy grinders were required, along with teams of horses to keep them in motion. There were mill foremen and strong workers in factories who undertook the task of kneading the tobacco in leaf-stripping and leaf-kneading troughs.[4] In contrast, all that was necessary to make cigars, that is, Cuban-style cigars, was the cigar workers' hands.

But as opposed to how things were done in Cuba, in Spain, female personnel were recruited to do that work. Even prior to the nineteenth century, cigars had begun to be rolled exclusively by female employees in the Cádiz Factory. Women were very productive workers; therefore, by the beginning of the nineteenth century, new cigar factories had begun to spring up, such as those in Alicante, Santander, Gijón, Bilbao, Madrid, and La Coruña. *The Tribune of the People* is based on La Palloza Factory, built circa 1820 in La Coruña.

The new factories no longer had the semifeudal quality of the old factory in Seville (which was renovated at the end of the eighteenth century). The old factory was like a fortified castle; there were a chapel and a jail on the grounds. Four soldiers with heavy bayonets guarded the entrance. The factory was known for its disciplinary code, and what is most interesting is that, as I have stated previously and based on Michel Foucault's study, strict discipline in the workplace and in prisons was based on the monastic model. In the renowned work *Carmen* (1847), by Prosper Mérimée (later immortalized by Bizet in 1875 in the opera of the same name), José Lizarrabengoa, a Basque who was a corporal in the army, "was put on guard at the tobacco manufactory of Seville," and thus he meets Carmen, who was a cigar roller for a short time in the factory. He falls in love with her.[5]

The factory introduced to us by the novelist is, no doubt, the modernized factory in Seville, because there is no longer a chapel or a jail on the grounds, and most of the personnel are female. In the novel, Carmen has a fight with another cigar maker, and "on that, criss-cross, she began, with the knife she used for cutting the cigars, to slash a St. Andrew's cross on the woman's face."[6] The Basque, José Lizarrabengoa, upon discovering evidence that Carmen has attacked the other cigar worker, says:

> The case was perfectly clear. I seized Carmen by the arm.
>
> "Sister," I said politely, "you must come with me."
>
> She darted a look of recognition at me, but she said resignedly: "Let us go then. Where is my mantilla?"
>
> She put it over her head in such a fashion as only to permit her fine eyes to be seen, and followed my two men as quiet as a lamb. When we reached the guard-house, the quarter-master said the case was a serious one, and that he must send the culprit to prison.[7]

Once outside the factory and on the way to jail, Carmen, cigar roller and gypsy, tricks the Basque by telling him that she is also Basque. She speaks to him in Basque, and in an alley in Seville, she turns around, punches him, and flees, and no one is able to catch her.

Factories in nineteenth-century Spain recruited mainly female personnel, which allowed thousands of women to gain autonomy and independence, because, before becoming *cigarreras*, many of them earned their pay by making lace or doing embroidery at home. Factory work allowed those women to earn as much as they could, since, as in Cuba, cigar making was paid as piecework. Securing employment at a factory was a very important step for women, since it practically assured their future and that of their daughters, as regulations required that priority in recruitment be given to cigar workers' daughters.[8]

In *The Tribune of the People*, the main character's mother has been a cigar maker for thirty years until, one winter night, she becomes permanently paralyzed. Her wish has always been that her daughter, Amparo, become a cigar maker, as she is a precocious child who has no interest in sewing, but, rather, takes pleasure only in strolling along the city streets. When asked at a party if she knows how to make lace, Amparo retorts: "Oh, they never *learned* [taught] me."[9] Therefore, Amparo symbolizes a break with tradition, because she does not want to earn a living making lace, as many generations before her have done.

In addition, she has another way of making money, by reading aloud to others: she reads the newspaper *La Soberanía Nacional* to the barber who lives across the street from her. The barber is a cultured person, as he is "well read and knowledgeable, and very pretentious."[10]

Amparo has gone to school for only a couple of years, as have most women in Marineda, but she is as proud as always when she says: "I know how to read very well and I write fairly well too. I went to school and the teacher said there was nobody like me."[11] During the nineteenth century in Spain, as well as in Cuba, it was not necessary to know how to read and write to be able to find work at a factory; the only requirement was that new workers behave well. In Amparo's case, knowing how to read and write well works in her favor, because when she starts to work at the factory, her coworkers ask her to read to them.

Reading aloud in cigar factories was an institution transplanted from Cuba to Spain, as I have noted. As José Pérez Vidal puts it: "This teaching institution, that is, reading, first took root in the factories of the northern part of the peninsula: La Coruña, San Sebastián, etc. And, no doubt, it was imported from the factories of Cuba."[12] As I have mentioned, the time frame of *The Tribune of the People* spans the years 1868 through 1873 in Spain. In Cuba, when the Ten Years' War broke out, also in 1868, thousands of people had to flee into exile, and many of them set out for Spain. Therefore, it is quite possible that in Spain reading aloud was established following the models implemented in what was then a colony.

There are several allusions to Cuba in the novel, beginning with the obvious fact that most of the tobacco was imported from the island. But there is more: Rosendo, the main character's father, lived in Cuba, where he served in the Spanish army. Although once back in Marineda, he was a simple *barquillero*, or pastry cone vendor, his years in Cuba had changed him significantly. Also, there are allusions to the steamers that sail to Havana and to Cuban music. For example, *habaneras* are listened to passionately in the literary circles of the wealthy and in the cigar factory on Shrove Tuesday. Ultimately, the city of Marineda becomes saturated with Cuban culture.

La Granera, the factory portrayed in the novel, is quite similar to La Palloza, the cigar factory in La Coruña. The building was once the Arsenal de la Palloza and was situated on the outskirts of the city. But what is most interesting is that most factories in Spain are located in places that once were arsenals, military barracks, or convents—institutions where discipline prevails.[13] As I have stated, in jails, military barracks, workshops, and factories alike, the monastic model was imitated with regard to firm rules and especially to strict schedules. Therefore, it is symbolic that when Amparo approaches the factory on her first day of work, she has the uncanny feeling that she is nearing a place that is not only imposing, but also sacred and to which entrance is prohibited:

> As she ruminated in this way, she crossed the roadway and found herself in the courtyard of the Factory, the former granary. The girl was overcome by a feeling of respect. The very size of the building compensated for its antiquity and its inelegant appearance, and for Amparo, accustomed to venerating the Factory since her most tender years, those walls assumed a halo of majesty, and a mysterious power dwelled within its confines, the State, and it would undoubtedly be a waste of time to fight against it, a power that demanded blind obedience and reached out everywhere and dominated everyone. The adolescent who steps into the classroom for the first time must feel something akin to what Amparo felt.[14]

The power that is exerted is reflected not only in the architecture of the building, which is isolated and secured by enormous walls, but also by the fact that the factory is government owned, which entails an even higher authority that demands greater subordination. In fact, factories in Spain were government property, not owned by private businessmen, as was the case in Cuba.

Amparo starts to roll cigars in the "*cigarros comunes*" workshop, in other words, where cigars are made with wrappers and filler that are not Cuban. The workshop is located on the first floor, and most of the cigar workers there are mothers.

It is interesting that the workshops in Spanish factories were not set up like those in Cuba. In Spain, workshop personnel were divided into "*ranchos*" [groups] of six to eight cigar workers who worked at a shared rectangular workbench. This allowed them to have coworkers on either side of them, and it was possible for them to see one another's faces. Each *rancho* had an "*ama*" [supervisor] who was chosen based on the perfection of her work. Each workshop was managed by a "*maestra*" [forewoman], who was in charge of both technical order and discipline. The *maestra* taught the new cigar workers and kept up with the quality control of finished cigars.[15]

In each workshop, as was the case in Cuba, there were hundreds of cigar rollers; nevertheless, Spanish factories operated with thousands of employees, as in the fictional factory portrayed by Pardo Bazán, where four thousand women worked. "There were one or two readers in every workshop; their companions would guarantee them the time they lost, and so things moved ahead," says the narrator.[16] Therefore, the practice of reading aloud began in Spain just as it had in Cuba: the cigar workers themselves were the ones who read to their coworkers.

Amparo starts to work at the factory just when the September Revolution of 1868 breaks out. Pardo Bazán presents political ideas in counterpoint in this way: "It was readily evident that the countryside and the cities in the interior were inclined to favor monarchic tradition, while the manufacturing and commercial centers of population, and the seaports, acclaimed the republic."[17] Marineda is located on the coast of Cantabria, and, as a result, there are an abundance of proclamations, clubs, juntas, committees, demonstrations, and newspapers. In the cigar factory, people promote the future Republic, and the workers are anxious to hear the latest news. It is in this context that Amparo's companions ask her to read newspapers to them. "Amparo was among the most esteemed, on account of the feeling she put into her reading," says the narrator, since "she had already acquired the habit of reading aloud, having practiced it so many times at the barbershop."[18]

We can conclude that there are at least two reading shifts in the novel: one in the morning and another around four o'clock in the afternoon. The afternoon shift is reserved exclusively for political readings. In general, the newspapers that the audience wants to hear are read, so the listening community makes the selection. Amparo reads local newspapers and those from Madrid, but the cigar workers prefer the former. The narrator says: "Naturally, the local papers tended to have an exaggerated style and overdid their depictions; their titles were generally of this sort: *The Federal Guardian*, organ of the republican Federal-Unionist democracy, or *The Representative of Democratic Youth*, or *The Redemptive Beacon of Free People*."[19] It is logical to conclude that the audience is attentive but not very refined. This becomes especially obvious when the "court press from the capital" is read; it is not the audience's favorite, although they are fascinated by Castelar's speeches. The *cigarreras* do not really understand the content of the articles, but they love the style:

> So many pretty words and how nicely one connected with another! They seemed to be poetry. It's true that the greater part of them were difficult to understand and that such strange names were dancing there that only that devil of an Amparo was able to read them fluently, but it made no difference: because as for being really pretty, all that was very pretty. And everyone readily concluded that the substance of the speech was in favor of the people and against the tyrants, and so all the rest was to be taken to be adornment, like a delicate flourish.[20]

The audience likes how these speeches sound, because they have a good *lectora* and speeches are written to be read aloud, not to oneself.

The way in which Amparo does her reading has a great impact on her audience. Her reading is no doubt accompanied by physical gestures, elements that are required for a good reading or speech. Pardo Bazán could not have described this *lectora* and her style of reading any more eloquently: "Her tongue was glib, her larynx untiring, her accent robust. She didn't really read, she declaimed, full of fire and expressiveness, stressing those passages that were worthy of stress, raising her voice for words in italics, adding the necessary mimicry when the occasion required it, and beginning the important paragraphs slowly and mysteriously, in a restrained voice, so that she could raise the anxiety to a loftier level and wrench involuntary shudderings of enthusiasm from her audience when she adopted a more rapid and vibrant intonation as she moved along."[21]

As is always the case, her audience is not completely passive and reacts not only to the content of the reading (when they understand it), but also to the emphasis and reading style. This becomes particularly evident when they listen to in-depth articles that address social justice and teaching. Then, the narrator says, "Amparo's voice would change and her listeners' eyes would grow moist with tears. A slight shudder would race through the rows of women. . . . It took a great effort on their part to suppress their desire to embrace one another as the feeling came over them again and again."[22] In another sense, the *lectora* knows her audience well and is aware of how important it is to keep them in suspense:

> It isn't easy to imagine how profound a sensation was produced among that gathering by a particular section of news items with a title like, "An Unspeakable Happening."
>
> "Let's find out, let's find out. Listen, everyone. Quiet. Silence, you chatterboxes."
>
> And a palpitant hush reigned throughout the place and all you could hear was the clinking of the scissors as they kept snipping the ends of the cigars.
>
> "An Unspeakable Happening," Amparo repeated. "We have been assured that it is very likely that two days ago three off-duty rural policemen went into the Café de la Aurora and an officer, who happened to be there, arrested them . . ."
>
> "It's possible he arrested them, that he arrested them . . ."
>
> "Keep quiet, you loud mouths . . ."
>
> ". . . arrested them for so terrible a crime . . ."[23]

The *lectora* inserts pauses on purpose in order to keep the audience simultaneously attentive and in suspense.

The novel portrays two kinds of cigar workers: urban dwellers, who are from the city of Marineda; and those from villages. Fierce rivalry exists between the two groups, since it is said that the small-town women are greedy and stingy, while the city women are generous. This dichotomy is set up intentionally to show the country's political divide in microcosm through this portrayal of the listening audience: "Spain was very close to a great struggle between traditionalism and liberalism, of the countryside against the cities, an epic combat that was represented in miniature in the factory in Marineda," the narrator tells us.[24]

But what is the reading's impact or influence on each of the groups? As I mentioned previously, if the reading deals with social rights, such as military conscription or the right to education, both groups agree. But in general, the women from rural areas are less radical, "the least inclined toward federalism," since "filled with skepticism and craftiness, they would shake their heads and say that as far as they were concerned, the republic 'wasn't going to raise them up from poverty' . . . You couldn't draw the slightest spark of patriotic fire from them."[25] But although the small-town women are not as zealous, they are still in favor of the Republic. For example, it is interesting to read the following ekphrastic passage from the press:

> Amparo's audience represented the two forms of government in contention at that very moment in Spain, in exactly the same way you could see them portrayed in the caricatures in the satirical newspapers; the monarchy was seen as an old woman wearing a mastiff's spiked collar, as wrinkled as a raisin, with a nose like a parrot's beak, a very tattered purple cloak, a scepter stained with blood, and surrounded by bayonets, chains, clamps and instruments of torture; the republic, portrayed as a healthy, robust young woman, wearing a white tunic, a splendid Phrygian cap of liberty, and by her left arm was the classic horn of plenty, from which a cascade of railroads, steamers and symbols of the arts and sciences were pouring out, all pleasingly wrapped in coins and flowers.[26]

The reading of all these political texts no doubt creates awareness in the audience, but especially in Amparo, which is why she is called by the nickname La Tribuna in the city where she lives. Amparo, or La Tribuna, becomes the cigar workers' spokesperson.

Reading political newspapers transforms La Tribuna and turns her into a speechmaker and avid defender of the Republic. Still, Amparo does not understand politics with any depth, but, rather, relies on a sort of intuition and conviction:

What the newspaper lacked in sincerity, Amparo made up for in credulity and concurrence. She was growing accustomed to thinking in the style of the editorials and to speaking in a like manner: the trite turns of phrases and the commonplace expressions of the daily press came to her lips easily, and she embellished and composed her language with them. She began to acquire extraordinary fluency of speech; it's true that she sometimes used words and even whole phrases whose exact meaning was not exactly clear to her, and that she even mixed up some others, but even in doing that, she was very much like the careless and anti-literary press of the time.[27]

The influence that the reading has on her causes La Tribuna to begin to interrupt what she is reading to make speeches. Suddenly, the readings are intermingled with rebellious oratory and political speechmaking:

"That is what I always preach to you," the reader exclaimed when she reached this point, taking control of the discussion. "The worst scoundrels are at the top, at the very top. If someone can't see it, he's blind . . . On the same day that liberty was proclaimed and the Bourbons were given the boot, I would have published a decree . . . , and you know what I would have said?" [T]he orator opened her left hand and made as if she were writing in it with a cigar. "I, the sovereign people, do decree that, in accordance with my individual rights, all the generals, ministers and other bigwigs be removed from the high places they now occupy, and that those places be given to others whom I shall name in any manner that may darn well suit me. That's what I have to say."[28]

The political arguments generated by the reading and speeches become noisy in the factory, and thus the reading begins to be viewed as a threat that must be controlled. The *maestra* of the *cigarros comunes* workshop exerts her authority and reprimands employees who talk too much.

Angered by the expression and watchful eye of the *maestra*, Amparo asks to be transferred to the "cigarette" workshop, that is, where they make small cigarettes of shredded tobacco wrapped in rolling paper, which is located on the floor above the *cigarros comunes* workshop.

II

The cigar workers carry / tucked behind their comb / a Havana cigar / for their Pepe at home.

Cigar factories in Spain have always imposed severe discipline.[29] As I indicated earlier, when personnel were recruited, preference was given to the daughters of the cigar workers, and, in this sense, the art of rolling cigars was somewhat of a secret that was passed down from generation to generation. Also, every applicant was required to submit a certification issued by her parish priest that established her age and habitual behavior. If the applicant showed proof of good habits, she was hired, and once she was working in the factory, her data were recorded in a book in which personal information was written on the right-hand side of every page of the book. The left-hand side was left blank to allow a space to write down how the cigar maker behaved toward the factory's management and her coworkers.[30]

The workshop's *maestra* was in charge of its discipline and prohibited singing and making noise. In *The Tribune of the People*, political readings and speeches get the whole workshop agitated; thus, Amparo's presence and her readings immediately become a threat. Interestingly enough, the discipline imposed in Spanish factories became public knowledge when *Carmen* first appeared. Prosper Mérimée portrays a violent gypsy woman who is capable of slashing her coworker's face with a knife used to cut cigars and of causing everyone in the workshops to freeze in their tracks and stop producing. Note also the description of the workshop from the point of view of the Basque man, one of the factory guards and, later, Carmen's lover:

> Two or three hours later, while I was still thinking of the incident, a porter arrived at the guard-house, out of breath and greatly discomposed. He told us that a woman had been assassinated in the great room of the factory, and that it was necessary to have the guard in. The sergeant ordered me to take two men and go and see what was the matter. I took the men and went up. Picture to yourself the sight that met my view when I entered—about three hundred women *en chemise*, or with as little as possible on them—screaming, crying, gesticulating, and making such a row that you couldn't have heard thunder. At one side a female was sprawling on the floor drenched in blood, with a cross—an X—cut on her face with a knife. Opposite the wounded woman, who was being tended by the rest of the females, I perceived Carmen, restrained by five or six of her associates. The wounded woman kept crying out that she was dying and wanted a priest.[31]

This piercing and cruel image of the workshop and the cigar workers could only occur in fiction, because in truth, the disciplinary rules were always very strict. This is why in the old Seville factory there was a jail on the grounds, and anyone who committed a crime was severely punished there. The British writer Havelock Ellis, who visited the workshops in the cigar factory in Seville, was surprised at how different the factory was from that described by Mérimée and by Pierre Louys, author of the novel *La femme et le pantin*.[32] Ellis writes:

> Bearing this in mind [as described by Mérimée and Louys], my own visit to the Fabrica, together with a small party, was planned not without some misgiving. So far, however, from being unpleasant, the Fabrica seemed to me one of the most delightful spots in this delightful city, and one of the most picturesque. The workrooms are vast chambers, supported by great piers and resembling cathedral crypts, airy, scarcely redolent even of tobacco, and occupied by girls and women, who have changed their out-door dresses, which hang all round the walls, but remain fully dressed in various costumes, and are so absorbed in their work, except when they turn to the babies some have brought with them, that even the hum of conversation is scarcely heard and but few workers look up as the strangers pass.[33]

The description of the workshops in *The Tribune of the People* and the code of conduct have more in common with the one that Ellis describes. In fact, in Pardo Bazán's novel, a cigar roller is found with stolen tobacco. This is a crime that always brought severe punishment.[34] That is why the old *seguidilla* verse says: "The cigar workers carry / tucked behind their comb / a Havana cigar / for their Pepe at home." As it was always forbidden to take tobacco from the factory, the cigar workers had to be patted down by forewomen before leaving the workshop. If anyone was found with stolen tobacco, she was immediately fired, which is what happens in *The Tribune of the People*.[35] But the fact that someone is fired for stealing is not very surprising. What is more astonishing is the discipline that is imposed with regard to reading aloud.

The reading of political texts definitively represented a threat to factory management, which is why "the reading from newspapers, manifestos, proclamations and handbills" was prohibited.[36] The most serious incident of all is a description of how Amparo and other cigar workers are punished: they are all fired. Suddenly, reading aloud becomes a crime as serious as stealing cigars or Carmen's attacking her coworker: it is a subversive act that has crossed the line and must be severely punished.

III

Before Amparo loses her position at the factory, her father, the other authority figure, warns her that he was going to break "one of her ribs if she ever again read any more newspapers at the Factory," but she pays him no mind and decides to continue her involvement in politics, although at the cost of her job.[37] In contrast to his daughter's subversive personality, Rosendo has learned to be subordinate during his time in Cuba; "the ugliest crime for him was insubordination" (137). Now unemployed, La Tribuna begins to make a name for herself as a political figure, and when a delegation comes to Marineda to promote the future Republic, she joins them during their assembly.

But what is most revealing is what occurs when the "pact," an official document that advocates for the Republic, is read aloud. When everyone is gathered, politicians and the listening audience, "[a]nd the voice of the reader of the pact flew high above the sea of heads," Amparo's father, Rosendo, who is selling *barquillos* to the crowd, is stricken, falls to the floor, and dies that night, silenced, "without making confession, without recovering his senses" (136–137).

The death of Amparo's father can be read as a metaphor for the danger posed by reading aloud. Her father knew well the risk of reading, which is why he warned his daughter, but she would not hear him. And, this time, when he saw her even more involved in politics, the elderly man could not tolerate it, could not listen anymore, nor could he say anything.

Only reading of political texts is portrayed in *The Tribune of the People*; Amparo reads no literature. In fact, when an army officer, Baltasar Sobrado, courts her and they meet at an outdoor lunchroom, she tries to read him novels, but cannot. The narrator says: "Reflecting on new ways to amuse themselves, Baltasar brought Amparo a novel so that [she] could read it to [him] aloud, but the cigarette maker tended to burst into tears so easily as soon as the heroes died of love or some other malady of that sort, that the officer, convinced that he was overdoing things, put an end to the books.[38]

Conversely, and in counterpoint to her lack of prowess with literature, her passion for political texts and her activity with political struggles transform Amparo into a strong character who truly believes in equal rights for men and women and in workers' rights. This is what allows her to go back to the factory: she is granted a reprieve and goes back to work as a cigarette maker.

Back at the factory, Amparo does not read aloud, but Pardo Bazán alludes to the texts that were heard. Once again, they are political newspapers that revolve around the context of Spain at the beginning of the 1870s, that is, at the time of the arrival of the constitutional monarchy of King Amadeo I in 1871.

Still, this time, what brings about chaos in the factory is nothing short of labor struggles between management and the cigar workers. Amparo does not necessarily read aloud, but she does protest the injustices suffered by the cigar workers, who are not paid for months due to the shortage of tobacco or its poor quality.

The Tribune of the People, therefore, not only portrays the political events in Spain, but also sheds light on labor difficulties that shook a number of Spanish cigar factories at the end of the nineteenth century. In the fictional La Granera Factory, the cigar workers strike because, as Amparo says:

> all they send us here is second-rate Philippine tobacco, and you have to wait a month or two even for that. The higher quality cigars, the *regalías* and the small tapered *conchas*, those they make in *Madrid* . . . As if our fingers weren't made of human flesh! Are we some kind of slaves here or just clumsy fools that we don't know how to *perfect* the work! And besides all that, over there they always get standard pay and consignments galore. . . . Citizen workers, we must shake off the yoke of tyranny with nobility and energy when that moment comes which we're all waiting for! Eh, girls?[39]

In the face of this situation, the cigar workers strike, but it does them no good, because troops are sent in. They lose the fight and have to return to work under the same conditions. These labor struggles, whether they were due to tobacco shortages, low wages, or working conditions, which are seen clearly in Pardo Bazán's novel, became reality in one way or another in all the factories in Spain.[40]

At the end of the novel, Amparo has a child by Baltasar, the army officer, but he abandons her without acknowledging his son or giving him his last name. Her child is born on the very day the establishment of the First Republic is proclaimed, February 11, 1873. Thus, the much-anticipated republic that Amparo had fought so hard for was born, but it was born without social or political support.

In reality, the First Spanish Republic lasted only a few months. The Republican parties had few followers, and the masses began to favor labor movements. In addition, in 1887, Spanish cigar factories underwent a financial and social transformation when the Compañía Arrendataria de Tabacos took control. The factories were no longer state property.

But this is not the worst of it. Cigar-rolling machines started to make their debut in Spain in the 1880s, and this entailed a drastic transformation. The cigar maker of yesteryear was almost completely displaced by the machine operator.[41]

The Tribune of the People shows, in a captivating way, why reading aloud in Spanish cigar factories was so short-lived. First of all, it was established sporadically and in only a few factories during a turbulent time in Spanish history. Second, the reading of almost exclusively political texts gave rise to its being seen as a threat, and it was sanctioned and even banned. Third, the spontaneous transformation of manual labor workshops to mechanized workshops must have made reading aloud impossible because of the noise generated by the machinery.[42] All this was taking place at the time that *The Tribune of the People* was being written, and although this extraordinary novel in one sense reclaims reading aloud in Spain's cigar factories, in another sense, it shows how inevitable its untimely death was. But thanks to literature, this cultural practice, which was brought to Spain from Cuba, remains as a testimony to the level of enrichment of the exchange between the colony and the homeland.

PART TWO

"WORKSHOP GRADUATES" AND "WORKERS IN EXILE"

Reading Aloud in the United States and Puerto Rico, 1868–1931

PREVIOUS PAGE: *Lector* in a Tampa cigar factory, circa 1930
(Courtesy of the University of South Florida Libraries Special Collections)

THREE

Key West

—|■■|—

The first cigar workers to come to Key West, whether voluntarily or involuntarily, arrived in 1868, that is, at the beginning of the Ten Years' War. Since Cuba was in conflict and in chaotic circumstances that did not lend themselves to cigar production, a number of owners opted to leave and establish their factories in the United States, mainly in Key West and New York.

The war did not affect exportation of raw material, because the Spanish government benefited from the income generated by tobacco sales. Under these circumstances, the establishment of the cigar industry in the United States was a great success, and the Havana cigar, especially in Key West, attained international renown. Leading factories such as Ybor y Manrara, Seidenberg and Co., O'Halloran and Co., and Bustillo Bros. were originally established in Key West.[1]

The prosperity of those factories made it possible for cigar workers to find immediate employment doing the very work they had been trained to do. Conditions were favorable for factory owners as well as cigar workers, because the warm climate was very much like Cuba's, and Key West was just ninety miles north of Havana. Additionally, Key West's climate was ideal for crafting a fine cigar, since it was hot and humid, both of which are key to keeping the leaf in good condition. As Key West also offered excellent channels of communication between Cuba and New York, several factories established in New York at the beginning of the war moved operations to Key West after just a few years.

Few people knew where Key West was in 1868, but by 1885, it had become one of the fifteen most important ports in the United States.[2] The factory owners were Cubans, Spaniards, and immigrants from other countries. A cosmopolitan culture was instilled from the very beginning, because many of the cigar workers and those employed in related fields were immigrants from Cuba, Spain, and other Latin American countries, as well as Jewish immigrants from the Bahamas and people born in Key West.[3]

Entire families came from Cuba; therefore, if the head of the household was a cigar worker, this ensured that the whole family would work in the cigar industry. Women worked as leaf strippers, and, whenever possible, they also put their children to work. Cubans did any kind of work in the factories: they were pickers, wrapper selectors, casers, and, of course, cigar rollers.

The culture that existed in Cuban factories was transplanted to the United States. At the factories, there were people who brought in coffee, rolls, sandwiches, sweets, and many other items for sale, which made for a warm, harmonious atmosphere, since everyone knew one another, and everything revolved around cigars. The Cubans who came to Key West turned the island into a dynamic entity, because they built their houses near the factories and opened cafés, restaurants, and pharmacies. Moreover, Spanish became the most-spoken language in both the public and the private spheres.

In 1869, one year after the Ten Years' War started, José Dolores Poyo, a journalist who had supported Cuban insurgents, took refuge in Key West. Colonial authorities had watched and pursued him all over Havana, and when he realized what a tight spot he was in, he had no recourse but to flee to the Keys. Immediately on his arrival, José Dolores Poyo began to work as a *lector* at the Príncipe de Gales Factory, the owner of which was Vicente Martínez Ybor. Martínez Ybor, who emigrated from his native Spain to Cuba at the age of fourteen, had become one of the most prosperous manufacturers in Havana by 1860. When the war broke out, the corps of volunteers (*voluntarios*) tried to murder him.[4] When Martínez Ybor was forced to flee, he moved his famous factory to Key West, where he took in hundreds of Cubans (and Spaniards) who arrived anxious to work and live in peace.[5]

José Dolores Poyo was the first cigar factory *lector* in the United States. Another distinguished Cuban journalist who became a *lector* after his arrival in the Keys was Juan María Reyes. Francisco María González, an educated, dynamic stenographer, also took on the task of reading aloud in factories.[6]

How was reading aloud done, and what was read in the factories of Key West? As I have previously stated, the first *lectores* in Cuba were cigar workers who took turns reading to their coworkers and, in turn, were compensated for the production time they lost. Over time, the *lectores* began to be people who had other full-time professions and occupations and read to cigar workers for an hour or two a day. Therefore, the position of "official" *lector* or "cigar factory" *lector* did not exist, especially in 1868, when reading aloud in Cuba had overcome so many obstacles.

In Key West, the first people who read in cigar factories were generally people who worked in the fields of journalism or education. Workshops, especially the *galera,* or main workshop, in which the *lectores* carried out their tasks were similar to the ones in Cuba: they had *vapores,* or rows of five or six workbenches, set up one behind the other, like rows of desks in a classroom. The *lector* sat or stood on a small platform—approximately two yards high, resembling a pulpit without a rail or canopy—located in the middle or at the front or side of the workshop, depending on the room's acoustics.

When reading aloud at the cigar factories began in Key West, *lectores* read from English-language magazines and newspapers in circulation, such as the *Light of the Gulf,* the *Key West Guardian,* and the *Democrat.* Spanish-language newspapers were sent from New York, but they arrived two to three days after publication; the same was true of newspapers that came from Havana. Obviously, the English-language press offered the latest news. In cigar factories, the majority of the listening audience was Spanish-speaking, so the *lector* often felt obliged to read the latest news in Spanish. However, since the Spanish-language newspapers arrived late, many times the *lectores* bought the English-language newspapers, reviewed the headlines, local, national, and international news, breaking news, classified advertisements, and obituaries and read them; that is, while *lectores* read, they translated the content into Spanish. Doing so must have been exhausting, as we must not forget that there was no microphone, it was hot, and the audience was made up of hundreds of workers who had to be able to hear everything.

The best account regarding what it meant to read from the platform (not to translate simultaneously as Poyo, Reyes, and González did) was written years later by Wenceslao Gálvez y Delmonte:

> My poorly trained throat resented the effort, and the more I tried to speak louder, the hoarser I grew. . . . So I had to shout more, to make an even greater effort when I thought even passersby could hear me. I did not feel good. An incessant burning in my throat caused me to have a constant cough, and I was close to losing my voice. . . . I read standing up, and halfway through a paragraph I would stand on tiptoe, making great efforts to project my voice. I felt as if the words were being extracted from my stomach and hurled a great distance, like a bowler throwing the ball at the pins, and in spite of that great effort, my voice did not come out strong or clear.[7]

If we add to the extraordinary effort described by Gálvez the additional effort translating entails, it is easy to imagine how laborious it must have been to work as a *lector.* A *lector* not only had to have an excellent speaking voice, but also had to be an educated person.

During the first two years, the Spanish-language newspapers that *lectores* read from came from New York and included *La América, El Avisador Cubano, El Boletín de la Revolución, La Voz de América, El Correo de Nueva York, El Demócrata, Diario Cubano, La Estrella de Cuba,* and *La Independencia.* Any paper that was received from Cuba was read, but mainly *El Diario de la Marina* and *El Siglo.*

Since Key West had no Spanish-language newspaper, one of the *lectores,* Juan María Reyes, started one, *El Republicano,* in 1870. The newspaper was read aloud, and there was much interest in hearing it in the factories, not only because it presented what was currently taking place in Key West, Cuba, and New York, but also because it was a tool for the clubs and associations that were beginning to be formed.

José Dolores Poyo later launched two newspapers, *La Igualdad* and *El Patriota*; both had the same features and function as *El Republicano.* The first two newspapers that Poyo set up were short-lived due to their limited circulation, but even with few subscribers, those newspapers were sent to Cuba, where people read and heard about what was happening in the Cuban community in the United States. In 1878, at the end of the Ten Years' War, Poyo launched the newspaper *El Yara,* which published anything having to do with Cuban immigration in the cultural and sociopolitical spheres. The newspaper remained in circulation until 1898, when the Spanish-American War ended. It was one of the most widely read newspapers in Key West. Also, *El Yara* was read in other parts of the United States, such as New York, where José Martí read it continually to learn of immigrant issues.

In the 1880s, other newspapers from New York that were read aloud included *El Avisador Hispano-Americano, El Avisador Cubano, La República,* and *El Ciudadano.* A newspaper that enjoyed wide circulation in Key West was the first bilingual daily, published in 1887, *The Equator: El Ecuador.* The Spanish-language section was edited by Ramón Rivero, who would later become a cigar factory *lector* in Tampa; Martín Morúa Delgado, a writer who was also a *lector* in Havana; and Carlos Baliño, one of the foremost labor leaders. In the 1890s, people read *Cuba, El Oriente,* and *Revista de Florida* from Tampa; *Patria,* managed by José Martí was the primary New York newspaper read aloud. From 1897 through 1898, *Revista de Cayo Hueso,* essentially a literary journal, was published. Writers who contributed to the publication included Eduardo Alonso, Esteban Borrero Echeverría, Bonifacio Byrne, Aurelio Ramos Merlo, and Dulce María Borrero, who was both an arts and a literary contributor.

The only account that exists about the books *lectores* read was written by Gerardo Castellanos, who points out that "a cigar factory is a civil encampment in active service. The *lector* read about wars of liberation, the French Revolution, Bolívar's campaigns, the ever-hopeful *Don Quixote*, Garibaldi's campaigns, *Les Misérables.*"[8]

Victor Hugo and cigar workers had something in common: both were living in exile. From the Channel Islands, on the Island of Guernsey, a small British territory situated between Great Britain and France, the French author wrote to Cubans in exile in the United States. Victor Hugo had lived in exile for nearly twenty years—in fact, he wrote his masterpiece, *Les Misérables* (1862), on Guernsey.

In 1870, Hugo received a moving letter written and signed by three hundred Cuban women in exile in the United States. There is no doubt that included among those who signed the letter were dozens of cigar workers or wives of cigar workers. The letter reveals the brutal savagery used by the Spanish government against Cuban revolutionaries and the extermination of entire districts carried out by colonial military forces in Cuba. The women were asking Victor Hugo to intervene in the bloody struggle. Hugo responded in an emotional letter "To the Women of Cuba" [Aux femmes de Cuba]:

Women of Cuba, I hear your lament, which you send me from the depths of your hopelessness. You, refugees, martyrs, widows, orphans, ask a vanquished man to help you. You, exiles, write to an exile. You who no longer have a home have asked for help from a man without a country. There is nothing left to you but your voice, and there is nothing left to me but mine. Your voice laments, mine informs. Who are we? Weakness. No, we are strength. You are moral strength, and I am conscience. Conscience is the backbone of the soul, just as conscience is the truth and the soul stands on its own. . . . I shall speak for Cuba as I have spoken for Crete. No nation has the right to trample another; neither has Spain the right to be in Cuba, nor England in Gibraltar. . . . Those who treat others with tyranny and the race that cheats another represent the monstrous suction of the octopus and its horrible power: this is one of the horrific acts of the nineteenth century. . . . Women of Cuba, who speak to me so eloquently of your agony and suffering, I kneel before you and kiss your most painful feet. Do not waiver, for one day your persevering homeland will be made whole for all its suffering; so much blood shall not have been shed in vain. Magnificent Cuba shall one day rise up free and sovereign among her august sisters, the Republics of the Americas.[9]

In fact, Victor Hugo had a great deal in common with these women and with the Cuban people in the United States, because both were writing from exile; both desired peace and social justice. But why write specifically to Victor Hugo? Perhaps it had to do with the fact that they had read *Les Misérables*, or had it read to them, and learned through the novel of the topics that most concerned the author, that is, social injustice, love and compassion, revolution, orphanhood, and refuge.

It is fitting to recall here that *Les Misérables* tells the story of the sorrowful life experiences of Jean Valjean, an unfortunate man convicted of stealing a loaf of bread and whose incarceration turns him into an evil man. Released from prison after nineteen years, Jean Valjean is given refuge at a bishop's house, but at night the ex-convict steals two silver candlesticks from the cleric and flees. He is apprehended by the police and returned to the bishop's home to be identified as the perpetrator. The bishop forgives him and makes a gift of the candlesticks to him, with the hope that Jean Valjean will change and become a righteous man. In the novel, the two candlesticks are the most prominent symbol of compassion, because they glitter with the light of promise. And Jean Valjean does indeed change his ways and struggles for the rest of his days to do right and to live a better life.

Also symbolically, the institution of reading aloud resembles the flame that illuminates and transforms countless people. Those cigar makers who were forced to live in exile took with them the light of hope, because they established reading aloud in cigar factories in a land not their own. Although there are few accounts about the literature that was read in Key West, it is widely known that the cigar workers fervently enjoyed *Les Misérables*.

Starting when they arrived in the Keys, Cubans set about establishing organizations that allowed them to carry out their artistic, literary, and charitable activities, as cigar workers in Cuba had done. They also established a variety of cooperatives and guilds. One of the most important and dynamic centers was the Club San Carlos, which served as an educational establishment (a girls' school and a separate boys' school) during the day and a cultural and patriotic center evenings and weekends. Cigar factory *lectores* played a pivotal role in the founding of this institution; Poyo and Reyes were in charge of the learning center. *Lectores* also generously organized literary conferences, *zarzuelas* (Spanish comic folk operas), music recitals, and concerts in their spare time. In addition to devoting themselves to reading, when literary conferences were held, they served as masters of ceremonies and also were responsible for hiring Cuban musicians, actors, and poets. Thus, the *lector* was viewed as a magisterial figure who read in the workplace and disseminated culture in social and cultural spaces.

In fact, the *lector* was seen and heard not only by the workers, but also by a wider audience, other communities of listeners. José Martí, who visited

Key West, called the *lectores* "workshop graduates": "assiduous readers of history and philosophy, who, during the course of an evening soirée, without any preparatory coiffure or the beads or chignons of the conference, speak, as if in an athenaeum of truth, of law and beauty, which make the world good, and the plans and methods by which man aspires to make it better. Those young people are a bonfire and an oath, not created at someone else's expense but, rather, through their own valiant efforts. Work: that is the spine of the book!"[10]

The platform for the *lector* in the workshop was like the platform at the Club San Carlos, because both provided space for culture. Regarding the Club San Carlos, Martí wrote the following:

> To San Carlos come the races which must live together, to be brought up together in the warm embrace of the school; to San Carlos, on the tide of opinion, come diverse ideas and interests, . . . to San Carlos people come to hear our poetry, our theater, and our music; to San Carlos, with equal rights, comes the white man of purest lineage, who was born among notables, and the eminent black man, with parchments of righteousness, and the country boy of the daring hat, who still doesn't know whether a vest is a bad thing or a tie a good thing. All are indignant together: they applaud together: they cry together. It is a sacred house.[11]

As it had in the Club San Carlos, the platform for the *lectores* in the workshop was transforming little by little, because *lectores* assigned themselves the task of making cultural presentations while the cigar makers worked. Thus, workers enjoyed the privilege of enriching their cultural landscapes without having to leave their workbenches.

When two Cuban musicians, Rafael Díaz Albertini and Ignacio Cervantes, who had just won first prize at the Paris Conservatory, visited the Keys, Francisco María González invited them to perform in a factory. When they entered, the cigar makers "applauded" by tapping their *chavetas* on their workbenches. Poyo wrote in *El Yara* that the "applause" seemed "like a wave, like a wave that was going to break contentedly on the pedestal of those two great artistic virtuosos."[12]

The musicians, accompanied by the *lector*, went up on the platform. Before the concert started, the *lector* let the musicians speak. Ignacio Cervantes addressed the workers as follows: "I have had only two sources of pride in my life: the first, having been born in Cuba; and the second, having received first prize at the Paris Conservatory, so that I could offer the prize as a token of my affection to my beloved country; and today, the third, this visit to the workshop where I have been welcomed in this way by my beloved compatriots, the honorable workers who gather here."[13]

After this brief introduction, the musicians began their debut performance. It is important to take into account that during this type of presentation, the cigar workers' production was not interrupted, just as production was not suspended or delayed while reading was taking place. Martí described the cigar workers as "children of their country, fettered to their work during unending hours," and he wrote about the concert in his newspaper, *Patria*:

> The complete men, the Cuban creators, the Cuban founders proudly climb the workshop steps—as our two great musicians, Albertini and Cervantes, had just climbed the steps of the Key West workshop. Neither the sovereign keyboard of the one nor the impeccable violin of the other was ever able to produce any harmony to equal that with which the workmen of the factory ascended during that visit, like a hymn of announcement, like a promise of peace, like a proclamation of accord issuing forth from the satisfied silence of those hearts. Though there be vipers born of Cuban soil, how many more beautiful eagles![14]

According to Martí's description, the platform in that workshop must have been quite spacious, like a kind of press box intended for several individuals. He alludes to a keyboard, so there certainly must have been a piano or an organ on the platform. The size of the platform demonstrates that a variety of cultural or other types of activities took place there, where a group of people could be present at the same time. In this case, the platform was not a kind of pulpit intended for one individual, but, rather, a spacious platform—a stage—that had a lectern where the *lector* stood to read, or a table with chairs where he could sit. Hence, the platform for the *lector* came to resemble the platforms in cultural centers where a variety of presentations took place.

It would not be an exaggeration to say that poets, poetry readers, actors, playwrights, novelists, choirs, and, ultimately, a panoply of artists crossed those platforms. As Martí said: "Art is work. Work is art. The workers love each other. Our people are not men who want to bring down grandeur, but, rather, men who want to rise up. There is no danger, there is nothing to fear, a people who join together moved by a common emotion, who unite spontaneously, their different trades, there where the people develop and move forward; there where the people mature and become sure of themselves; there where the people learn the habit and the methods of creation: in the workshops!"[15]

Thus, cultural events that took place on the platform in the workshop were an extension of the artistic expressions that were presented in cultural centers. The idea of bringing culture into the factory through presentations shows how creative the *lectores* were, as well as their social commitment to the community.

At the Club San Carlos the *lector* organized raffles, soirées, and dances to raise funds and thus defray educational expenses. His work as organizer, leader, and teacher, if you will, situated him in such a public domain that he was repeatedly asked to attend all kinds of ceremonies and civic events, such as meetings, processions, and patriotic parades at cigar factories. For example, a commemoration was held each year on October 10, the date that the Ten Years' War broke out in Cuba, and hundreds of people gathered at Club San Carlos headquarters. It was a holiday, and a day off from work both in cigar factories and other businesses. If we examine that day's agenda, it is easy to conclude how the *lector* was involved with and committed to the entire community.

In the morning, people went to church and then the cemetery to visit someone's grave (usually someone who had been involved in the war), where the *lector* said a prayer. Then everyone knelt and prayed. In this case, the *lector* took on the role of a priest or of a very trusted person who could cast out sorrow. Once this event had concluded, the procession returned to club headquarters, where the needs of the community were discussed and collections were taken up. Here the *lector* acted as a liaison between the community and the board of directors.

At night a party was usually held, and the *lectores* served as masters of ceremonies. For example, at one of these parties, Juan María Reyes first introduced a cigar worker, Antonio Ríos, who recited the verses "Desahogos del alma." The *lector*/master of ceremonies was so caught up in the moment that he spontaneously recited poems that he knew by heart. Later, he introduced a number of other people who also recited poetry. Next, a group of people sang a hymn, and, finally, a patriotic allegory, *Cuba: Su pasado y porvenir*, was staged.[16]

At any sort of celebration, there was never a dearth of speakers, artists, poets, children who were art and poetry aficionados, and, of course, musicians. In fact, there was a musical group called La Libertad made up of cigar workers who played free of charge at all festivities. In their spare time, the members taught music at an academy that they founded.

Religious holidays were also celebrated in Key West, including the feast days of San Juan and San Pedro, Midnight Mass, Holy Week, and even Epiphany. Ultimately, in all civic, social, and religious celebrations, it was expected or, rather, mandatory that the *lector* participate.

Those who took on the task of reading aloud in Key West's cigar factories came to the United States to flee the brutality and horrors of war. The factory owners, Cubans or Spaniards, and a vast number of cigar workers who were employed in Key West had come to Florida for the same reason. They shared the common ground of having been dispossessed, of being refugees in a land not their own, of working in the same industry, of being, as Martí said, "workers in exile."[17]

Politically, they were all in favor of the nationalist cause and aspired to see Cuba become an independent republic. We must not forget that José Dolores Poyo had been an insurgent; Vicente Martínez Ybor, one of the most prosperous industrialists and owner of the factory where Poyo had been a *lector,* had fled because a group of mercenaries had tried to murder him. Add to this the arrival in Key West of Eduardo Hidalgo Gato, a fervent Cuban revolutionary and cigar maker who started a *chinchal* (a small cigar shop where a minimal number of employees rolled and sold cigars) and ended up with a factory that made him one of the richest and most powerful men in the history of the state of Florida. Thus, the *lector* read to a politically savvy audience that had experienced firsthand the sparking, igniting, and combustion of the war—an audience that had made the voyage from Havana to Key West, and their journey was not in vain. Cigar makers, foremen, factory owners, businesspeople, and politicians all shared a common ideology.

The establishment of reading aloud coincided with the formation of clubs and associations that functioned as both patriotic and political entities, and of cultural and charitable organizations. Secret societies and Masonic orders were also founded. The work of cigar factory *lectores* in these establishments was important, as seen in the case of the Club San Carlos. In 1869, the cigar workers at the Martínez Ybor Factory founded the Asociación Patriótica de Cayo Hueso [Key West Cuban Patriots' Association] with the goal of sponsoring events and raising funds to assist those who were being affected by the Ten Years' War. José Dolores Poyo was named president, and Juan María Reyes was the association's first secretary. That same year, the Sociedad de Artesanos Cubanos [Cuban Artisans' Society] was founded in New York, made up of nationalist leaders such as Cirilo Villaverde, Ramón Rubiera de Armas, Carlos and José Gabriel de Castillo, José J. Govantes, Miguel Bravo, and José F. de Lamadriz, who, like the cigar workers of Key West, were advocating for Cuban independence.[18] In 1870, on behalf of the Club Patriótico Cubano [Cuban Patriots' Club], Poyo organized collections in different factories to support the Sociedad de Artesanos, and from that time forward, it became obvious that the cigar workers of Key West supported the nationalists not only ideologically, but also financially. The clubs' efforts were reported in newspapers, reached the ears of the cigar workers in the United States, and were read at the same time in Cuba.

As they were such important public personas, *lectores* were also viewed suspiciously, since all *lectores* were first and foremost journalists. If their work was not read aloud in cigar factories, their writing was read, especially in Cuba, by their staunchest enemies. For example, the newspaper *El Republicano*, for which, incidentally, Poyo wrote, reported on the immigrants' social, political, and cultural activities while simultaneously criticizing the activities of the Spanish colonial regime in Cuba. As was the norm, the newspaper was a battlefield where ideological struggles were written about in extremely strong words. Therefore, the cigar factory *lector* was exposed to public criticism and accusations.

Nothing could have been more dramatic or as much like something out of a work of fiction than the arrival in Key West of Gonzalo Castañón, a Spaniard who ran the newspaper *La Voz de Cuba*. His arrival had been reported beforehand in his newspaper; his mission was to challenge Juan María Reyes, the *lector* who managed *El Republicano*, to a duel to the death, because Reyes had written a critical piece about him and about the activities of *voluntarios*, the brutal organized militias that were sowing the seeds of terror in Cuba. It was January 1870. Castañón's plan could not have been more melodramatic: he wanted to confront Reyes face to face, slap him, and launch his attack. All of Key West knew what was coming because *La Voz de Cuba* had been read aloud in the cigar factories.

Castañón called Reyes out, took from his pocket a copy of *El Republicano*, and asked him whether he had written the article in question. Reyes answered that he had. Castañón shoved the newspaper in his face and slapped him. The crowd that surrounded them got agitated, word spread like wildfire, and factories and businesses shut down and all the townspeople went out into the streets. Mateo Orozco, a baker, angrily swore to confront Castañón at the first opportunity, and the next day, when Castañón tried to flee to Havana, Orozco hunted him down and killed him with two gunshots.

This confrontation was symbolic because, from that time forward, the *lector* began to be seen not only as a charismatic being with a grandiloquent voice, like a teacher, priest, or politician, but also as a figure capable of creating work stoppages and conflicts. This latter opinion circulated mainly among those who did not have direct contact with the cigar-making workforce and knew of *lectores* only through secondhand information. Castañón's death surprised the Cuban community in both Cuba and the United

States. A chronology and all the details pertaining to the incident were reported in *El Republicano*. The newspaper became more well known and gained much wider circulation. In another sense, the function of the journalist/*lector* caught the suspicious eye of both Cuban and U.S. authorities.

But all was not politics, be it colonial, national, or Cuban. As in any workplace, there were labor struggles that directly harmed the *lectores*. We must recall that it was the cigar workers who paid the *lectores*. Thus, when disputes arose between owners and employees, and production was delayed for one reason or another, the *lectores* were stuck in the middle of the two groups, helpless. They could oppose neither the cigar workers, as they paid them, nor the owner, who could fire them. In 1873, amid a national financial crisis, the owners of the largest factories, that is, Martínez Ybor and Seidenberg, began to terminate the employment of many cigar workers. Faced with this situation, *lectores*, still-employed cigar workers, wealthy businesspeople, and political leaders set up a fund so that the unemployed could count on some income. In this case, the *lectores* were affected, because their salary was reduced, as the number of employees determined their pay.

The situation deteriorated in 1875, when the factories announced wage reductions. This time, Reyes and Poyo could not hold their tongue: they published an attack on the manufacturers in *El Republicano* and called on workers to leave Key West unless the owners paid them a fair salary, and they were able to reach a mutual agreement. There were no labor unions at that time (the first was organized in 1884). These were difficult years for the entire community, and in what was then the homeland, the unjust Ten Years' War had no end in sight.

But in 1878, the Ten Years' War came to an end. Poyo hurried to launch his newspaper, which he symbolically named *El Yara*.[19] "The belief that the Spanish mother country can give Cuba what it needs to prosper is pure fantasy," since "there is but one way for us to save ourselves," and it is by way of "establishing a Cuban Republic in which Cubans and Spaniards can find peace, work, and progress," he wrote.[20]

Despite the labor struggles and the crisis they had endured in the mid-1870s, owners as well as cigar workers and *lectores* were of one mind in terms of politics. *Lectores* concurred with the school of thought of nationalist leaders, for whom it was imperative that they preserve their cultural integrity. In other words, it was important to them to maintain their Cuban identity wherever they were. As a result, *El Yara* also reported on the cultural activities that took place throughout Key West. However, of even greater importance was that reading aloud in cigar factories, a manifestation of Cuban culture brought into exile, had remained afoot throughout the war: in Cuba, reading had been banned and did not take place for ten years, while in Key West it continued slowly and steadily.

Obviously, the war brought with it severe consequences; in Cuba, it brought about a financial crisis that caused waves of people to emigrate from Cuba to the United States. During the first half of the 1880s, Cubans in Key West, whether newly arrived or not, continued to back the nationalists. The war had affected each of them in one way or another, and they held the conviction that a free, sovereign Cuba would offer them the peace and progress they sought.

In October 1885, Máximo Gómez and Antonio Maceo appeared in Key West for one simple reason: they wanted to raise funds for future expeditions to Cuba. It is no exaggeration to say that, without the presence and participation of the *lectores*, they would not have been able to raise the sum that the cigar workers contributed. The *lector* was the one who led them by the hand from one cigar factory to another. He was the first to appear on the platform, spoke to the audience about the purpose of the visit, introduced the guests, and gave the guests the floor. These events were no doubt accompanied by a presentation during which someone recited poetry or sang.

On occasions such as this, *lectores* did not read, but, rather, made use of their natural gift of oratory, which Martí himself admired:

> Neither memorized oratory nor those expanded and transposed sentences, emerging rounded from the bellows, with which the Narcissuses of eloquence face off against their rivals of everyday emotions, would have been worth anything: because to those wooden workshop floors, raised with struggle through the excess contributions of the enthusiastic workers, and firmly anchored by their hardworking hands—symbolizing that the platform of truth will endure forever, when all other platforms have fallen . . . to those floors ascended, in the light of the moment, and with a discourse seeming anointed and angelical, the men who have adorned it, their culture recognized by only a few, the whole truth they themselves discover through life's adjustments and hardships, and it flows from their lips in stanzas of limpid beauty, in new and happy images, in wise and essential ideas, and in torrents of that brotherhood which I will not allow anyone to deny exists in the exemplary Cuban soul.[21]

Lectores had to win over their audience, so they varied the volume of their voice and were conscious of their tone, gestures, and pronunciation— basic elements for doing a good reading or giving an eloquent speech. Martí, orator par excellence, noticed the eloquence of those *lectores*/orators. Reading from the platform and its entire corollary of cultural and political activities continued even as difficult years for *lectores* and cigar workers approached.

In the mid-1880s, some cigar workers began to show their disagreement with the nationalist cause, as they started to become more concerned with the reality of their day-to-day life: they had lived through several financial and social crises and felt that their political leaders had not lent them support. Many turned their backs on the nationalist movement and were drawn to anarchist ideologies. Additionally, a succession of strikes took place during the latter half of the 1880s.

At the end of 1885, due to those labor struggles, Vicente Martínez Ybor transplanted his factory to northwest Tampa, and *lector* José Dolores Poyo lost his job. On the night of March 30, 1886, a fire broke out near the Club San Carlos and spread to many parts of the island. Dozens of cigar factories, businesses, and homes were in ashes by the following morning. The victims of the catastrophe were forced to abandon everything to seek refuge.

Just a year before, Tampa was nothing more than a small village, but with the building of the Martínez Ybor and Sánchez y Haya factories, the latter of which had been transplanted from New York, Tampa now seemed like the Promised Land for unemployed cigar workers. Among those who boarded the steamer that took them to Tampa was José Dolores Poyo, who, as soon as he set foot on the ground in Tampa, resumed his work as a *lector* at the Martínez Ybor Factory.

Poyo was the first cigar factory *lector* in Tampa. But he did not resign himself to reading alone, and in Tampa once again launched *El Yara*, which was the first Spanish-language newspaper published there. Before discussing the role of the *lector* in Tampa, a recap of *lectores* in Key West is warranted.

The cigar industry in Key West was quickly rebuilt. After spending a few months in Tampa, Poyo returned to the Keys and was hired as *lector* at the Ellinger Factory, which had just been rebuilt.[22] Martí referred to Poyo as "the humble pilgrim," about whose travels through Florida (in 1894) he wrote the following:

> It is beautiful to see an honorable man fight, to see him suffer, since from the spectacle of his pain arise forces which oppose evil; to see him rise up triumphant, with his face to the sun, from all the road's crossings; to see him defend without recompense, and at the cost of his own blood, and his children's medications, and his grandchild's shoes, an idea which will triumph only when its defender, at the mountain's slope, finally glimpses the welcome splendor of the tomb. The spectacle of these invincible men burns in faith

and in love. José Dolores Poyo is like that; his newspaper, when everything
was collapsing in Key West, and the deserted houses were like the somber
and silent trees of the cemeteries, and everything was changing or becoming
chaotic, ceased publication, while the humble pilgrim traveled through the
new towns of Florida.[23]

Back in Key West, Poyo resumed publishing *El Yara*. Still, labor struggles continued, and strikes were becoming widespread. In 1887, La Alianza
Obrera [Workers' Alliance] was founded in Cuba by leaders who had been
influenced by the ideals of Spanish anarchism. As I mention in Part I, one of
the most influential leaders was Enrique Roig de San Martín, who was the
spokesman for La Alianza through his newspaper, *El Productor*, which he
began in 1887. "Socialist Revolutionaries" was what Roig called his followers, who in general terms rejected the concepts of traditional labor movements, which emphasized study, education, and cooperative production
among workers as the basic tools needed to achieve progress. La Alianza
and its members advocated for the socialist concept of class struggle and
became known as anarchists, due to their militant nature and because they
rejected all political movements.[24]

In Key West, La Alianza and Roig de San Martín managed to attract supporters, since a number of cigar workers read *El Productor* or had it read
to them. Between 1887 and 1889, *El Yara* and *El Productor* waged a bitter
ideological battle. The anarchists, such as Roig de San Martín and his labor
militants, relying on socialist ideology, believed capitalists, who advocated
a liberal nationalist movement, had exploited them. Poyo and the editors of
El Yara had always supported the nationalist movement and openly rejected
anarchist political goals. As far as Poyo was concerned, anarchism favored
Spain, because it railed against Cuban nationalism. To Roig de San Martín's way of thinking, nationalists such as Poyo were nothing but "agents of
the factory owners" who did not concern themselves with the needs of the
workers.[25]

Enraged by ideological debates, Poyo refused to read *El Productor* at
the Ellinger Factory, where he worked. Since a significant number of cigar
workers there were followers of Roig de San Martín and his anarchist
thinking, they simply decided to fire the factory's *lector*.[26]

This incident shows the power and control the cigar makers had over
reading and the *lector*. As I stated previously, the *lector* read to an educated
audience that had deeply ingrained cultural and political awareness. Therefore, *lectores* could not just read what suited them, much less could they
manipulate cigar makers to favor one doctrine over another. Beyond the

microcosm of the factory, the workers listened, read, informed themselves, and participated in patriotic and cultural events.

It is obvious that, at the Ellinger Factory, the cigar workers chose what they wanted to hear; therefore, the ones in control were the majority of the employees. It would be naïve to think that all of them had anarchist leanings. Thus, in spite of the respect and influence the *lector* enjoyed both in the workplace and in the community, he was essentially just another worker who was told what to do. It is important to point out that, in this case, neither the owners nor the foremen could do anything about it; after all, since the cigar workers paid the *lectores*, they were their bosses.

José Dolores Poyo continued to read at a different factory. After all, despite how widespread the anarchist movement had become, deep down, most of the cigar workers in Florida, as well as the majority of immigrants, supported independence.

By the early 1890s, Key West had recovered from the fire that years earlier had destroyed nearly half the island. The cigar industry in Tampa was booming. In Cuba, the financial situation was worsening, mainly due to the decline in the sugar industry caused by massive destruction of plantations during the Ten Years' War. As a consequence, Florida received waves of Cuban immigrants who arrived in search of better living conditions.

In Key West, José Dolores Poyo and Francisco María González were the *lectores* at the island's most prosperous cigar factory—Cuban magnate Eduardo H. Gato's factory—which employed more than seven hundred workers. As was the norm, reading material in the factory included newspapers from Cuba, Key West, and Tampa. A popular paper was *El Porvenir*, in which José Martí reported on his independence ideology and his plans to mount an insurrection against Spain in Cuba. Martí, for his part, avidly read newspapers from Florida and Cuba, which kept him up to date with regard to the cigar workers' labor conflicts and, needless to say, the bitter disputes between the anarchists and the nationalists. For the revolution to take place, he knew it was necessary first and foremost to unify the cigar workers, since in the past they had worked together unconditionally in behalf of the independence movement. Military veterans of the Ten Years' War needed to join forces with the cigar workers, as most of these veterans were living in Key West.

José Martí was not very popular in Key West. Although people read his writings in *El Porvenir*, to them, he was a politician who lived in New York. Martí had to win over the Florida cigar workers and hence the war veterans to be able to set his campaign in motion. The winds were in his favor when the members of the Club Ignacio Agramonte de Tampa

[Ignacio Agramonte Club of Tampa] decided to invite him in November 1891 to participate in an artistic-literary celebration. Martí knew this was one of the most desirable and coveted opportunities of his lifetime; he had to hurry.

He arrived in Tampa on November 25. "Cubans: For suffering Cuba, the first word. Cuba must be considered an altar for the offering of our lives, not a pedestal for lifting us above it," he said at the beginning of his speech before a crowd of cigar workers at El Liceo Cubano in Tampa.[27] This speech is known as "With All, and for the Good of All," the phrase with which he ended his talk. Martí was asking everyone to unite in the cause of the war for independence.

Francisco María González, a highly reputable stenographer and the *lector* at the Eduardo H. Gato Factory, attended Martí's speech in Tampa, transcribed the presentation, and as soon as the session ended, rushed to send Poyo details of the visit and portions of the speech.[28] *El Yara* immediately published a supplement that contained a minutely detailed account of Martí's visit to Tampa, the exceptional welcome the whole town had extended to him, the rounds he made of the cigar workshops, and his talks at different clubs. "Everything was ready" in Tampa, said Martí at the conclusion of his visit.[29]

In another sense, he knew deep down that there was still much to be done, because he had to win over Key West. Poyo, like the Cubans in Key West, had shown himself to be somewhat indifferent to the plans Martí was promoting from New York. But when he learned how well Martí had been received in Tampa by cigar workers, *lectores*, businesspeople, and politicians, it awoke in him an unusual interest. Everyone wanted to meet Martí and hear him speak.

The supplement published by *El Yara* could not have suited Martí better, because it was immediately heard by the cigar workers in Key West. It became readily apparent that Martí was promoting unity to carry out the insurrection, and that the Tampa cigar makers were more than willing to support his efforts. Needless to say, a speech is written to be heard. More specifically, since a speech is written or given so that it will achieve the goal of reaching those who hear it, Martí had the good fortune to be heard in cigar factories, where the audience that was unable to go see him was able to hear him by way of the voice of the *lector*. We must not forget that most *lectores* were orators, and their voices were already graced with the gift of persuasion. Martí's speech had such an impact on his audience that it bears including the ending:

Out of the torn entrails we are building an unquenchable love of country without which no man, good or bad, can live happily. There she is, calling to us. We can hear her moan; she is being raped and mocked and turned gangrenous before our eyes. Our dearest mother is being corrupted and torn limb from limb! So let us rise up at once with a final burst of heartfelt energy. Let us rise up so that freedom will not be endangered by confusion or apathy or impatience in preparing it. Let us rise up for the true republic, those of us who, with our passion for right and our habit of hard work, will know how to preserve it. Let us rise up to give graves to the heroes whose spirit roams the world, alone and ashamed. Let us rise up so that some day our children will have graves! And let us place around the star of our new flag this formula of love triumphant: "With all, and for the good of all."[30]

One of the persuasive elements Martí employed was the use of voice as a metaphor for repression, exile, and freedom, which is why his homeland is "calling to us. We can hear her moan." As Jorge Mañach observed, this speech was "a model of perfect public speaking," since "in short, he had to mobilize that diverse and somewhat youthful mass, not only for the initial rapport, but also for immediate action; so as to neither betray himself, nor to sacrifice the doctrine of the 'foundation' to revolutionary diligence."[31]

Hearing this speech was all it took to convince the cigar workers to support the revolutionary cause, although it is especially symbolic that the workers in Key West had heard the speech from the mouth of the *lector*. This demonstrates the power of the word and, in this case, more than anything, the power of reading aloud. Without the involvement of the *lectores*, Martí's speech would not have made such a great impact, since for the *lector*, champion of the people that he or she was, it was not difficult to recite a speech eloquently.

In some factories *lectores* read while standing, a position that allowed them to function much like someone giving a speech. The inflection of the *lector* must have been of utmost importance when he read a speech by Martí. In essence, the work of the *lectores* was indispensable in the efforts to have Martí's message reach the cigar workers of Key West.

Back in New York, Martí read what Poyo had published in *El Yara* with regard to his visit to Tampa. A surprised Martí hurried to write to him, thanking him and letting him know that he wanted to be invited to Key West. In the letter he lamented:

But how can I go to Key West of my own volition, like a well-known beggar who searches for friends, or as a supplicant, when I would go as a simple, tender man who trembles to think that his brothers might fall prey to the deceptive and authoritarian politics of evil republics? It is as sweet to obey the mandate of one's countrymen as it is improper to ask for it. It is my dream that each Cuban be a completely free political individual, as I understand the Cuban of Key West to be, and that all his acts be engendered by wise affection and by independent choice, without the harmful influence of some hidden motivation. For although one may die of desire to enter a beloved house, what right does he have to show up, as an intruder, where he has not been invited?[32]

By then, Martí was aware of the importance and impact of reading aloud in cigar factories. Thus, when he wrote to Poyo, he knew very well that his letter would probably be read to the cigar workers, which is why this letter intentionally included rhetorical questions that disguised how convincing Martí wanted his epistle to sound. He purposely asked a question and subtly demanded the answer he anticipated. Martí was a master of rhetoric and knew that the cigar workers were first and foremost a listening audience, a fact he had just learned in Tampa, because before he traveled to Florida, he was unaware of the institution of reading aloud in cigar factories. Therefore, if he was to win over Key West, he had to make an appearance there and make use of the platform of the *lector* to lay out his plan.

It was almost a dream come true. Poyo published Martí's letter. The letter was read and heard. Martí was immediately invited to Key West by a committee made up of Serafín Bello, an old friend of Martí's; Francisco María González, a *lector*; and a group of cigar makers, because everyone in Key West also wanted to see and hear him speak.

On the evening of December 25, 1891, Martí arrived in Key West on the steamship *Olivette*. Strategically, he had asked the leaders of the revolutionary movement from Tampa to accompany him, and they obliged. Although he was ill during the first five days of his visit, he had the opportunity to give several revolutionary speeches. For example, he visited the Club San Carlos for a political gathering, at which he addressed the members of La Convención Cubana [Cuban Convention of Key West], whose members included José Francisco Lamadriz, Fernando Figueredo—another cigar factory *lector*—and José Dolores Poyo. La Convención Cubana was the flagship patriotic and revolutionary organization in Key West and had two dozen members whose sole responsibility was to form a small club that would operate under the direction of La Convención Cubana. As Néstor Carbonell observed during a visit to Key West: "Martí explained his plans, based mainly on the unification of exiles, that is, by promoting a party that, in a broader sense than La Convención, would join all exiles' associations," and thus he proposed the platform of the Partido Revolucionario Cubano [Cuban Revolutionary Party].[33]

The next day, El Círculo Cubano [Cuban Club] offered to hold a public literary, musical, and artistic soirée for Martí. As I have noted, the *lectores* played a very important role on those occasions, because they were the organizers and masters of ceremonies. In honor of Martí's visit, members of the community gathered at the Teatro de San Carlos [theater at the Key West San Carlos Institute], where boys and girls played musical selections on the piano; there was a violin performance; patriotic songs were sung; melodies were played on the zither; poetry was recited; a one-act comedy titled *La casa de campo* was performed; and Martí was presented with a framed portrait of himself inscribed with "One of the glories of Cuba."[34]

At artistic soirées, Martí was asked to speak; thus, he had the privilege of having a broader community listen to him. On this tour, Martí also visited private homes, schools, and associations, but the most important visits were those he paid to cigar factories.

On the morning of January 3, 1892, Martí and his entourage made their way to the Barrio de Gato, as the cigar workers called the place where Eduardo H. Gato's factory was located. It was a huge wooden building surrounded by hundreds of small houses that the owner had had built for his employees. Martí arrived at the cigar factory in the company of revolutionaries from Tampa and public figures from Key West. The factory comprised two floors, like many factories in Havana, and more than seven hundred workers were employed there in the various departments. José Dolores Poyo, Francisco María González, and a group of cigar workers met him just outside the factory. Everyone knew that Martí would be visiting them, and they anxiously awaited his arrival.

The main workroom was located on the second floor and housed dozens of rows of *vapores*. As I have previously stated, the rows of workbenches were lined up like students' desks in school; thus, the space resembled a classroom or auditorium. At Gato's factory, approximately five hundred cigar makers sat in the same workroom. The platform for the *lector* was in the middle of the workshop, off to one side. With Martí's visit in mind, the cigar makers decorated the workshop with multicolored curtains and banners. So, symbolically, the work space had a civic-minded and educational appearance much like a school setting.

When Martí entered with his entourage, the cigar rollers could not see him because they were on the second floor, but when they heard he was arriving, they began to tap their *chavetas* on their workbenches. The group came upstairs. Poyo went up on the platform for the *lector* and introduced the guests, then Martí gave his speech: "The Republic is the people with the worker's *chaveta* in its right hand, and the rifle of freedom in its left!"[35] This was one of the utterances of which Martí was most fond.

The *chaveta*, as we have seen, is the cigar roller's main utensil, because it is the knife, the implement, with which the leaf is cut and the cigar is shaped. Without the *chaveta*, it is impossible to make a proper cigar; therefore, the lack of the tool would symbolically represent the lack of support, of refuge, and of protection. Conversely, the *chaveta* is literally a double-edged sword, because, while it serves as an implement for cutting tobacco leaves, it also can be used as a defensive and fighting weapon. This is why Martí gave his phrase a double meaning, because if a republic were to be created, while it would be important to have financial support through the *chaveta* and the cigar-making workforce, at the same time, it would be important to form ranks and fight.

Martí received such a warm welcome from the cigar makers at Gato's factory that, by the time he left the building, he knew that everyone was on his side. Additionally, the owner, millionaire Eduardo H. Gato, was more than willing to contribute to Martí's campaign. During that visit, Martí made the rounds of all the factories in Key West, and his revolutionary entourage accompanied him to all of them. But first and foremost, the cigar factory *lectores* were his standard bearers.

Three days after his visit to Gato's factory, on January 6, 1892, an order was signed establishing the platform of the Partido Revolucionario Cubano.[36] Cigar workers from Tampa, Key West, and a variety of Cuban immigrant associations in the United States would be united by the party. This would be the body that would lead the insurrection for independence against Spain in Cuba. Martí had achieved what he had set out to do: he had won over Key West.

Martí returned to Key West with the goal of continuing his campaign. Between 1892 and 1895, the year in which the revolution started, the cigar workers were more than willing to offer him financial backing. On one occasion, Martí would recall "beautiful Key West, when six hundred souls from Gato's house, to the beat of tapping *chavetas*, which pierced the soul, greeted with gentle madness the poor gangly man who had just asked them for another contribution, which they gave, out of the goodness of their hearts, more than what was asked of them."[37] Martí asked Eduardo H. Gato for thousands upon thousands of dollars, and Gato always supported him.[38] On April 10, 1893, Martí wrote in his newspaper, *Patria*:

No. Not *Patria*. Some rogue must be putting on his tie and tails to show up as a lackey, there at the parties in Cuba, the parties at which, under the pretext of the centennial of Columbus, face powders and fancy trinkets are brought out so that the Spanish government of Cuba and Puerto Rico may shine like a new rotted wig . . . *Patria* prefers to that activity that of celebrating Cubans, who, after working all week to provide for their households, work, just as on many other occasions, during their day of rest, their Sunday, for the treasure with which they will obtain their honor as men and that of their brothers. Some little dancing man, recently come from who knows where, at his lieutenant's elbow may look down on those "cigar workers" of Key West between one brandy and the next; *Patria* prefers, from the heart, to send greetings to the cigar workers of the house of O'Halloran.[39]

It was common practice for cigar workers to work overtime and to donate their earnings to the Partido Revolucionario Cubano. Moreover, literary gatherings and conferences were held at which donations were collected for the revolutionary cause.

As far as Martí was concerned, platforms in social settings (clubs and recreational organizations) and those in workplaces (cigar factories) served a dual purpose, as both functioned as platforms that were as much cultural as political. The cigar workers were "agents" who contributed to their own "cultural capital," because they paid the *lector* to read to them and educate them.[40] At the same time, those cigar workers helped to shape cultural capital for their children, because they were the ones who kept the schools afloat. Likewise, through their work, they supported the revolutionary cause, and in the evenings and on weekends, cultural presentations were held at the school, where once again cigar workers donated money.

Again, we must keep in mind that *lectores* played a very important role in all these activities, and if they donated anything to the cause, it was their time. Martí held the investment Cubans made in education (and in the war) in very high esteem:

What the artisans of Key West are doing now with the schools of San Carlos should be written in the heavens; the stars should be that: virtues which shine in the blue firmament. Just yesterday, in response to the voice of a man who never confused them with flattery, or courted their passion, in response to the voice of the anguished homeland, they gave up, as on a holiday, the work of a whole day for the treasure which, despite intrigues and betrayals, will be salvaged whole entirely and will buy the just republic through independence . . . Just yesterday the artisans of Key West gave the product of one

day of work to the revolution; and today, when the free pupils of San Carlos
sit at their table, the pupils of the public good, which the public maintains
and the public administers—because when it comes to harmony and liberty,
the Cuban needs few lessons—those generous heads are raised attentively,
the *criollo* heart gives birth again, and once more the workers' hands are
opened so that the children are not left without a teacher; all the children:
those of African heritage, and those of Spanish color.[41]

Education at school and in cigar factories was just as important as the
support given to the nationalist movement. Conscious of this, Martí suggested to the cigar factory *lectores* what kind of conferences to organize
and what kind of texts to read. "Key West has everything, and she can
give all she has," Martí told the Partido Revolucionario Cubano Advisory
Board, of which Poyo was president. In a letter dated August 18, 1892, Martí
asked the board to hold low-budget monthly gatherings in all the clubs to
include dramatic readings, lively depictions of Cuban traditions, selected
passages from works by local writers, readings of poetry written in Cuba,
stimulating accounts about Cuban poets, and "another day, as part of the
program, a well-prepared interactive session in which the presenters tell
the audience—by way of acting and performing, to stir enthusiasm—war
stories."[42]

Suffice it to say, Martí was an old-school nationalist whose agenda was
to maintain Cuban cultural integrity, and to that end, the voice of the *lector*
was indispensable. Note that what he asked of Poyo was that, before all else,
he take on readings and presentations in which the spoken word was kept
alive.

Ultimately, reading aloud and cigar factory *lectores* were essential to the
cultural development of Key West. But of even greater importance was the
fact that the practice had been established in the United States at precisely
the time when it had been interrupted in Cuba, where reading aloud did
not take place between 1868 and 1882. Reading aloud in cigar factories in
Key West not only laid the foundation for a practice that would be carried out for decades outside Cuba, but also contributed to a Cuban cultural
phenomenon becoming firmly rooted in the United States. Also, reading
aloud helped to keep the native tongue alive and well in a foreign land.

Surprised by what he had seen in Key West, José Martí told a group of
Cubans who heard him speak in New York:

I will show you the house of the people [Club San Carlos,] which is paid for
and administered by all the people, and where all the people are educated

and join together; I will show you those workshops where men, putting real life aside in favor of books, practice politics, which is the study of public interest, in the work which purifies and moderates it, and in the truth which roots it firmly; I will show you those humble and happy abodes, with so much light and so many smiles and so many roses, where the new wife welcomes home her worker with the baby in her arms, and the books on the shelf serve as witnesses.[43]

In Key West, Martí found an educated audience that supported its education at work and at school avidly and enthusiastically. The work of the *lectores* as teachers, leaders, and cultural facilitators was remarkable. As I indicated earlier, Key West had an educated populace in the political sense. "Don't forget me, because I want to learn!" a sobbing child exclaimed to Martí when he embraced him.[44] The people of Key West reached out to Martí because, deep down, they supported the movement for independence, and, after all, children are educated both in school and at home. Thus, the cigar factory *lectores* were the cultural facilitators and the cigar makers were the newly inducted members who in turn expressed their concerns, their political and labor differences, and their ideological and intellectual preferences.[45]

Just about to saddle up and leave, two months before he died, José Martí wrote a brief message to one of his closest friends. The Apóstol was in Santiago de los Caballeros, in the Dominican Republic, and was on his way to Monte Cristi in 1895. In that message, he tells his friend from the heart: "Let me take to the sea now and leave you. One day we will see a day of peace, of humble, honorable peace."[46] This time, Martí did not have time to sign off in his usual way: "Do not stop loving me."[47] He wrote this message to José Dolores Poyo.

On February 24, 1895, the Spanish-American War broke out, and for the next three years, reading aloud in cigar factories in Key West decreased dramatically. On May 19, Martí ended his days in Dos Ríos, in his beloved Cuba, whose independence he did not live to see.

FOUR

Tampa

—┤▪▪▪┤—

I

On the morning of December 22, 1903, two men were having a heated argument in the bar of the Restaurante Lorenzana in Tampa, Florida. The dispute reached such proportions that both drew their guns and fired at each other. The shooting continued as each of the rivals tried to escape from the other. Once they were outside, however, one of them, having taken bullets to the chest, stomach, and leg, fell to the ground; the other was wounded on the right side of his chest.

Jesús Fernández was from Spain; Enrique Velázquez was from Mexico. The fight had carried over from the previous day at the José Lovera Cigar Factory in Tampa, where both men were cigar workers. Their argument started when the cigar factory *lector* introduced a novel published in Spanish as *La canalla*, by Émile Zola, as one of the possible works to be read aloud. There were a number of women working in the factory, and some objected to the work's being read because they considered it to be immoral.[1] All of a sudden, everyone in the workshop started to argue about whether the work was of an obscene nature or not.

Irate at not being of one opinion about *La canalla*, Fernández and Velázquez continued to argue when they left the workshop, and in front of the crowd that surrounded them, they both vowed that, if they saw each other again, they would do one another in. No one thought that the next morning the two would still be inclined to fulfill their promises, but when they saw each other in the bar at the Restaurante Lorenzana, the drama continued. Five days after the incident, Velázquez died as a result of the wounds he sustained.[2]

How can reality end up being more like fiction than fiction itself? This incident seems to come straight out of a novel, and, to be more precise, it reminds us of the narrator's statement in *Chronicle of a Death Foretold*, by Gabriel García Márquez: "There had never been a death more foretold."[3]

But the fact that the crowd that surrounded the rivals in the bar was not able to do anything about the matter is not as surprising as the way a work of literature can ultimately affect readers and listeners. That incident reflects how important reading aloud was in Tampa, where it was the cause of murders, kidnappings, strikes, high hopes, and disenchantment.

On April 12, 1886, the steamship *Mascotte* put into port in Tampa. The boat had sailed from Key West, and most of the passengers were cigar makers; all of them were very discouraged and distressed by the bad luck that had obliged them to board the ship. They had lost everything they had in Key West; they were homeless, and their jobs had disappeared. They were victims of the fire that razed the city on April 1 of that year and which destroyed more than half the island.

In 1885, a year before the cigar makers' nearly accidental arrival, Tampa had only 720 residents.[4] That year, Vicente Martínez Ybor, owner of the Príncipe de Gales Factory in Key West, decided to transplant his factory to Tampa due to the frequent interruptions that were taking place because of labor struggles promoted by his personnel. Martínez Ybor had confronted the cigar workers in his factory several times when the workers demanded better working conditions and higher salaries. A series of strikes had threatened the welfare of his factory, and, as a result, he decided to leave Key West and establish himself in Tampa. To that end, he bought a vast expanse of land in northwest Tampa. This area, located on the outskirts of the city, is what later would be called Ybor City.

In October 1885, construction in Ybor City (which was not really a city, but, rather, a neighborhood in Tampa) got under way. Priority was given to the establishment of workshops, housing for employees, and businesses selling household goods and basic necessities. At first, two factories were built: Martínez Ybor and La Flor de Sánchez y Haya. The owner of the latter was Ignacio Haya, who transplanted his factory from New York because it was better for him to be in a more appropriate climate, with more physical space for his employees, and especially where he would have a Cuban workforce. Martínez Ybor's factory was set up on Seventh Avenue between Twelfth and Thirteenth streets. It was a wooden building and was a sort of two-story house built on brick columns.

Both Martínez Ybor's and Haya's factories began operations in February 1886, but they did not have enough staff. Tampa or, rather, Ybor City was a deserted, nearly desolate place. The streets were not paved, so people had to walk on sand, and there were no streetlights. Eligio Carbonell [y] Malta, an Ybor resident during that year, described the city as follows:

> In order to go from one place to another in town, the [traveler] had to prepare himself for an ordeal as if it were a hard trip across a desert. . . . Sidewalks or any other kind of paving which facilitated public traffic did not exist then. . . . The settlement lacked public lighting. Therefore, it was indispensable that the night traveler prepare himself with a lamp or lantern which would permit him to see his way. The streets were not exempt from danger, and one also had to go prepared with a rifle or a revolver in case of a disagreeable encounter with dangerous animals. . . . Added to all of this was the constant threat of the deadly malaria fever, whose germs infected the air because of the nearby swamps and mudlands.[5]

So when the cigar workers from Key West, used to a dynamic social and cultural life, arrived in Ybor City, it seemed like a small hamlet in the middle of nowhere. This is the context in which reading aloud started in the cigar factories there.

But things did not happen by chance. When the *Mascotte* left Key West on April 11, 1886, a key person was on board—José Dolores Poyo, who introduced reading aloud in that part of the United States. Moreover, Ramón Rivero Rivero, who would become the most important *lector* in Ybor City until 1900, made the same voyage.

In 1886 in Ybor City, there were no newspapers, schools, libraries, theaters, or social or recreation centers. In a cultural sense, it was necessary to populate the city. Thus, the establishment of reading aloud in cigar factories was an extremely important accomplishment because, while the cigar makers were working, they could listen to news from other places as well as what was happening in their immediate environs.

At first, the *lectores* in Tampa faced the same obstacle that the *lectores* in Key West had: newspapers came from New York, Key West, or Havana two or three days after publication. Also, most of the time, English-language newspapers had the greatest circulation; that is, the local papers, the *Morning Tribune* or the *Tampa Daily News*, or even the *New York Herald* or the *New York Times*, reached Tampa more quickly than, for example, *El Avisador Cubano* or *Novedades* from New York, *La Propaganda* from Key West, or *El Diario de la Marina* from Havana. Under those circumstances, the *lectores* had to translate the news from English to Spanish.

Thus, as the *lector* at the Martínez Ybor Factory, José Dolores Poyo took the initiative in Ybor City of restarting his newspaper, *El Yara*, which he had been forced to suspend in Key West. Poyo read his newspaper enthusiastically to the cigar workers. He also took on the task of translating any newspaper he could get his hands on. His time in Ybor City lasted only a matter of months, from April to approximately October, as he decided to return to Key West, but his work as the founder of reading aloud in that desertlike place was transcendent.

Ramón Rivero Rivero, who had been a journalist in Key West, replaced Poyo at the factory, and, in light of the fact that the publication of *El Yara* had been suspended due to Poyo's having left, at the end of 1886, Rivero started to publish *Revista de Florida*, which, like *El Yara*, dealt with international, national, and local issues.

Other newspapers gradually began to be published, but they were very short-lived because of the lack of subscribers. So the cigar factory *lector,* the primary spokesman in Ybor City, was the one who ran to the port to wait for the arrival of newspapers from other places, and if an important news item was reported late at night, he showed up on any street corner or at any gathering place to read the latest news aloud. At the very beginning, the *lector* established himself not only as an essential figure in the workplace, but also, by extension, as a fundamental person within the community.

By the end of 1886, the cigar industry was flourishing in Tampa, as evidenced by the construction of a three-story brick building with room for eight hundred employees. It was Martínez Ybor's new factory, which included extensive space for the various departments. The upstairs housed rows of hundreds of workbenches for the cigar rollers, and of course, a platform for the *lector*. The lavish building stood on Fourteenth Street between Eighth and Ninth avenues.

What is most intriguing is Martínez Ybor's decision to donate the building that had housed the original factory to the cigar workers, so they could hold their parties and meetings there. The interior of the simple two-story wooden building was completely remodeled. The second-floor workshop became a huge room with a stage and a proscenium intended for artistic performances. Symbolically, the transformation of the platform from a sort of lectern to a stage was nothing short of a reflection of the tasks and activities that the *lector* undertook in the workplace and the community.

In 1887, *lector* Ramón Rivero took the initiative of founding an educational and recreational club called Flor Crombet. In addition to reading aloud, he was an active member of the club and organized literary gatherings as well as serving as master of ceremonies. The *lector* was concerned with the promotion of harmony both inside and outside the cigar factory, and with the cigar workers enjoying a worthwhile social and cultural life.

Rivero was convinced that Cuba should be a free, sovereign country; thus, he supported the ideology of independence. Since the Flor Crombet Club did not last long, in 1888, Rivero founded La Liga Patriótica Cubana [Cuban Patriotic League], which was a secret society where the most noteworthy revolutionary immigrants gathered. All of them worked in the cigar trade. La Liga organized meetings, gave classes, and held parties and a wide variety of social events in which most of the cigar workers participated. Although La Liga was a political organization, it provided residents with a social and cultural life that would otherwise not have been easy to achieve. The society's board of directors believed "that the labor movement should be kept apart from the struggle and from political and religious matters, so that it would show unity in its objectives and methods."[6] As a result, La Liga had many followers, especially among the nationalist cigar workers who had come from Key West and who wanted Cuba to free itself from Spain.

In 1890, a new organization was founded in the former Martínez Ybor cigar factory. El Liceo Cubano was described as an artistic and literary society. The building was decorated in the style of the Club San Carlos in Key West, as Cuban coats of arms and flags were hung, as well as portraits of erstwhile patriots, teachers, politicians, and scientists. In addition, a night school was established at the club's headquarters, and its principal was Néstor Leonelo Carbonell, a veteran of the Ten Years' War who had first emigrated from Cuba to Key West, where he was a teacher. Only having just arrived in Ybor City in 1890, he was more than willing to continue his career as an educator and to direct his energies toward the fight for Cuban independence. Thanks to his initiative, as well as that of Ramón Rivero and several prominent cigar workers, El Liceo Cubano was founded. More important, Néstor Leonelo Carbonell also worked as a *lector* in cigar factories.[7]

La Liga Patriótica Cubana was the first association established in El Liceo Cubano, and since the artistic, literary, and patriotic gatherings that its leaders organized attracted crowds, a close connection was formed between the cigar workers who were members of other clubs and associations that had come into being in Ybor in its barely four years in existence.

Between 1886 and 1890, Tampa made remarkable progress. From the 720 people who lived there in 1886, by 1890, the figure had climbed to 5,532.[8] The number of factories that had been transplanted from New York, Philadelphia, and Key West had also increased considerably. Ybor City's physical appearance had changed; by 1889, main thoroughfares were paved, wells had been dug to supply the city with water, and electric lighting came into use.

The prosperity of that part of the United States attracted other industrialists, such as the brothers Manuel and Fernando J. del Pino, Cubans who, with the establishment of their cigar factory to the west of Tampa, gave rise to the small town of Pino City. Dozens of Cuban families established themselves there, and for years that suburb of Tampa was almost entirely populated by Cubans.[9] By 1890, reading aloud had spread to other cigar factories in Ybor City and Pino City.

Tampa's progress attracted cigar workers from Havana, Key West, and other parts of the United States, such as Philadelphia, New York, and New Orleans. Not all cigar workers were Cuban; many were Spaniards. There were also Italian immigrants born in southwest Sicily but who came to Tampa from a small town near New Orleans, where they had lived for a few years.[10]

Both Cubans and Spaniards worked in the cigar factories, and within the workplace there was little dissension among them, because they were all part of the same workforce. In 1890 in Ybor City, there were 233 Spaniards, mostly single men, and 2,424 Cubans, counting men, women, and children. There were some political differences, but it would be imprecise to say that all Cubans were against the Spaniards, or vice versa. Likewise, it would be an exaggeration to say that all Spaniards who lived in Ybor City were against Cuban independence; after all, many of them had fled Cuba in search of better working conditions, or had escaped because Cuba was at war. The clearest example of this was that Vicente Martínez Ybor was a Spaniard, and he supported Cuban independence.

In 1891, Néstor Leonelo Carbonell, his son Eligio Carbonell [y] Malta, many veterans of the Ten Years' War, *lectores*, journalists, and cigar workers decided to found El Club Ignacio Agramonte, a Cuban revolutionary organization whose project was fund-raising for a future war of independence. Néstor Leonelo Carbonell was the club's first president.

As in Key West at clubs of this ilk, the job of cigar factory *lectores* was organizing artistic, literary, and patriotic functions to raise funds. In the cigar factories, the *lectores* were the ones who announced a variety of activities at the clubs and at their headquarters (in this case, at El Liceo Cubano).

II

The cigar worker with his artistry
makes his camp in the roots of history;

with Martí he destroyed all tyranny
in Tampa's magnificent factories.

GUILLERMO VILLARONDA, "IN PRAISE OF THE HAVANA CIGAR"

To commemorate El Grito de Yara, Néstor Leonelo Carbonell and the board of directors of El Club Ignacio Agramonte decided to invite José Martí to Tampa to participate in a literary gathering.[11] The commemoration was belated, but on the evening of November 25, 1891, Carbonell, Rivero, and other members of Tampa's Cuban neighborhood made their way to the train station to meet Martí. As I indicated previously, that invitation was extremely important to Martí, because his goal was to attract followers who would help him carry out the revolution for independence.

The next morning, accompanied by Ramón Rivero, Martí visited the Martínez Ybor Factory. As I have stated, the factory was a three-story brick building with large windows measuring more than two yards on the sides. There were ten mosaic-tiled steps at the building's entrance and an ornate rectangular gate that stood at least four yards high. Eduardo Manrara, a Cuban partner of Martínez Ybor's, was waiting for Martí at the entrance.

When Martí entered the factory, the *lector* who was substituting for Ramón Rivero stopped reading and gave the platform to Rivero. This was the first time Martí had seen a *lector* and learned about the practice. Accustomed to speaking to crowds from a platform, on this occasion he occupied the work space of the *lector*, and he spoke to the cigar workers about how important it was to start a revolution for independence, and how crucial it was that they unite in that cause.[12]

In the afternoon, Martí made the rounds in Pino City and gave a speech at Céspedes Hall, where most of the audience was Cuban. That evening, hundreds of cigar makers heeded the call to go to El Liceo Cubano to hear Martí: "The immaculate Cuban, the very distinguished thinker and excellent speaker, José Martí, has now arrived. In coming here he has scorned his need for rest, perhaps brought forth tears in the beloved wife who saw him depart, interrupted his own many projects and courteously complied with the request of his fellow countrymen from Tampa."[13] Then Martí began his speech with its now well-known first sentence: "For suffering Cuba, the first word."

As evidenced by what we have seen thus far, the work of the *lectores* was indispensable during Martí's visit. In fact, without them, Martí would not have gained the popularity he was able to achieve among the cigar workers. The *lectores* were the ones who took the initiative of inviting him to

Tampa, of introducing him in the cigar factories, and of accompanying him on his visits to the various clubs and associations. From the moment Martí set foot in Tampa, he realized that in the future he would not be able to make inroads in any part of Florida if he were not accompanied by those *lectores*. Indeed, when later that same year Martí was invited to Key West, he made sure to go first to Tampa and leave for the Keys from there, accompanied by Ramón Rivero, who never left his side during his entire visit to Key West.

The same held true on their return. When Martí traveled from Key West to Tampa, he asked José Dolores Poyo, a *lector* at that time in Key West, to accompany him. One of Martí's other constant companions during his trips to Florida was Francisco María González, *lector* and stenographer in Key West.

In the introduction to his famous speech, known as "With All, and for the Good of All," Martí strategically thanks Néstor Leonelo Carbonell and Ramón Rivero and mentions reading in the workshops:

Cubans: For suffering Cuba, the first word. Cuba must be considered an altar for the offering of our lives, not a pedestal for lifting us above it. And now, after calling forth its most cherished name, I shall lavish the tenderness of my soul upon these generous hands that come to give me strength—surely not inopportunely—for the agonizing task of building. Now, with our eyes placed higher than our heads, and my own heart torn out of my body, I shall not egoistically thank those who think they see in me the virtues they desire both from me and from every Cuban. Nor will I merely thank the genial Carbonell or the fearless Rivero for the magnificent hospitality of their words and the fervor of their generous affections. But I shall give all the gratitude in my soul to them, and through them in all those here who have set their hands to the task of creating; to these loving people who have stood up in the face of the ambitious landowner who spies upon us and divides us; . . . to these cultured people whose writing desks stand beside their work benches, and for whom the thunderings of Mirabeau stand beside the arts of Roland—answer enough for the contemptuous of this world; to this temple bedecked with heroes and built upon men's hearts.[14]

It was of critical importance to start the speech by alluding to reading aloud, which is why he used the symbol of the altar as a metaphor for a pulpit or table from which one read and disseminated the truth. Likewise, he mentioned the *lectores* (and not the factory owners) to show his solidarity with them. Martí knew that, if he were to win over the cigar workers of Tampa, he first had to establish an extremely close connection with the *lectores,* because they were the linchpins of the cigar factories.

Martí admired the task of reading aloud, which is why the *lector* was to him like a priest or teacher in a temple, who reads from an altar or pulpit to the souls there present. Martí's speech is, in itself, a sort of prayer or supplication directed specifically to a listening public, and since all the people gathered were adept at the art of listening well, they truly appreciated what he had to say.

The speech he gave the following day, known as "The New Pines," given at the soirée-homage to the students who were shot in 1871, was also one of the most eloquent he had ever given.[15] Here Martí uses the image of the pine trees as a metaphor for unity, fraternity, and freedom. He alludes to Tampa's landscape, starting with the view a traveler arriving by train sees: the dynamic trajectory of an ever-changing panoramic view. The landscape and pine trees function as a symbol of what the Cubans could achieve in the end if they mobilized and fought for independence. The speech ends with exquisite persuasive prose:

> Today, let us sing the hymn of life before the memorial of their [the students'] graves. Yesterday I heard it coming from the earth itself, when we came to this gracious town. The landscape was damp and shadowy; the streams ran turbulent and muddy; the sugar cane, sparse and withered, did not move sorrowfully like the one far away that seeks redemption for those who nourished it with their death. Rather, its blades entered, rough and sharp, like daggers through the heart. In defiance of the storm clouds, one pine stood with its top raised. Suddenly the sun broke through a clearing in the forest, and there in the midst of the shimmering light, I saw growing over the yellowed grass, next to the blackened trunks of fallen pines, bunches of new pines. That is what we are: the new pines![16]

Oddly enough, the previous afternoon, Martí had visited the suburb known as Pino City, where all the residents were Cuban, and there was very little disagreement among them. It would not be a stretch to say that Martí used the metaphor of the new pines to allude to the population of Pino City, a new town united in solidarity that served as an example of what could be done in the Cuba of the future.

It must be reiterated that the speeches given by Martí in Tampa were immediately published and read in cigar factories there and in Key West, thanks to the work of Francisco María González, *lector* and stenographer. Likewise, the work of Ramón Rivero was quite remarkable because he wasted no time publishing all the speeches given by Martí during his first trip to Tampa in his newspaper, *El Crítico de Ibor City/Ybor City Critic.*

When Martí returned to New York, he said the following about his trip to Tampa at a talk given at Hardman Hall on February 17, 1892:

> The columns adorned with flags enclosed borders of new pines. The sun shone, and with it unaccustomed love, sudden knowledge, the joy of being together in the dawn of a new age, the pride of seeing and showing off the happy family—the school with its luxuries—the counselor who comes and goes, spreading balm on any wound he sees, and books and newspapers and lessons at the workers' attentive table; the orator who plucks from his natural greatness the fiercest and most deeply felt eloquence which can be heard from any platform; . . . the elegant and gentlemanly artisan, a source of love and a model for youth, who would appear to advantage in the most exquisite salon; . . . the little boy who goes, dressed as if for a party, to his work table, where, between the knife and the cuttings, one can see the poetry he just completed, or his storybook, or his physics book; and the old lady of the workshop, who through the labor of her hands feeds the homeland's prisoners in the castles and the patients in the hospitals, and with her most eloquent pen flagellates or gives advice.[17]

Here he alludes to the *lector* as a teacher, a counselor, and an orator, and to the workshop as a source of work for all and as a cultural nucleus. All generations are represented in this passage: the "old lady" who is a leaf stripper, a woman endowed with wisdom and who is hardworking and educated; the cigar worker, also educated thanks to the *lector*, who provides him with newspapers, books, and lessons; and, finally, the youth who uses the workbench in the cigar factory as a desk. As far as Martí was concerned, beams of culture flowed from the cigar factory, thanks to the example and participation of the *lector*.

III

In February of 1895, before the war started, revolutionary clubs in Tampa numbered forty-six, thirty of which were in Ybor City and the remaining sixteen of which were in West Tampa (previously known as Pino City). In Ybor City, the revolutionary organizations were completely autonomous from the cigar factories, while in West Tampa they were exclusively made up of workers from each of the manufacturing plants; this is why West Tampa was also called "Cuba City."[18]

On February 25, 1895, when Tampa residents learned that war had broken out the previous day, people took to the streets to celebrate. They hoisted Cuban flags, sang *El Himno de Bayamo*, and listened to revolutionary speeches given from the platforms at the clubs. In the cigar factories, the latest news about the war and all the details of what was happening in Cuba were announced from the platform of the *lector*.

In Ybor City and West Tampa, two action committees were formed and took charge of raising funds to be able to send military equipment and medicine to the insurgents. Ramón Rivero took charge of the agency in Ybor City, and the one in West Tampa was led by Fernando Figueredo Socarrás, a veteran of the Ten Years' War who would later become the secretary of the treasury of the Republic of Cuba.[19] Incidentally, Figueredo Socarrás was a cigar factory *lector* at the O'Halloran Factory.[20]

During the Spanish-American War, from 1895 through 1898, reading in Tampa's cigar factories was not suspended. Wenceslao Gálvez y Delmonte, a cigar factory *lector* in Tampa who practiced his profession during the war, was saddened to see the extraordinary efforts being made by Ramón Rivero, who was a teacher, minister, journalist, political figure, and *lector* all at the same time. Unfortunately, said Gálvez y Delmonte, Rivero "cannot even devote himself entirely to his newspaper [*Cuba*]; instead he is in turn a *lector*, and he devotes to his patriotic enterprise the time others devote to resting."[21] And he also pointed out how exhausting the work of the *lectores* was: "Time waits for no man, and repetitive labor oppresses him cruelly and tyrannically. He must be in the workshop, reading aloud to hundreds of men."[22] But in spite of all obstacles, during the war and after it ended, the practice of reading aloud prevailed.

Between 1886 and 1900, reading aloud was gradually established, but not in a uniform manner. Each workshop operated according to its own codes and regulations. To a certain extent, some modeled themselves after the factories of Havana, making reading aloud into an entity with a president and a set schedule during which the news was usually read for an hour and forty-five minutes in the morning, and works of fiction were read for one and one-half hours in the afternoon. Additionally, a system was established whereby employees submitted works of fiction that they would all vote on. Most notably, the profession of *lector* came into being as a full-time position. The *Tampa Tribune* stated in February 1890 that some *lectores* were required to stay in the factory throughout the workday even though "scarcely more than half their time is occupied in reading."[23]

One of the first people who was a full-time *lector* was Wenceslao Gálvez y Delmonte, who, before he came to Tampa in the 1890s, was the first historian of baseball in Cuba as well as a standout player and manager. He had also been a journalist and had written works of fiction.[24] Due to the scarcity of jobs during the Spanish-American War, Gálvez y Delmonte had emigrated from Cuba to Tampa, where he had no choice but to work as a door-to-door salesman. He made the rounds of all the suburbs on foot until he decided to apply for a position as a cigar factory *lector*. Since he was not offered the job, he went back to selling trinkets, until one day, when he was offering his wares at one of the few bookstores in Tampa, he was convinced to go take the test at a cigar factory where there was an opening. On his second try, he passed the test, and from then on he worked as a cigar factory *lector*.[25] Thanks to the account in his book, *Tampa: Impresiones de emigrado*, published in Ybor City in 1897, it has been possible to recover crucial references with regard to reading aloud, and as may be apparent, this part of my study owes a great deal to his extremely important publication.

The fact of the matter was that anyone could apply for the position of *lector*. On the day of the test, the candidate went up on the platform, or stood at the head of a row of workbenches. In some workshops, candidates were asked to bring a text to read, while in others they were provided with a passage from a novel or an article from the press. Aspiring candidates then introduced themselves to the audience and began reading on hearing a bell signaling the beginning of the test. After ten minutes, the bell rang again. After all the candidates finished the test, the cigar workers voted by secret ballot for the candidate they preferred.

Most factories had a reading president, who was an employee elected by coworkers. The reading president was in charge of greeting the applicants, organizing the candidates' introductions and testing, counting the votes, and informing the winner. Also, the reading president kept order in the workshop and kept the time (the small bell was always on the reading president's workbench). If someone interrupted the reading while it was in progress, the president rang the bell to restore silence. Also, the president served as mediator between the workshop and the *lector*, since he told the *lector* which newspapers the audience wanted to have read to them and which books they wanted to vote on.

As I indicated previously, when reading aloud began in Tampa, the dearth of Spanish-language newspapers presented an obstacle for *lectores*, who had to translate the news from English to Spanish. Some *lectores* did not speak English, but even so they attended gatherings with the hope that someone who did speak English would update them on the latest news. In the face of this situation, the number of Spanish-language newspapers began to burgeon in Tampa, starting with *El Yara* (1886), edited by José

Dolores Poyo; *Revista de Florida* (1886–1887), edited by Ramón Rivero; *Heraldo de Tampa* (1887), by Constantino Díaz; *Emigrado Cubano* (1889); *La Contienda* (1890) and *Liceo Cubano* (1890), by Néstor Leonelo Carbonell; *Revista de Tampa* (1890); *El Patriota* (1890), by E. Planas; *El Esclavo* (1890), by Manuel Fuentes; *El Crítico de Ibor City/Ybor City Critic* (1890–1893), by Ramón Rivero; *Revista de Cuba Libre* (1892 and 1898), by Clemencia Arango and Justo Carrillo; *Cuba* (1893–1898), by Ramón Rivero; *El Combate* (1894), by J. H. Hernández; *El Mosquito* (1895), by Eligio Carbonell [y] Malta; *El Español* (1895); *La Opinión* (1896–1897); *Nueva República* (1896–1898), by Pablo Rousseau; *Eco de Martí* (1897); *Expedicionario* (1897); *Libertad* (1897), by Fidel Aragón; *Oriente* (1897); and *Cuba y América* (1898). In short, there were a great many newspapers.[26]

The short lives of the various newspapers were due to the lack of sponsorship and subscribers. An example of this is the newspaper *Cuba*, the official paper of the Partido Revolucionario Cubano in Tampa. In 1897, it was published only three times per week, and the editor kept it going "out of sheer patriotism, since far from making him a profit, it left him in debt."[27]

Lectores had to buy the newspapers they were going to read. As Gálvez y Delmonte said: "In the workshop where I read, there are no regulations. I may bring in any newspaper I might acquire; as I earn very little, they do not wish to insist that I spend a great deal of money on newspapers, which are rather expensive."[28] The minimal circulation of newspapers, logically, caused the price to increase, a fact that presented another difficulty for the *lector*.

With regard to the reading of newspapers, the *lector* enjoyed a certain level of freedom. He bought the newspapers he liked: "I try, of course, to vary the reading as much as I am able, not only to please the workers in the shop, but also in order to treat myself with kindness. And I read newspapers from Cuba, New York, Mexico, Madrid, and Tampa," wrote Gálvez y Delmonte.[29] In fact, *El Imparcial* from Madrid, *El Heraldo* from Asturias, *El Eco* from Galicia, and *Madrid Cómico* arrived regularly from Spain.[30]

Conversely, the *lector* was always required to read one or more newspapers that were to the cigar workers' liking. In this case, whether the *lectores* liked it or not, they had to read it:

There is, however [a newspaper] that to me is sheer torture: *La Lucha*. Not because I am opposed to its way of thinking in terms of the issue of Cuba— each person has every right to believe as he will about public issues—but, rather, because of how badly their inland correspondents write. Blessed be the name of the Lord! I must always out of necessity read those reports for which I have no use. They are all cut from the same cloth and make today's

issue of *La Lucha* look just like yesterday's, always the same, never any different, utilizing the same descriptor of valiant for every soldier, dripping with
adulation for official functionaries.[31]

As a great number of *lectores* were journalists and were accustomed to editing newspapers, no doubt many of them faced the challenge of reading
what was not to their taste.

Another factor that must be taken into account is the diversity of the
listening audience. In any given workshop, there were usually employees of
all ages; Cubans, Spaniards from Galicia and Asturias, and a few Italians;
women, who were mostly leaf strippers, from Cuba, Italy, and the United
States. Those who did not speak Spanish learned the language quickly so
they could understand the *lectores*. The cigar workers' nationalities varied
from workshop to workshop; therefore, *lectores* always had to be receptive
to the varying tastes of the audience, the level of tolerance of the owners
and foremen, and the number of workers in the factory.

Due to the lack of libraries, *lectores* in Tampa depended on getting literary works that arrived on ships from New York or Havana. There was a
small bookstore in Ybor City that sold books by Zola, Daudet, Bourget,
Hugo, and Galdós. Néstor Leonelo Carbonell was the owner of the bookstore, and he rented books to *lectores*.[32] Cigar workers also lent their own
books to the workshop.

Various clubs and associations that were springing up established reading rooms (or small libraries). El Centro Español de Tampa, founded in
1891, served as a model for future associations such as El Centro Asturiano (1902), El Círculo Cubano (Tampa's Cuban Club, 1902), and L'Unione
Italiana (Italian Club of Tampa, 1894).[33] A library was set up in El Centro
Español in 1893, and by 1897 it contained seventy-one literary and informative works, made up of ninety-four volumes. Among the treasured works
were the *Diccionario etimológico*, by Barcia; *Obras poéticas*, by Espronceda;
Vidas y opiniones, by Diógenes Laercio; *El parnaso español*, by Quevedo;
and *Obras completas*, by Campoamor. The club members donated the
books available in these reading rooms or libraries, and the majority of
those club members were cigar workers.[34] Thus, those libraries reflected
what was read aloud at other cigar factories. Ignacio Haya, owner of La
Flor de Sánchez y Haya Factory, was one of the founding members of El
Centro Español. At the cigar factory where Gálvez y Delmonte worked, he
read Dumas, Galdós, Zola, Flaubert, Paul de Kock, and especially all works
by Armando Palacio Valdés, as they were his audience's favorites.[35]

The cigar workers determined the books that would be read in the workshop by way of a vote. Almost all were novels, but there were some exceptions, since now and then *lectores* read histories or books about travel. Both the *lector* and the cigar workers brought in books. The text that got the majority vote was the one the *lector* would read. Only those who paid the *lector* could vote. The *lector* announced the names of the authors and the titles of the books under consideration from the platform. Afterward, the *lector* went from workbench to workbench and collected the vote of each cigar worker (it was a secret ballot). The *lector* would then read each novel's title and the number of votes it received and announce the winning work.

Although it was a democratic election, factions formed. Some liked one author more than any other, and their choice was obvious. But in many cases, neither the works nor the authors were familiar to the workers, and voters abstained or simply voted with the majority.

During the voting process, competitive politics came into play, because if a group preferred an author or a work, it would try to persuade the others in order to gain more votes. Sometimes elections were so contentious that voters threatened the *lectores*, telling them, for example, that, if a certain work won, they would not pay for the reading. To make matters worse, during the reading of the winning work, the faction that had favored it would yell out: "We won!" Losing factions often did not pay for the reading because they had not won, and they complained constantly. However, once a work was chosen, the *lector* had to read the entire thing.[36]

There was generally discipline in the workshop when the reading was taking place. With the exception of the sound of the *chavetas* against the workbenches when the tobacco leaf was being cut, the sounds of the mold in which the just-rolled cigar was placed before its outer wrapper was applied, or someone's coughing or sneezing, the workshop remained silent. According to Gálvez y Delmonte, when the novel was interesting, some workers fell behind because, when they were paying attention to the reading, they could not roll properly. Conversely, when they were not enjoying the novel, everyone in the workshop was in a bad mood, especially the *lector*. Someone might even say: "*Lector*, skip two or three chapters."[37] But these were idle words, because the reading was always respected, and although the listeners might get restless, the *lector* continued reading. One time was all it took: if the reading was not to the taste of the cigar workers, both the author and his or her work were banished for a long time.

The manner of reading aloud, that is, tone, enunciation, inflection, and even body language, played a very important role in the reading process, and they still do. When Gálvez y Delmonte started to work as a *lector*, he suffered through passages written by Alexandre Dumas:

The only thing I resented, and this was because I was a novice, were Dumas'
dialogues:

"Have you seen him?" said the viscount.

"I have," the page answered.

"Blonde?" the viscount gave back.

"Very blonde," replied the page.

"Was he wearing boots?" the viscount added.

"He was," said the page.

The two figures regarded one another.

"That is all," said the viscount. You may go.[38]

The manner of reading no doubt had a marked effect on how the work
was received. In this case, for example, the *lector* attributed bad reading to
his lack of experience as a *lector*, but at the same time he was intuitively cri-
tiquing the writer's style, which is why he says that, compared with Dumas,
Pérez Galdós was "a delight."[39]

The audience was very demanding and insisted on good reading
approaches. They paid attention to gesture, tone, enunciation, and, at the
same time, they expected that both the content and the style of the text
would be to their liking. Moreover, the *lectores* had to keep in mind audience
diversity as well as divisions between male and female workers. Women, for
example, preferred some texts over others that were geared more toward a
male audience. The *lector* was always working under pressure from his audience. As Gálvez y Delmonte so wisely says: "It is the case that one does not
read for oneself, but, rather, for the workers in the shop, and since they pay
for it, it is only fair that one reads purely to please them."[40]

In 1890, the *Tampa Tribune* reported that the *lector* usually earned a
minimum of $20.00 per week (during that year, the weekly fee per cigar
worker was twenty-five cents). The profession of *lector* was "lucrative,"
wrote the editor, since there were *lectores* who earned as much as $125.00 a
week.[41] The article refers to the editor of the *Revista de Tampa*, who worked
part time as a *lector*. But that was truly an exception.

In some workshops in Tampa, paying for reading was not mandatory.
Cigar workers who did not contribute toward paying the *lector* did not
have the right to vote for candidates applying for the position of *lector*,
nor could they vote for books or comment on the text being read. *Lectores*
were charged with collecting their own salaries. On payday, usually Saturday, *lectores* sat by the door of the workshop to collect their salaries. By
1897, the reading fee was still a set rate—twenty-five cents per week per
worker—but cigar workers often gave *lectores* only ten, fifteen, or twenty

cents. Those who worked only four days per week, the so-called discounted ones, often refused to pay because they only worked a short time. Others did not pay because they claimed they had not liked the reading. As Gálvez y Delmonte says, when it came to collecting pay, "the *lector* in this sense ends up as the workshop's scapegoat, the whipping boy," since "the reasons why people do not pay for the reading are unique: I won't pay because I didn't care for the article from a certain newspaper, or because that work was read, or because people laughed when the *lector* read such and such a passage. Unfortunately, the excuses abound for not fulfilling one's duty of camaraderie."[42]

Not all cigar workers were that way; some truly admired the reading and respected both it and the *lector*. There were, in fact, cigar workers who refused to work in workshops where there was no reading. In short, each workshop was different, each had its own guidelines for payment, and each had varying numbers of cigar workers, which directly affected the weekly pay of the *lector*.

From 1886 through 1900, reading aloud was not practiced with uniformity, but what is essential to understand is that the profession of *lector* emerged in Tampa. Also, rules were adopted that made the practice more democratic, such as the reading schedule, the selection of a president, and voting on the works to be read. Still, each workshop had its codes, and the *lector* had to respond and adjust to the diversity of his audience, to their taste, to the tolerance of owners and foremen, and to the number of employees in the factory.

Although reading aloud was not uniform, it transformed the cultural, political, and social life of Tampa. The *lector* was the people's spokesman. He disseminated information and at the same time was a sort of priest or teacher. His vocation and the pleasure he took from his work—which was by no means easy—was that of an educator who rejoices when he sees the achievements of his pupils. For that reason, *lectores* were instrumental in the founding of educational centers and cultural associations.

In great measure, those *lectores* changed the course of history. Politically, they were convinced that Cuba should be a free country; as a result, they committed all their efforts and energy to the revolutionary cause. Thanks to them, Martí was invited to Florida, as we have seen; in fact, the *lectores* took up collections in cigar factories to finance his trip from New York to Tampa. The *lectores* were Martí's supporters and his standard-bearers. With his usual brilliance, Martí realized that the platform of the *lector* was nothing less than a teacher's desk, and he hoped for the day when Cuba would be free, because "when a new land is opened to the worker, business to the *criollo*, newspapers to the truth, and the platform to teacher, which is its true use, oh, Cuba! The American university of the future!"[43]

The century drew to a close, and the practice of reading aloud, that sort of "American university," continued on its way. The new century was about to get off to a roaring start, with lots of surprises in store.

IV

In October 1902, a piece of news shook all the residents of Tampa: Francisco Milián had been abducted in West Tampa. The kidnappers had taken him to a remote part of Hillsborough County, where they stripped him and beat him severely. They threatened him there, telling him that if he did not leave Tampa once and for all, they would kill him. In fact, they challenged him, saying that he was being deported and that he had to return to his native Cuba. The abductors were vigilantes and proudly appeared before the press to say that Milián was "an agitator, a dangerous character, that he must leave [Tampa], never to return."[44] Francisco Milián was a cigar factory *lector* who worked at the Bustillo Brothers and Díaz Factory, and he was also the mayor of West Tampa.

It all started when Mr. Bustillo, the owner of the factory where Milián read, prohibited him from collecting his salary inside the workshop; he asked him to go outside to collect his pay. Outraged, the *lector* refused to do so and quit his job on the spot. Days later, the *lector* mysteriously went missing. He was in the hands of kidnappers. When they beat him and pronounced their own death sentence on him, he wasted no time in boarding the next ship to Key West. Once he arrived there, he wrote a moving letter to the cigar workers, his colleagues:

> Comrades:
>   The firm having ordered me not to make my collections anywhere in the shop, and as it is impossible for me to do it on the outside, because it would be a sorry spectacle in regard to the position I now hold [as mayor] in this town as a servant of the people, I feel myself compelled to lose my wages. I am unable to understand how a human being can exact from another the condition of exposing himself to get a bad cold or some similar malady during this season of the year. Even if I were willing to do it, I do not believe I would be able to resist it. The other readers, so far, have not been made to collect their wages out of the shops. If the firm cannot accede to it, and having in mind that it is an exceptional case and that a reader only collects the price of his personal efforts and by that means in no manner to offend the proprietors

of the business, then, Comrades, you can appoint another reader, if he is willing to accept. If you want to send me some money as payments for the readings of a few days I served you, it would be gladly received, but if you do not, be sure I would bear you no ill will for it.

Comrades, it seems the Committeemen did not expect such incident and by this reason they said nothing to me about it. I hope you would look at this from a dignified standpoint and will not consider it is a sudden determination on my part.[45]

When the four hundred cigar workers heard Francisco Milián's letter, they immediately called a strike. The committee representing the workers issued a manifesto in which it made the following demands: "First, the firm is not to antagonize the readings nor to molest the reader when he is collecting his wages," and "second, the proprietors shall build a platform for the reader to read from."[46]

The details of the incident, as well as the letter and the manifesto, were quickly published in other newspapers. All of Tampa was in an uproar because the news had reached the cigar workers of Ybor City, and no doubt it had been heard in Key West, where Milián had taken temporary refuge. In fact, when Milián arrived in Key West, he immediately met with cigar workers to relate his tragedy to them. Wasting no time, the cigar workers mobilized and went to the police to request protection.[47]

The incident sent such shock waves through Tampa that the residents called a general strike. The whole city stopped in its tracks. There was unanimous opposition to Francisco Milián's deportation and a demand for his unconditional return. The protest was made public, and the responsible parties were accused of having committed "an unlawful act," of having caused "an act which establishes a precedent by which private citizens are denied the right and liberties guaranteed them by the Constitution, where private citizens are denied the right of free speech, their liberty, their home and family."[48] Public officials "prostitute their offices," and their actions are nothing short of a "disgrace and blot on the fair name of Tampa," says the manifesto issued by the strike committees.[49]

But the general strike caused by the Francisco Milián incident was not the first. The previous year, in 1901, there was a strike that lasted four months. The Sociedad de Torcedores de Tampa [Society of Tobacco Workers of Tampa] union, known as La Resistencia, whose membership numbered five thousand, organized a massive strike that caused violence and firings. After four seemingly endless months, the union failed, and in the settlement there were two clauses which read as follows: "that nothing should be read in the factories pertaining to the management of the business"; and "that collections of any kind or for any purpose would be prohibited in the factories or at their doors."[50]

But the restrictions on reading were short-lived, because the *lectores* continued to collect their income inside the factory, and they had the freedom to read essentially whatever the cigar workers wanted to hear. They had the last word after all.

Mr. Bustillo, the owner of the factory where Francisco Milián was a *lector*, did not allow Milián to collect his pay inside the workshop because he had not liked a work that had been read.[51] The content of what had been read is unknown; thus, to say that it was something antiadministration or "anarchist" literature, which had a very bad reputation in those days, would be to fall into the trap of what scholars call the "sociology of misinformation."[52]

The *lectores* were always under scrutiny, for reasons I have repeated often here: they were important public figures who disseminated information quickly. The fact that they were political made them into the perfect target, the newest scapegoat of accusations that easily stereotyped them as agitators, as was the case with Francisco Milián.

"The Cuban simply has got to talk unless there is something going on to rivet his attention. And when he talks it is equally imperative that he gesticulate until his hands and arms are a mere [sickening] blur about his head and body. Now this characteristic . . . is not conducive to the rapid manufacture of cigars. To meet this peculiarity of temperament on the part of the Cuban, it is the custom to employ for each room in the factory a reader," wrote a hurried and careless North American journalist who did not even speak Spanish.[53] And that was not all. He accused the cigar workers of being "fanatical exponents of the trade union idea carried to extremes, with also a strong tincture in their make up of socialism of a semi-militant type" who "are excitable, easily led by their demagogic agitators."[54]

Conversely, Milián told the press: "I have always been with the good people of Tampa, against all agitators and disturbers, and my character can be vouched for by the most prominent citizens of Florida. . . . My record is too well known for me to fear any harm from the citizens of Tampa."[55] It was not sheer chance that Milián had been the mayor of West Tampa for eight years (1901–1908). He was an honorable and educated person who always advocated for the well-being of the residents of his city. It was his reputation, but not his money—because he truly was poor—that caused him to make enemies.[56] The platform of the *lector* was the ideal target for attacking an individual.

On November 12, 1902, Francisco Milián returned victoriously to Tampa. He sailed in on the *Olivetti,* and two officials went onboard to greet him. When he got off the steamship, more than two hundred people were anxiously waiting to see him. Surrounded by the weeping crowd, members of which embraced and applauded him, he made his way to the railway station. When the train reached West Tampa, more than four hundred people were awaiting his arrival. That evening he was taken to the International Cigar Makers Hall, located on Sixth Avenue in Ybor City, where a reception had been organized, with approximately two thousand in attendance. Everyone wanted to pay their respects and shake his hand.[57]

Milián's return was one of the most symbolic events in the history of reading aloud, because it shows how important the institution was and, especially, underscores its power and vulnerability. Two days after Francisco Milián's return, the cigar workers resumed their labor. The agreement reached by the workers at Bustillo Brothers with its owner called for the *lector* to be able to collect his wages inside the factory.[58]

On November 11, 1902, the *Tampa Morning Tribune* noted that word of the incident had reached large numbers of people near and far, and since Milián's deportation had not been an action taken by all citizens, but, rather, by only by a couple of kidnappers, and since the citizens had not approved of the action, it was time for everyone to put the matter behind them: "Milián is at home; he is assured of protection; the sentiment of the community has been expressed; the trouble is all over. There is no occasion for further reference to the subject. Drop it, and drop it at once!"

Ironically, at the beginning of the century, strikes and violent deaths were due not only to the policy regarding the *lector*'s collecting his compensation, but also to what should or should not be read, as was the case with the duel to the death between the Spaniard and the Mexican to whom I referred earlier. On March 2, 1901, an intriguing event took place at La Paz & Parsons Factory in West Tampa. According to the *Morning Tribune*, the male cigar workers in that factory had voted for a book by Paul de Kock, a French author who wrote more than sixty novels; the book was published in Spanish translation as *El cornudo*. When the women who worked in the factory found out that the men had chosen that work, they immediately objected, saying that the work was "immoral." The men defended their choice, saying that the women had no way of knowing whether the text in question was immoral because they had not had it read to them yet; they asked them to be so kind as to reconsider.

Unconvinced, the women went to the owner, Mr. Paz, and threatened to call a strike if the work was read. The owner said that in no case would he allow the reading of immoral material, and when they heard this, the women calmed down and left.

Then the men showed up in the cigar factory office, demanding that either the work be read or they would go on strike. The owner tried to reconcile both sides, but all his efforts were in vain: both groups called a strike and production was completely paralyzed.[59] "Now, the perplexing question arises, as to how this war of 'sex against sex' may be overcome. The labor leaders of the various bodies, male and female, have an enormous task on their hands," said the *Morning Tribune*.[60] Later that day, the *Tampa Tribune* stated that the women's decision to go on strike showed "not only that they had adequate protection, but knew how to manage a 'crisis' of the kind, occurring with them, with inspiring capacity." It also emphasized, almost sarcastically, that "the women must win this present strike. They cannot help doing so, for with the women on strike, the life of the poor, unfortunate [male sex] would be unbearable."[61]

Some weeks later, operations at the factory resumed. The women had won the case. It was also made known that "the objectionable book . . . has been 'put under the ban' in the local factories."[62]

It is unknown to what extent the women had the right to vote for the work that was to be read, since in this case, they did not find out until after the text had been selected. Most of the women worked as leaf strippers, and, surprisingly, more Italian women worked in the factories than of any other nationality: the Ybor City census of 1900 states that 191 Italian women, 75 Cuban women, and only 2 Spanish women were working there.

Working as a leaf stripper was one of the least-desirable positions. As a workers' newspaper in Tampa wrote: leaf stripping attracted only "orphan girls, maids who have no male helper, widows with young children, the victims of divorce, the daughters of large families, the victims of vicious men, or of sick and disabled men."[63]

Most of the Italian women came to the United States with little formal education. In 1910, only 45 percent of the Italian women—and men—knew how to read and write, while all the Hispanic women were educated.[64] Consequently, the Italian women hurried to learn Spanish so they could understand the reading and feel integrated into the community of listeners.

In general, the women of Tampa (and Key West) played an extremely important role within the community, because they volunteered in all kinds of activities, and they served as teachers and organizers of events at the different educational and recreational societies. In contrast, in the factories, they held lower-level jobs. Seldom did leaf strippers sit in the main workshop, where the *lector* read to the workers. The distance of their work space from the *lector* and the cigar rollers reflects the amount of power they had with regard to choosing or suggesting reading matter. Still, the fact that they won the strike in March 1901 shows that they were gradually gaining power within the factory and, specifically, a voice with regard to the reading.

The reading aloud of newspapers at the beginning of the twentieth century continued despite its challenges. The Spanish-language press did not achieve, through circulation or immediacy, the levels of the English-language press. For this reason, when breaking news arrived, the *lector* who could speak or read English well would go that same day to several workshops, as Francisco Milián ended up doing. For example, when news of the Dreyfus trial in Rennes, France, was published, the *lector* had to go from workshop to workshop to bring the workers up to date about what was taking place. While the trial was in session, he read in four factories. The following are his weekly schedules and compensation in each of them: from 7:30 A.M. to 8:30 A.M. at the Ellinger Factory, $28.00; from 10:30 to 11:30 at the Bustillo Brothers Factory, $23.00; from 12:00 to 1:00 P.M. at the O'Halloran Factory, $12.00; and from 2:00 P.M. to 3:00 P.M. at the Barranco, Rico y Guerra Factory, $11.00.[65] This shows that some factories had more than one *lector* and that they took turns with others who arrived with the news in English, or with *lectores* who read only literature. "Mr. Milián not only translates the press dispatches, but he readily reads and translates the editorials of such papers as the *New York Herald*, the *Sun*, and the *American*, and the best speeches made in Congress by our ablest statesmen." He is a "talented and gifted reader." He is "the best translator at sight that there is in the city today," says an article in the *Tampa Tribune*.[66] In 1904, each cigar worker's contribution was still twenty-five cents a week, and according to a newspaper article, the *lectores* who did not speak English collected only fifteen cents per worker.[67]

There were also cigar workers (rollers) who took turns reading when they were not rolling cigars, as was the case with Fermín Souto, a Spaniard born in Galicia. In 1870, he left for Havana and from there moved to Santiago de las Vegas. In Santiago he worked in a general store where the owner bought old newspapers to wrap his merchandise in. Fermín always reviewed those newspapers and read what he could. From Santiago he first immigrated to New York and later moved to Key West, finally settling in Tampa. Souto said in an interview:

> When the factory of Lozano Pendas & Co. had been destroyed by fire, I went to work with Mr. Cuesta. He was then part owner of the Cuesta-Ballard & Co. which was situated where Hav-a-Tampa is today located: corner 22nd Street and 10th Avenue. While working here the cigar-makers

requested that I read to them. I took up these duties willingly, making cigars part time and reading at other times. I used to translate for them the *New York Herald, The Citizen* of Jacksonville, and *The Tampa Daily Times*. Later Mr. Cuesta separated from Mr. Ballard and myself, a friendship that had started in New York.[68]

We do not know how much the *lector* was paid compared with a *lector* who was not a cigar maker. Nor do we know whether the rate of pay Souto received was fair, since he also translated.

In 1903, it occurred to Ramón Valdespino, a *lector* who read in a certain cigar factory, to start a newspaper that would publish the latest news translated from English into Spanish. Before he came to Tampa, Ramón Valdespino lived in Key West, where he was a cigar worker, a journalist, and an active member of the Club San Carlos.[69] When he got to Tampa, he became a full-time *lector*, and that is when he realized how necessary it was to publish a concise newspaper that included the latest news items from the national and international press. For that reason, in 1903, he took on the task of launching a newspaper that would be a digest of the news translated from English to Spanish. His newspaper was called *La Traducción*. At night or in the wee hours of the morning, Ramón Valdespino would sit at a table in his home, at 1908 Eleventh Avenue, and would translate and type an English summary. On occasion, he also condensed the news that arrived in a timely manner from Havana.[70]

When he started he did not use a mimeograph, but, rather, carbon paper, which allowed no more than five reproductions at a time. He usually translated summaries of articles from the *New York Herald, Saturday Evening Post, Tampa Tribune,* and *Tampa Journal*. His method for choosing articles was neither simple nor casual, since after the massive general strike provoked by La Resistencia in 1901, one practically "could not write anything. Any silly thing would take on tinges of anarchism as far as the people of Tampa were concerned," wrote J. de la Campa González, a *lector* who knew Valdespino.[71]

Valdespino had to be very cautious about what he translated because, while the American press circulated very freely, in his case, the selection of one article to translate and not another, as with everything, was seen as an ideological or political act. This being the case, he was a thinker who worked with care and whose style was well liked by both *lectores* and listeners.

From Monday through Saturday, Valdespino left his house with a package under his arm and an umbrella he used as a cane. At ten o'clock in the morning, he met with a number of *lectores* at the Café Novedades, and that is where the conversation started. He sold each *lector* a carbon copy of what he had translated. When J. de la Campa González was a *lector* in a small workshop, he translated orally, because there were not many workers, and those there were not very demanding. When the number of employees increased, however, the cigar workers asked him to buy *La Traducción*. Faced with that situation, the *lector* walked over to the Café Novedades and appeared before Valdespino:

> "How much do you charge per week for *La Traducción*?" asked the *lector*.
> "There are first copies, which cost three pesos; second copies, which cost two, and third copies which cost one and a half pesos," Valdespino answered.
> "What's the difference?"
> "The third copy is blurrier because it's the last page of the carbon."
> "Let me have a third copy: I have good eyesight," replied the *lector*.[72]

Valdespino was so generous that he gave the *lector* a first copy of the translation, but charged him for a third copy: "The good old gent knew how to distinguish between those who live off *café con leche* alone, and those who are well-fed," thought de la Campa.[73]

La Traducción was successful because people liked the choice of news items as well as Ramón Valdespino's style. Over time, *La Traducción* began to be published in a mimeographed format, and years later, in 1922, the newspaper became a four-page printed publication with greater circulation than other Tampa newspapers.[74] But its policies remained unchanged; the newspaper was informative in nature and was devoted to summarizing for cigar workers news from the English-language press or from the Havana press.

Ramón Valdespino sold his newspaper to sixty *lectores*. As a result, what was generated by *La Traducción* was a community of listeners to which uniform material was read. It became the most widely circulated daily in Tampa, which is why it prided itself on being "the oldest local newspaper published in Spanish" and on providing "the latest news from the American press."[75] The daily continued to be published years after Valdespino's death in 1922.

Since Valdespino was a *lector*, he was familiar with the tastes of his listeners. Several people tried to imitate him, but they failed. As J. de la Campa González said, the style of the others was not well liked because, "concerned that there were those who would give their eyeteeth to hold the position of translating for workshops . . . I recall one who used every trick in the book and failed."[76]

Like other *lectores*, Valdespino wrote for other publications, such as the Cuban newspaper *La Época* and *La Revista* (of Tampa), and he even wrote a poem, "A Italia," which was recited by his daughter, María Valdespino, at the grand opening of the building that housed L'Unione Italiana Society. The poem was recited in Italian by Eulalia Valdespino and was also published in that language in the weekly magazine *Tampa Ilustrado*.[77] His passion for languages was so great that he left poems written in English on loose leaf paper, such as the one he dedicated to José Martí, which is titled "On a 24th of February":

Twenty fourth of February,
Beautiful which inspires love!
Steel striking steel is heard
A dawn's light is seen.

It's that the hour has arrived
For the fatal fall
Of criminal rule,
From fear the tyrant trembles,
And by the push of the Cuban,
He rolls from his pedestal!

Contempt has ended!
Lesson, honor, and warning,
The explosion of feeling!

Freedom of thought
Which now is oppressed no more,
Pain of a mother who moans,
Redemption and glory's light,
Martí, recording in history
A people who redeems itself.[78]

Valdespino was not a poet, but his work as a translator transformed him. For nearly two decades, he worked in the service of the *lectores* not only as a journalist, but also as a colleague, since he was also a *lector*. His solidarity with the community of *lectores* and listeners was quite remarkable. He, like Martí, believed in harmony and peace, but he especially believed in the platform of the *lector*, because to him, it was a sort of "pedestal."

During the first decade of the twentieth century, there were few changes in the institution of reading aloud. As we have seen, in spite of disputes that it caused, the selection of works was democratic, Spanish- or English-language newspapers were read, there was generally a reading president, and, surprisingly, salaries remained unchanged.

Conversely, listening audiences became more demanding all the time, because they wanted to stay up to date with what was taking place abroad, nationally, and especially in the social, educational, and recreational spheres within the dynamic, modern city. By 1910, Tampa's population had grown to 37,782 (from, in 1900, 15,839 residents). In the cigar industry, the workforce was made up of 6,961 men and 1,793 women: 3,545 Cubans; 2,008 Spaniards; 1,649 Italians; 1,419 Americans (including 1,016 whites and 90 blacks); and 133 people of other nationalities.[79]

As a consequence, responsibilities for meeting demands gradually increased. Since there were no radios, the *lector* had to announce what was going on locally. On September 25, 1908, *lectores* Eliseo Pérez Díaz, Fernández de Velasco, José Berardo García, Rafael Domínguez, Honorato Domínguez, Rogelio Barrios, Gerónimo Amat, Manuel Cádiz, Cándido Menéndez, Pedro Leira, R. Rivas, Luis M. González, Miguel Díaz, Antonio Hevia, Eduardo Bernardos, Leopoldo Fernández, Daniel Hierro, Ramón V. Pages, Sandalio Romaella, Ramón Valdespino, and Melquiades Calvo thanked Mr. La Presa, director of a theater company, who had admitted them free of charge to all the functions put on by his company at the theater in El Círculo Cubano. This was the first time that such an honor was granted to cigar factory *lectores*. "[T]he *lectores* are no doubt the best 'spokesmen' or announcers of all theatrical functions or other types of shows that take place throughout the city, and usually the *lectores* are forgotten by businessmen," wrote the *lectores* who signed the article.[80]

Thus, demands were made not only by listening audiences, but also by organizations that were interested in promoting their activities and that knew they could gather a large number of individuals at one time. A journalist who wrote under the pseudonym "Abel Kain" wrote: "Since performing companies, whether they be theatrical productions, or equestrian events, etc., visit this hamlet with some regularity, their agents must have realized that the most appropriate and *positive* way to announce their *functions* resides on the platforms in cigar factories."[81] And the *lectores* said: "Companies of performers being the way they are, there is no reason why we should read their programs to them without the benefit of free admission."[82]

The same article includes a sort of manifesto that is symbolic because it is one of the few documents the *lectores* ever wrote as a joint effort:

Therefore, from this day forward, be it resolved:

First: That no *lector* be obliged to read programs of companies that do not make to us the same concessions that the company of the most notable artist Mr. La Presa has justly made us. Second: That the magnanimous example of La Presa Company should become a precedent for the rest of the organizations that visit Tampa. And Third: That this resolution made by us shall not be construed as a threat to said companies, but, rather, a simple demonstration that, if our services are utilized, we have the legitimate right to the concession, and if they are not utilized, no one is obliged to us.[83]

As we have seen, demands were increasing, and the *lectores* were becoming more and more unprotected, because now they had to adjust and respond to the wishes of different groups. Also, it was taken for granted that they would participate free of charge in a variety of events at the *sociedades*. By way of example, El Círculo Cubano evolved from El Club Nacional Cubano [Cuban National Club], founded on October 10, 1899, as a recreational society. The club had three hundred members in 1902, and by 1909, almost one thousand. In 1907, El Círculo Cubano celebrated the grand opening of an opulent two-story building on Fourteenth Street and Tenth Avenue, which included a nine hundred–seat theater. Dances, patriotic ceremonies, and meetings related to labor issues were organized there. But even before the celebration of the grand opening of the magnificent building, *lectores*, especially if they were popular, made appearances at all types of events.

On May 21, 1903, the interior of El Círculo Cubano was decorated with flowers and flags. Red roses festooned the chandeliers of the luxurious rooms, and in the main room, portraits of Martí, Gómez, and Maceo were hung and decorated with white flowers. In the corner was a table set with drinks and hors d'oeuvres, and in the middle a platform had been set up. At eight that evening everyone was ready to celebrate the first anniversary of Cuba's independence. Of course, the *lector* could not miss the occasion. This time, Rodolfo Blain y Bustar occupied the platform.[84] Blain was one of the most prominent *lectores* in Tampa, and therefore his participation at patriotic and social gatherings was nearly mandatory. Like most *lectores*, he was a charismatic person and had a way with words.

On June 26, 1905, the bases and branches of the candelabra in the parlor of El Círculo Cubano were covered with black satin. A stage was set up in the middle of the room in the center of which a coffin was placed and covered with black velvet with a pattern of muskets and sabers on it on the left and right sides. Two torches were lit, which cast the image of a white cross on black fabric hanging on the wall. The casket was escorted by four guards on each side, and they were replaced at specific times. Other rooms in El Círculo were decorated with the flags of Cuba and the Dominican Republic. All day long, homage was paid and the death of Gen. Máximo Gómez was commemorated. That day, consuls, mayors, judges, and cigar factory *lectores* such as Rodolfo Blain and Sandalio Romaella (a Spaniard) gave "eloquent speeches."[85]

The camaraderie and respect Blain felt for the cigar workers and the community knew no bounds. On May 20, 1904, Blain held one of the most splendid banquets in the history of Tampa.[86] He announced in the newspaper in advance that he would hold an open house at his home and that he was extending the invitation to all his friends, whether they were American, Cuban, Spanish, Italian, or German.[87] He put up tents and decorated the house with Cuban and American flags, hired a band, served food, and offered beer, wine, champagne, imported desserts, and French creams. That day he celebrated Cuba's independence with his guests; it was "their Fourth of July," as it was reported in the *Tampa Tribune*. Several speeches were made, mainly by the host.

Rodolfo Blain was a brilliant interpreter whose presence became necessary at political sessions. When Robert W. Davis ran for governor of the state of Florida in 1904, he visited Tampa and called for a gathering at the old Criterion Theater building. On that occasion, Blain served as his simultaneous interpreter.[88] Blain was also a correspondent for the Cuban newspaper *La Lucha*; thus, he was involved in all spheres in Tampa. "Rodolfo Blain . . . scored a great 'beat' on rival Havana papers in reporting the dedication of the Centro Español Sanitarium [of Tampa] Sunday. Blain got off his story of the event on the day of its occurrence," the *Tampa Tribune* reported.[89] When the Florida State Fair was held in 1906, Blain took on the task of writing a series of articles for *La Lucha* in which he described (and illustrated) the most prominent citizens, the buildings, and the associations and different businesses, especially the cigar factories. During that type of fair, people visited cigar factories, and usually the *lector* was greatly admired by the visitors.[90]

Blain's work as a journalist and his profession as a *lector* were closely linked, since in both he had to disseminate information in a timely manner. Even before he became a journalist, he showed at the factory how bright he was, because he made prudent use of strategies to obtain news before others did. In 1903, when the baseball championship in which the All-Cubans were to face off against the All-Americans at De Soto Park was coming up, Blain already had the scoop. That year's October 3 issue of the *Tampa Tribune* said:

A letter to Roldolpho [*sic*] Blain, the popular Cuban factory reader, from a friend at Havana, received yesterday, stated that the All-Cubans had gotten together the best bunch of ball-players on the island for the present trip. They will bring five pitchers, headed by Carlos Royer, better known as "Bebe," the best pitcher of Cuba, who has a record superior to that of any League pitcher in the United States. Other members of the twirling staff will be Salvador Rosado, Juan Violat, Jose Munoz, and Miguel Prats.

The fact that the *lector* learned the news before the newspaper did shows how important spoken news was in the cigar factories. Also, since the *lector* was a correspondent, this indicates that a number of news items, before they were published in newspapers, had already been read (although they may have been read from rough drafts) and heard in the workshop. This exchange between the *lector* and his audience underscores the demands made by the listeners. Perhaps that is why Blain was so masterly in anticipating what item would turn into a great piece of news, as was the case when the Spaniard José Fernández Vázquez, who was a musician and cigar worker, stabbed and murdered the Mexican Pedro Pablo Bazagoitia in a restaurant on Seventh Avenue.

The fight started out of simple jealousy: Fernández Vázquez was married and kept a blatantly jealous eye on his wife. When the Spaniard got the feeling that his wife fancied the Mexican man, he decided to confront him publicly and killed him.[91] Blain attended Fernández Vázquez's trial and stated to all the newspapers in Tampa that he intended to publish the news item with photos of the court, the attorneys, the defendant, and the jury. "Mr. Blain declared the case of great interest in Havana."[92] Without a doubt, Blain knew more than enough about his reading audience and especially about his listening audience.

On the morning of August 5, 1908, hundreds of cigar workers put aside their tasks and showed up on Seventh Avenue. Hushed and with their heads bowed, they watched the funeral cortège pass, followed by the Santa Cecilia musical group, which also proceeded slowly, playing a mournful dirge. Dozens and dozens of people accompanied the procession to Woodlawn Cemetery, where a series of rituals took place and a white dove was released. Rodolfo Blain had died of asthma at age thirty-six. The *Tampa Tribune* noted that "one of the most popular and highly respected members of the Cuban colony in Tampa" had been lost.[93]

In the *Diario de Tampa*, Jacinto Bombín wrote: "In Tampa there are a few men who, without being rich, live as such," and "they never get up early, they get up at nine o'clock in the morning, a couple of hours later than any member of the Rosdchild [*sic*] family."[94] He went on to say: "In the case of a former *lector* . . . all the *lectores* meet between 9:00 and 10:00 to get the newspapers and novels that are, along with their voices, their only tools of the trade." There is no question that the writer did not understand the arduous work of the *lector*, as he added the following:

> After chatting a while (the *lectores*, by dint of having read speeches and newspaper articles, end up thinking they are orators and learned men), after chatting a while, as I said before, they spread out like the ribs of a fan and each goes off to his factory, where they read at most three hours, choosing regularly the most insubstantial novels they find in print. Only thus can it be understood that the cigar workers, the only laborers in the world who have the good fortune to listen to three hours of daily reading, should be the mental inferiors of the mailmen of Paris, or the cobblers of Barcelona, for example.

Obviously, the writer understood neither the social dynamics of reading aloud nor its value. Few of those who did not work in the cigar milieu understood the working conditions faced by the *lectores* and therefore thought that reading three hours a day was inconsequential.

The best descriptions of the workshops' conditions were written by Wenceslao Gálvez y Delmonte, who said: "Workshops are not made for reading, nor do they even have a sounding board or any kind of acoustic modification."

> There are a few castoffs from the workshops around, *lectores* who have gotten themselves laryngitis in their struggle for a livelihood. The *lector* is predestined to that, to come down with an illness of the larynx at any time, to lose his voice, to be forever sucking on potassium chlorate lozenges. They cannot tolerate the work and soon quit, defeated, to look for something else, even here where it is so difficult to find that something else. The *lector* at a large factory, in order to be able to tower over the workshop, has his head near the ceiling, and there, the smoke of so many cigars being puffed on at the same time, since there is no air circulation, rises and envelops him like a bluish cloud.[95]

Those work conditions were not exceptional and continued for the first two decades of the twentieth century.

Another issue was that, in 1910, paying for the reading was still voluntary in some workshops. The *lectores* protested this, and it was not until

February of 1911 that a regulation regarding reading aloud was written. It said essentially that all cigar workers were required to pay for the reading whether they liked it or not.[96] Still, it is unknown how long that regulation lasted, or if it was truly put into effect in any uniform way. The *lectores* were never able to form an organization that would look out for their rights, although the effort was certainly made.

Between 1900 and 1920, Spanish-language newspapers and magazines (and also those in Italian) were abundant in Tampa. Weekly or monthly magazines were published with topics in literature, beauty, business information, the cigar industry, the various *sociedades*, and so on. The following is a partial list: in 1900, *El Independiente* and *El Mensajero del Hogar* were published; in 1901, *La Federación* and *L'Alba Sociale*; in 1902, *El Federal* and *Observador*; in 1903, *El Boletín Obrero, La Justicia, La Revista,* and *La Traducción*; in 1904, *El Internacional*; in 1905, *Hojas Nuevas* and *La Tribuna*; in 1906, *El Progreso de Tampa*; in 1907, *El Audaz*; in 1908, *El Boletín Mensual, El Diario de Tampa,* and *Ecos de Fiesta en Tampa*; in 1909, *El Intruso, Echo di Tampa,* and *Lunes del Diario de Tampa*; in 1910, *Cubano* (the magazine of El Círculo Cubano); in 1911, *El Comercio, Alegría* (the annual publication of El Centro Asturiano) and *El Progreso*; in 1912, *Tampa Ilustrado* and *Hojas Nuevas*; in 1913, *El Quijote*; in 1914, *El Heraldo Dominical* and *Voce della Colonia/Voz de la Colonia*; in 1916, *Bohemia, Defensa, La Prensa,* and *Suplemento del Círculo Cubano*; in 1917, *Luz y Verdad*; in 1918, *Cheruto* and *La Raza*; in 1919, *El Buen Público*; and in 1920, *Organizzatore*.

As had been the case at the end of the nineteenth century, some publications were very short-lived because of the lack of subscribers. Still, since the readings were in Spanish, those texts are a good indication of what was heard in workshops. Some magazines and newspapers published short stories, chronicles, poetry, and even serialized novels, which suggests that literature was also read aloud.

Lectores Rodolfo Blain, Francisco Milián, Eliseo Pérez, and Ramón Valdespino contributed to *La Revista: Semanario de Literatura, Ciencias, Artes y Sport* (1903–1905; in 1904, its name was changed to *La Revista: Semanario Hispano Cubano*), which was edited by Rafael M. Ybor. Novels were published in installments in the magazine, including *La novela de los celos,* by Eduardo Bustillo; *Dolores,* by Carlota M. Braeme, translated into Spanish by Vicente Becerra; *Resurrección,* signed by F. C.; short novels, such as *Un beso,* signed with the pseudonym Championet; and *Diario de una recién casada,* by an anonymous author. Short stories were also written (some of which were published in installments), such as "En el crepúsculo," by Rafael M. Ybor; "En el manicomio," by Daniel Ureña; "Viaje a Monte

Gloria," by Tomás Camacho; and "El verano," by Benito Pérez Galdós. A story titled "Epifania," by Manuel A. de Carrión, was sent for publication from Cuba. What predominated were chronicles about Tampa that dealt with funerals, dances, private and public parties, conferences at the various *sociedades*, and even histories of the Russian-Japanese War and travel logs about distant places such as the Philippines or about closer places. For example, Ramón Valdespino wrote of his trip to Cuba on board the steamship *Miami* in the company of the All-Cubans baseball team. He asked them for money to help a poor woman aboard the ship who was suffering because of separation from her husband, who, in turn, had been confined to a psychiatric facility.

The chronicles of Rodolfo Blain were distinguished by their style and eloquence. In fact, he wrote the section "Crónica," which discussed in detail El Círculo Cubano, weddings, illnesses, banquets, theatrical works, baseball, travel, picnics, patriotic celebrations, international affairs of all kinds, and even *la charada* (a numbers game called *la bolita*).[97]

But the most talented writer at *La Revista* was Eliseo Pérez, who wrote editorials and chronicles and was a poet as well. Pérez was a cigar factory *lector*. His brilliance is obvious when one reviews the editorials he wrote about newspapers and the importance of education and secondary schools. In 1904, he asked the labor and recreational *sociedades* to fund the schools:

> There are very few in Tampa, so few that they can be counted as very unusual cases, at least in our language; and I wish I were mistaken when I make this statement, but, unfortunately, according to the accounts I have, it turns out to be true. . . . Right now in our country, everyone laments the horrible case of the child murdered in order to extract her heart to cure her from "troubles" and other illnesses with which a member of that barbaric association had been "cursed," an association whose fanatical beliefs cannot be based on anything but the most incredible ignorance. Education, which sheds so much light on human understanding, is charged with helping the society of the future to avoid those terrible spectacles that bring such sorrow to the soul of whosoever contemplates them ever so slightly! . . . Through the continued pounding of the hammer of science, castles in the air tumble down, truths held as incontrovertible; this progress is achieved only with the generous mellow breeze of education. Shall we do something in Tampa? That remains to be seen.[98]

With regard to Tampa's progress, the perceptive *lector* and writer said the following in exquisite prose worthy of comparison with that of Martí:

The moment that it occurred to Jules Verne to choose this part of the planet as the point of departure for the famous travelers who embark on their imaginary excursion through space in search of the "moon" was the end of the obscurity of this corner of the "Florida" peninsula known as "Tampa." We know not what to admire more, be it the fertile imagination and the world of knowledge possessed by the illustrious geographer, or the verisimilitude and confirmation of his original predictions. . . . Tampa, small, obscure hamlet, little known, lost on the "Florida" coast, achieves celebrity when it is selected by the incomparable novelist, and as if it meant to contribute to the materialization of all of the brilliant author's musings, it causes political dissension to spring up in the Pearl of the Antilles. Cuban chests swell with the love of freedom, it blinds the Spanish government, which allows its most abundant colonial industry to be snatched away, and all the necessary elements in play, all the fertile elements of work, come together at the appointed place. The barren land is populated by factories, and the forlorn shantytown is transformed into a thriving city that the inspired Master hinted at in the visions of his fantastic imagination. . . . Here, where immense stands of pine trees once towered, sprinkled here and there with orange groves that perfumed the atmosphere when in bloom, filling the spirit with that melancholy caused by rough landscapes, where today haughty and proud posts rise up, crisscrossed by wires that transmit human voice and thought. . . . The immigration attracted by the stimulus of equitable remuneration flows from all points on the globe, and the motley combination constitutes a rare spectacle that befits this cosmopolitan city. An electric streetcar is "Babel" in motion. Add to the diversity of clothing the difference in languages, and he who observes and examines is also examined, is at once actor and spectator in this brief play that is performed every five minutes.[99]

Eliseo Pérez wrote better prose than poetry. And, as we will see, *La Revista* allotted quite a generous amount of space to poetry.

Anyone could send material to *La Revista*. In fact, the mission statement published in the first issue notes that "the editors of *La Revista* desire the contributions of people who are aficionados of literary endeavors; therefore, we are setting up the publication as an open forum to disseminate the criticism and discourse of anyone who enjoys this type of work."[100] Thus, the editors published the creative work of a series of authors (who were not necessarily writers by trade). They also included poetry by Cuban poets and those from other countries, and, as it could not be otherwise, poetry written by *lectores* was included as well. Among the poems published were "Tributo" (to José Martí), by Mercedes F. de Barranco; "En un álbum," by

R. M. de Mendive; "La muerte del poeta," "Temor," "A Panchita Acosta," "Tú y yo," "Transición," "La mañana," "Diálogo inocente," and "Otoñal," by J. C. Labra; "La orgía de los esqueletos," by Salvador Rueda; "La poesía," by Domingo Perdomo; "El oro," "Junta de médicos," "Poesía química," "Gaita y sermón," and "Los específicos," by Vital Aza; "Los cangrejos," by Mariano Martín; "Flores," by Ramón Zambrana; "En el circo," by Guillermo Valencia; "Dogma inédito," by R. de Campoamor; "¡Amémonos!" by José M. Carbonell; "A la juventud cubana," by Emilio Thuillier; "El desertor," by Rafael Díaz Mirón; "Lo más negro," by Carlos Rodríguez Díaz; and "Restitución," by Federico Balart. Rodolfo Blain wrote "Mi madre y tú" and "Mi madre," and Ramón Valdespino published a poem in prose form with the title "Poemita." Eliseo Pérez wrote "¿Poeta?" and "Dos épocas" [Two eras], the content of which is two sonnets that were recited by the author at the gathering that took place on the evening of May 20, 1905, to commemorate the third anniversary of the proclamation of Cuban independence:

TWO ERAS
—October 10, 1868—
Auspicious day! We see now from afar
The sun of Independence shine its light
With brilliant beams as of a sovereign star,
As brother with brother in hope unite.
Céspedes, the immortal patriot, calls
To summon his people to join the fight;
Defending his homeland, in death he falls,
Still holding high the Cuban banner bright.
Brave martyrs everywhere have met their fate,
The blood of heroes soaks the anguished fields
And creates liberty; Oh, Cuba, wait!
The seed now fertilized ere long will yield
Abundant crops of fruit surpassing fair
To reap this harvest, Cuba, now prepare.
—February 24, 1895—
The fruit has ripened now, and gloriously
A new day dawns for Cubans everywhere
And in the fields waving once more we see
The battle-scarred tricolor in the air.
Sublime Martí goes forward desperately
And valiantly he joins the battle's strife
And in Dos Ríos meets exaltedly

His death, which to his people brings new life.
Our hearts are filled with warlike ardor now
A burning torch in every hand held high
With fateful horror now rings out the shout
"Down tyranny, whether we live or die!"
The Master from his tomb is looking out!
America's will no longer denied![101]

Both the Ten Years' War and the Spanish-American War were intimately linked to the history of immigration of cigar workers to Tampa. As best they could, *lectores* like Eliseo Pérez were the founders of the history of Cubans in Tampa through literature. Thus, it is no surprise that the same *lector* dedicated a sonnet to a woman who was a cigar worker:

THE GIRL FROM TAMPA
The girl from Tampa passes happily
along the street and through the morning mist,
agile, attractive, of her fate, mistress,
from worries and from disappointments, free.
Just like the tide, within her noble breast
Her sweet devotion to her suitor flows,
And deep within her heart the longing grows
for this long-dreamed-of union to be blessed.
At work, she attacks her task soberly;
Triumphant now, she smiles at her success,
Now broken are the bonds of poverty:
Back at her home, of which she is goddess,
She greets her pretty mother and softly
Kisses her cheek with loving tenderness.[102]

This is one of the few poems dedicated to female cigar workers in Tampa, and the fact that a *lector* wrote it shows the extent to which the writer and, in this case, also the *lector,* was committed to his listening audience. *La Revista* was one of the publications that were sold inside cigar factories by volunteer distributors who were cigar workers.[103] This type of distribution was no doubt imitated by other publishers. Thus, the dissemination of newspapers and magazines in Spanish is a very accurate indicator of what was heard in cigar factories.

In newspapers and magazines, usually weeklies, there was a great deal of serialized literature, whether short stories or novels. For example, in 1907,

El Audaz: Semanario Popular de la Familia published the short stories "El hechicero," "El fugitivo," "El jorobeta (historia de un tabaquero)," "Dos amores," "El osario," and "Bodas trágicas" in installments. The weekly also published a series of poems and a section titled "Por las fábricas" in which the feature writer described his travels among all the factories in Tampa. The weekly gave space to Italian authors, and Arthur D. Massolo contributed chronicles and articles of general interest.[104]

El Diario de Tampa (1908–1912) was one of the most dynamic publications, as it contained articles about women in Tampa and Europe; about Tampa society in general, such as literary contests, parties, theaters, schools, mutual aid societies; baseball; Cuban politics; news from Spain and Latin America; and also a section titled "Notas Tabacaleras." The newspaper included a section titled "Biblioteca del Diario de Tampa," where short stories and chronicles by a variety of unknown and known authors, such as Blasco Ibáñez and Gutiérrez Nájera were published. *Marianela*, by Pérez Galdós, and *Flor de mayo*, by Blasco Ibáñez, appeared in installments in June and November 1908, respectively.

The weekly magazine *Tampa Ilustrado* (1912) also published literature, such as the chronicles "Cuadro del hogar" and "La catástrofe de Bilbao," by Manuel Gutiérrez Nájera, and the poems "Muñeca" and "Tu hermano," by Manuel Cádiz; "En un álbum," by Salvador Díaz Mirón; "Composición póstuma," by Juan Clemente Zenea; "Canción de amores," by Catalina Rubalcaba; and "A Italia," by Ramón Valdespino. *Una mujer*, a novel Manuel Cádiz was working on, and the short novel *Esto, esto y esto*, by Ricardo Becerro Bengoa, were published in installments. Surprisingly, *La novela de los celos*, by Eduardo Bustillo, which had been published in *La Revista*, also appeared in *Tampa Ilustrado*.

The magazine *Bohemia* was published in Tampa from 1916 to 1917. It distinguished itself through publishing eloquent feminist articles in its section "Museo Matrimonial," written by María Valdespino, the daughter of Ramón Valdespino. The novel *La rica hoja*, by Gonzalo G. Rivero, and the play *Imbécil* appeared in installments. Quite a few short stories were published every week, including "El primer beso (cuento mexicano)," by Arturo R. de Carri Carte; "Celos" and "La decepción," by Raúl F. Roces; "Amor y paz," by José Miró; "La primera cana," by I. Huertas; "La fiera," by A. Muñoz de Diego; "El extranjero," by Víctor Fernández; "Vuelco sentimental," by A. Monteavaro; "El anillo del indiano," by Arizna Varreta; and "La noche buena de Nicky," by R. Álvarez.

The biweekly magazine *El Cubano* (1915–1919) published poetry and all the activities of El Círculo Cubano, as well as detailed information about baseball. In December 1918, *La Raza* was published, but it was very short lived, since it published only poems by Aurelio Bay and essays about Cuba and "the New Russia," as well as "Después de la guerra," a short story written by Miguel de Zárraga.

In short, a whole world of literature was read aloud in cigar factories from newspapers and magazines that the cigar workers wanted to have read to them. But what else was read?

As I have stated, the shelves of the libraries in the diverse *sociedades* were filling up, thanks to donations from their members, the majority of whom were cigar workers. On July 3, 1908, la Biblioteca de la Delegación del Centro Asturiano [the Library of the Local Branch of El Centro Asturiano] was founded. The cigar rollers at the Menéndez Factory wrote a letter to the president of the Education Division of El Centro Asturiano: "Dear Sir: We, the undersigned, employees of the Menéndez Bros. workshop, have the distinct honor of forwarding 4 works to you, which we wish to contribute to the establishment of the library of the local branch of El Centro Asturiano. We request that the Section over which you preside accept this humble offering, which will satisfy our wish to contribute to the creation of an institution that highly dignifies the *sociedad* that gives life and honor to those it represents."[105] The cigar workers donated five large, "lavishly bound and beautifully illustrated" volumes of *La historia de México a través de los siglos*; *La agricultura en general*; *Los grandes inventos* "in eight volumes, illustrated and with extremely useful information about all branches of science"; and "the monumental work *Las ruinas de Palmira* by Volney."[106]

El Centro Asturiano set up one of the best libraries in Tampa and contained a large variety of authors from all eras and from all over the world. The most-circulated books in the first two decades of the twentieth century were *Don Quixote*, by Cervantes; *Episodios nacionales* and *Fortunata y Jacinta*, by Pérez Galdós; *El conde de Montecristo*, by Dumas; *La Araucana*, by Ercilla y Zúñiga; *Los miserables*, by Hugo; *Los tres*, by Gorki; *La divina comedia*, by Dante; *La piedra angular*, by Pardo Bazán; *La iliada*, by Homer; *Rimas*, by Bécquer; *La vida es sueño*, by Calderón; *Las argonautas* and *La barraca*, by Blasco Ibáñez; *Novela de un novelista* and *Años de juventud del doctor Angélico*, by Palacio Valdés; *Romancero espiritual y rimas sacras*, by Lope de Vega; *Los desgraciados*, by Pérez Escrich; *Tardes de la granja o las lecciones*, by Rodríguez de Arellano; *Pepita Jiménez*, by Valera; *El motín de los retablos*, by Vargas Vila; *Las ruinas de Palmira*, by Volney; *Confesiones de un niño decente*, by Zamacois; *La taberna*, by Zola;

and *Leyenda de Al-hamar*, by Zorrilla.[107] El Círculo Cubano had collected the following:

> *El Diccionario de la Academia Española*, which had belonged to El Apóstol, José Martí, and then a thousand more volumes, among them *El Diccionario enciclopédico* . . . *"Biblioteca internacional de autores famosos"* and universal history and geography books about Cuba, Spain, and Latin America, a medical science dictionary, speeches by Mr. J. A. González Lanuza, *Evolución de la cultura cubana*, a collection of *obras estimulantes*, the collection of works by Don Manuel de la Cruz, and *El diccionario botánico*, written by Cuban writer Juan Tomás Roy, printed by the government and sent to all farmers on the island. Several works in English and other languages . . . [works] by Sanguily, Mari-Blanca, Carlos Martí, Antonio Iraizos, and other Cuban authors.[108]

El Círculo Cubano also had *Comedias*, by Lope de Vega; a full set of *Autores españoles desde la formación del lenguaje hasta nuestros días* (1918); *Obras completas*, by Alberto del Solar; *El conde de Montecristo*, by Dumas; *Los miserables*, by Hugo; twenty volumes of *El tesoro de la juventud o enciclopedia de conocimientos*; *Colección moderna de conocimientos universales*; *Tesoro de novelistas españoles antiguos y modernos*, in forty volumes; *Biblioteca internacional de obras famosas*; *Colección de los mejores autores españoles*, in twenty-one volumes; *History of the World War*, by Francis A. March; *Nueva geografía universal*; and *Los países y las razas*.[109]

Likewise, cigar workers nourished school and public libraries, such as the Carnegie Library of West Tampa. Still, the libraries at the *sociedades* are those that most reflect the cigar sector's preference of written works.[110] Also, cigar workers constantly visited these libraries so they could consult maps and encyclopedias and learn more about the works that were read to them. Similarly, the clubs were an extension of the cigar factories, because different aspects of works of fiction were enthusiastically discussed there.[111]

As we have seen, reading aloud in Tampa continued to take place throughout the First World War. Tampa's economy, however, gradually weakened. Between 1912 and 1919, the cost of living rose 135 percent, but the cigar workers' salaries went up only 12.5 percent. Consequently, the cigar sector organized a strike that started on April 17, 1920, and did not end until February of 1921. Obviously, reading aloud was suspended during the strike; moreover, when the employees returned to work, one of the clauses of the agreement provided for a ban on reading aloud.

The cigar workers could not abide not having a *lector* in the factories, and in November 1921, more than four thousand people went back out on strike; they demanded a pay raise and the return of the *lectores* to their platforms. "Readers, declared the owners, had abused the practice and used the tribune to inculcate radical ideas."[112] Some labor leaders were kidnapped, and others were forced to flee Tampa. The workers had to return to work, but without their *lectores*, as reading aloud was banned from 1921 through 1926.

As I have emphasized previously, the platform of the *lector* was always vulnerable. As far back as 1900, the *Tobacco Leaf* had said that,

> instead of the reader now being an entertainer, he has become an agent for the dissemination of the wildest anarchist ideas, of mob rule, incendiarism, and personal abuse of everyone and everything that is the bane of those who engage him. Reading proceeds from 10 o'clock in the morning until 3 P.M., and during all this time the hands are kept in a constant state of excitement listening to the exposition of red-eyed anarchy, certain of their oppressors. Discipline under these circumstances is out of the question. . . . The other feature referred to is the unresistable publication of anarchist newspapers in Tampa. Two of the type, the *Esclavo* and *Resistencia*, openly preach the right of the men to destroy the property of all who oppose their cause, and advocate without hesitation the adoption of violence. These papers are read out by the factory readers, and in this way the propaganda is maintained. The sheets are being published in Spanish, apparently to escape the scrutiny of the authorities, but nonetheless they are a source of perpetual annoyance and danger to the community. In a way, they should be wiped out and the office of the reader abolished, and the sooner they are, the better it will be for Tampa and Tampa's interests.[113]

It is certainly true that few were the *lectores* who professed to be anarchists, as was the exceptional case of Luisa Capetillo, a Puerto Rican cigar factory *lectora* in Tampa during the summer of 1913.

Still, as history shows, the *lectores* read essentially what the cigar workers wanted to hear; the platform of the *lector* was also the platform for labor leaders. From there, leaders spread their ideas, whether they were radical or not. Thus, the platform was dangerous not only because of the reading, but also because of the spread of labor issues by the employees themselves.

But the law pardoned neither the cigar workers nor the *lectores*, since in 1911, Juan Vilar, an educated cigar worker who was born in Caguas, Puerto Rico, was incarcerated, having been charged with being an associate of V. Grillo, an anarchist who had murdered one of the heads of the West

Indies Trading Company. The detective who brought the charges against Juan Vilar based them on literature he found in the library at the educational center that the cigar worker ran.[114] The U.S. Bureau of Investigation had zealously maintained a list in which José Millares was described as "a reader and socialist," Agustín Sánchez was an "admitted anarchist and reader," Abelardo Hernández was a "reader at Cuesta Rey . . . a Spaniard . . . and a radical."[115]

The government also took it upon itself to deport Maximiliano Clay, an anarchist who worked as a *lector*, as well as Manuel Salinas, a Cuban who was the editor of *El Obrero Industrial*. Panic over Communist influence was especially obvious after the First World War, and that was one of the factors, in addition to the obvious economic slump, that led to the suspension of reading aloud.

When reading aloud was suspended in 1921, Victoriano Manteiga, one of the most prominent *lectores* in Tampa, found himself unemployed, like many of his peers. Manteiga had come from Cuba in 1913 with barely ten dollars in his pocket and a suitcase that held two linen suits. Immediately on his arrival, he started to work as a *lector* and continued to do so until the time came when he had to live through the labor crisis in the flesh. Out of work and with no passion for anything but journalism, learning, and reading, he published *La Gaceta* for the first time in 1922. *La Gaceta* continues to be published in Tampa at the time of this writing. Leafing through the 1922 editions of his newspaper, one observes Manteiga's enjoyment of literature and his enthusiasm for publishing works in installments, such as the novel *La confesión de un bohemio*, by Xavier de Montépin; poems by Juana de Ibarbourou, Gabriela Mistral, and Ramiro de Maeztu; short stories by Leopoldo Lugones; and scholarly travel chronicles such as "Crónicas de Portugal," by Julio Camba, or chronicles from Russia, by Ricardo Baeza; essays on English literature; book reviews; in short, a veritable world of literature and culture. Reading aloud was suspended, but publishing was not, although, in fact, after 1914, publications in Spanish gradually declined, due in part to the state of the economy and in part to the labor struggles.[116]

The absence of reading aloud between 1921 and most of 1926 transformed factory culture. What is more, radio came on the scene and set out to partially substitute for the *lector*. In October of 1922, hundreds of cigar workers stopped working at 2:00 P.M. Everyone wanted to see the results of the World Series. To that end, Spanish-language newspapers put up a huge electric board in a public place where everybody could see it. On it, metal balls representing baseball players and scores moved according to how the game progressed. Since the cigar workers could not stand to miss the Major League games, they simply abandoned their workbenches to go and witness the championship by way of the public sign board.[117]

But interest in baseball was nothing new. The first baseball clubs in Tampa were established as early as 1887. Baseball player Al López pointed out that "the games started at 3:15, so by 2:30 they would leave the factory and come out and see the ball game. . . . And the people, the cigar makers, were great. I think that was our greatest draw."[118] On one occasion, *Tobacco Leaf* said: "Cigar manufacturers generally breathe a sigh of relief at the close of the local baseball season which, throughout its duration, kept a large number of cigar makers away from their benches for two or more afternoons each week. Most of the players were cigar makers and their friends and admirers followed them to the games, thus losing the entire afternoon's work."[119] In October of 1922, the owner of the Cuesta, Rey & Co. Factory made a drastic decision with regard to the matter:

> Cuesta, Rey & Co. got busy and installed a radiophone with an amplifier which gave the games play by play to their big force and [the cigar workers] also got reports on the features from the two papers and called these out. [The system] is working well, though there are still some of the more rabid fans whom nothing but the board will satisfy. The radio at Cuesta Rey seems the solution as it practically does away with the need for the board and they are not losing any time at all. It may solve the problem perpetually and if production is in great demand by another series it is probable that every large shop will install the radio.[120]

The installation of a radio was related not just to baseball but also to the absence of reading aloud in the factories. Accustomed to listening to someone's voice for hours, the employees no doubt had to suffer through the silence (or the monotonous noise of their work implements). Likewise, the absence of reading aloud in the workplace contributed to the cigar workers' cultural dearth. Although music on the radio provided cultural enrichment, depriving them of literature represented a step backward.

Still, there are indications that the practice of reading aloud was to a certain extent transplanted from public spaces to private ones, such as the home, since newspapers like *La Gaceta* continued to publish serialized literature without interruption. There were even occasions when they published two novels at the same time, which suggests demand on the part of the reading public.[121]

Reading aloud in factories resumed at the end of 1926, although this time the price was very high. However, to get a sense of the context of Tampa at the end of the 1920s, we should turn to *Anna in the Tropics*, one of the few literary works that focuses on a cigar factory *lector.*

V

Anna in the Tropics (2003), written by Cuban playwright Nilo Cruz, focuses on the reading aloud that took place at a cigar factory in Ybor City in 1929, just before the start of the Great Depression. The small workshop belongs to a family of Cuban immigrants, and all the family members work at cigar making. The play is about events that occur in the workshop on the arrival of a cigar factory *lector* who comes from Cuba, and how his readings influence and transform the people's lives.

At the beginning of the play, the female factory workers are anxiously awaiting the arrival of the ship on which the new *lector* is to arrive. They are Ofelia, the mother, a matriarch who is a great admirer of reading aloud and who pays the passage from Cuba for the *lector*; Conchita, her married daughter; and Marela, her younger, unmarried daughter. The *lector*, Juan Julián Ríos, comes bearing recommendations, as he has the reputation of being among the best *lectores* in Havana.

His arrival from Cuba is symbolic because it represents, among other things, the establishment and tradition of reading aloud. At the factory in Ybor City, the workers have already listened to other *lectores*: Teodoro, who read to them for ten years; and another, who stayed only a short time. Juan Julián arrives from Havana with a few books in hand, and he is the one who makes the decisions about what will be read in the factory. As I have mentioned previously, in the context of Tampa, the *lectores* usually did not choose the works; rather, the workers themselves did the choosing, but in *Anna in the Tropics*, Juan Julián decides to read Leo Tolstoy's *Anna Karenina*. How interesting that of all universal literature, the Cuban *lector* chose to read a Russian work.

The context of *Anna in the Tropics* is one of the most turbulent in the history of cigar making in Tampa. In the first place, it is an extremely difficult period in the financial sense, because of the Great Depression. Between 1929 and 1931, there was a 17 percent decrease in cigar production, and employees were forced to accept a 30 percent reduction in wages.[122] In the second place, the play deals with how the industry started to undergo a transformation, because in the 1920s, a number of owners began to buy cigar-rolling machinery to speed up production. Hundreds of cigar workers were let go because their labor was no longer necessary; now just a few people could operate a machine that produced cigars very quickly. The introduction of machinery into the industry directly affected cigar factory *lectores* in Tampa, because when the workforce was reduced, there was no longer anyone to pay their salary. Furthermore, it was practically impossible to hear the voice of the *lector* over the noise of the machinery.

As I indicated previously, reading was banned in Tampa from 1921 through 1925. By the end of 1926, however, it had begun to be reestablished with a few conditions. This time it was imperative that two committees be formed: one was to be made up of officers from the Cigar Manufacturers' Association, and the other of the reading president and a handful of other members, all cigar workers, selected by their coworkers. Consequently, the texts that were submitted to a vote had to pass the scrutiny of both an internal and an external committee.

The state of the economy and the transformation of the cigar industry between 1926 and 1931 reflect a crisis that also manifested itself in the cultural realm, since the number of publications in Spanish had already been drastically reduced. During those years, the only ones to debut were *Revista Tampa Latina* (managed by cigar factory *lector* Honorato W. Domínguez) and *La Tribuna* in 1926; *Latino-Americano*, which was first published in 1929; and *El Resviglio*, which came out in 1930. At that time, *La Gaceta*, which was managed by former cigar factory *lector* Victoriano Manteiga, continued to publish literary works, which, once again, are a good indication of what was heard in cigar factories. From 1926 through 1931, the following works were read aloud: *El sepulcro de los vivos*, by Dostoievski; *La hijastra del amor*, by Picón; *La Virgen del Líbano*, by Renault; *El hijo abandonado* and *De tales padres, tales hijos*, by Germain; *La amaba con locura*, by Cases; *La esposa coqueta*, by Burton, translated by Soloni; *Carina*, by Enault; *Almas que sufren*, by Anonymous; *El hijo abandonado*, by Anonymous; *Los ojos de Alicia*, by Pearce; *Currito de la Cruz*, by Pérez Lugín; *Las tragedias de París*, by Montépin, translated by Pedraza y Páez; *La prodigiosa*, by Alarcón; *Si yo fuera rico*, by Larra; and *Historias extraordinarias y aventuras extraordinarias de Arturo Gordon Pym*, by Poe. *Revista Tampa Latina* was very short lived, but, very interestingly, published the same texts in installments as did *La Gaceta*, such as *De tales padres, tales hijos*, in addition to a series of poems by Amado Nervo and Jacinto Benavente.

Those texts are merely clues to what was heard in the cigar factories. Still, due to its vulnerability, reading aloud was more threatened than ever before because, at the end of the 1920s, *lectores* were being accused of spreading leftist ideas.

Anna in the Tropics presents two opposing sets of surroundings. In the first, we find ourselves in a small, dark factory located in Ybor City during a period of time beset by financial crisis. It is summer, and the cigar workers are complaining of the suffocating heat. There are two couples in the play: Santiago, the owner of the factory, who is married to Ofelia; and Conchita, their daughter, who is married to Palomo. Santiago views life bitterly and has lost hope. As a result, he is a drunk who gambles and loses. His daughter, Conchita, is also discouraged, because her husband, Palomo, has a mistress. Another vitally important character is Cheché, Santiago's half-brother, who is also bitter because his wife has left him. The lives of all these characters are transformed by the arrival of the *lector* and the reading of *Anna Karenina*.

The second set of surroundings, which is gradually introduced through the reading, is that which is portrayed in *Anna Karenina*. The Russian novel deals with the aristocratic society of the impressive cities of Moscow and St. Petersburg. The countryside is shown with its frozen winter scenes, covered with snow.

Anna Karenina, which deals with marital infidelity, was published in installments in the newspaper from 1875 through 1878. Anna Karenina is married and has a child, but she allows herself to be seduced by a military man. Despite everything, her husband is willing to forgive her in order to keep up appearances. In the face of this reaction, Anna's lover attempts suicide, but is unsuccessful and merely wounds himself. After a time, he resumes his relationship with Anna. A short time later, Anna becomes pregnant with her lover's child. Both flee the country in shame, although Anna's husband has forgiven her again. Anna decides to return, but is shunned by society. These circumstances, that is, the refusal of her husband to grant her a divorce, and the suspicion that her lover is growing tired of her, lead Anna to suicide.

Thus, Tolstoy's work portrays the classic theme of infidelity: that it is impossible for the adulterous couple to establish a socially acceptable relationship, which commonly engenders a more burning desire in the parties, and which can result only in their experiencing greater difficulties. When they encounter obstacles, the lovers feel the irresistible need to continue to love each other, although usually one or both go crazy, become ill, run away, die, or commit suicide. Or, at least, that is what happens in literature.

At the beginning of *Anna in the Tropics*, we meet Santiago, the owner of the factory, who is a drinker, a man who bets on cockfights, a person who is generally disillusioned with life. In Tampa during the first decades of the twentieth century, people passionately bet on *la bolita*, cockfights, and *la charada*, as a poem, "The Gamblers," published in *El Bombín* magazine and written by Vital Aza, says:

Until a gambler he became
Vicente was a wealthy man
And then within a two-year span
He had not a cent to his name.
Now wretched and in rags arrayed
Vicente suffers every day
And when they see him people say
"He is a gambler! How depraved!"
Compare him to the banker Ponte:
Born to a humble family
He contrived to become wealthy
By playing roulette and monte.
Now he enjoys life without a care
A life of luxury and play
And when they see him people say,
"How lucky! He's a millionaire!"
With this the world can clearly see
Though gambling always is a sin,
They are condemned who do not win,
While those who do are called lucky.[123]

Just as the poem describes, Santiago is a person given to vice who has lost a lot by gambling. Conversely, he is an honorable and dignified man and refuses to return to work at the factory until he has paid back the money he has borrowed from his half-brother, Cheché, money he has lost to betting. Since Santiago has stopped working for a time, he listens to the *lector* from above the factory, where he and his family live, and he immediately becomes engrossed in the plot of *Anna Karenina*. Through the story of the characters in the Russian novel, he begins to reflect on his own existence.

Anna in the Tropics presents an extraordinary portrayal of the impact a literary work can have on its listeners. There are three women at the factory in Ybor City, but it is intriguing how each of them forms a different opinion with regard to the love triangle portrayed in *Anna Karenina*. Conchita and her mother feel that, although Anna has a lover, her life must be miserable. To them, Anna's situation is inescapable, since she is trapped by the power of love, and in this case, love does not necessarily bring her happiness. This is made clear especially when Ofelia reflects on Anna's situation and says that "she has no choice. It's something [love] she can't escape. That's why the writer describes love as a thief. The thief is the mysterious fever that poets have been studying for years. Remember Anna Karenina's last words."[124] During this scene, the cigar workers begin to change gradually because of the effect of the reading.

Captivated by *Anna Karenina* and fascinated by the presence and the voice of the *lector*, Juan Julián, Conchita becomes his lover. After all, the *lector* shares her passion for literature, which is capable of filling the void and easing the loneliness and the uncertainty that her married life is causing her to feel. Thus, the two lovers in *Anna in the Tropics* start to live the life of the characters in Leo Tolstoy's novel. In an analogous way, Conchita experiences what Emma Bovary, the main character of *Madame Bovary*, goes through.

Madame Bovary, the great novel by Gustave Flaubert, was published in installments from 1856 through 1857 in *Revue de Paris*. The novel tells the story of Emma, who is married but bored by married life. She longs to imitate the heroines of romantic novels. Thus, she decides to embark on an adulterous life.

Anna in the Tropics deals with the same subject, a subject that is not new to literature, as the main focus of *Don Quixote* is how the protagonist tries to imitate or live the life of fictional characters. Cervantes introduces the reader to an idealistic character who, carried away by the adventures he had read of in novels of chivalry such as *Amadis of Gaul*, tries to re-create and live in an anachronistic world.

There are many similarities between the novel by Cervantes and that of Flaubert, as the French author confesses: "Je retrouve mes origins dans ce livre que je sauvais par coeur avant de savoir lire" [I trace my origins to that book, which I knew by heart before I could read].[125] It has even been said that Emma Bovary is a female prototype of Don Quixote, because both are seduced by novels; they dream of being fictional heroes, and both have an unrealistic view of their abilities and possibilities.[126]

Anna in the Tropics is a link to the corpus of classical literature and raises once again the issue of the extent to which literature is capable of influencing the individual. As far as Emma Bovary and Don Quixote are concerned, the fantasies they have read about are part of their reality but not part of the reality of others. In the play, Conchita comes across what is known as "Bovarysm," the ability to imagine oneself to be someone else. This ability, however, becomes distorted in Emma's case, because she is incapable of taking advantage of only the positive qualities of Bovarysm, of imagining the world in different ways. Instead, she goes too far, is ruined, and commits suicide.[127]

An important difference between Emma and Don Quixote and, in this case, Conchita, is the way in which most of their readings are carried out.

In other words, both Emma and Don Quixote read to themselves, while Conchita is a listener, although I would not call her a *chaperone*, a term that carries the connotation of a corollary of meanings associated with observation.[128] Obviously, what *Anna in the Tropics* reclaims is precisely the tradition of reading aloud.

As I indicate in Part I, *The Tale of Inappropriate Curiosity* in chapter XXXII of part I of *Don Quixote* is first scrutinized by the priest before he reads it aloud to those present. The plot of that interposed novel is too subversive to be read by a priest; nevertheless, his reading it aloud confers on it the authority of the church to filter through enunciation what can be heard and what cannot. In chapter VI of part I, when the priest and the barber enter Don Quixote's room to review "the authors of mischief," that is, the books which are the cause of Don Quixote's madness, the barber passes the volumes one at a time to the priest, who reads their titles aloud. They discuss which ones to burn and which ones not to. In *Don Quixote*, reading aloud signifies authority while reading to oneself represents a sort of threat, which is especially evident in Cervantes' masterly exemplary novel "The Dialogue of the Dogs," which is read silently.[129]

In *Anna in the Tropics*, the person who selects which novel will be read aloud is the *lector*. In this case, he represents authority, although, ironically, it is he who is drawn into the intrigue of the plot of *Anna Karenina* and who begins to live the life of Vronsky, Anna's lover. Thus, in the play, the reading aloud of fiction is portrayed as a double-edged sword: one side represents provocation that can cause individuals to do bad things, as is obviously the case in the adulterous relationship between Conchita and Juan Julián; the other side, as we have seen, induces others to do good things.

The first passage of *Anna Karenina* the *lector* reads is the following:

Looking at him, Anna Karenina felt a physical humiliation and could not say another word. Her beloved felt what a killer must feel when he looks at the body he has deprived of life. The body he had deprived of life was their love, the beginning of their love. There was something dreadful and revolting in the recollection of what had been paid for by this awful price of shame. The shame Anna sensed from their spiritual nakedness destroyed her and affected him. But in spite of the killer's horror when he faces the body of his victim, the killer must cut the body to pieces and conceal it, and he must make use of what he has gained by his crime. And with the same fury and passion as the killer throws himself upon the body and drags it and cuts it, he covered her face and shoulders with kisses. "Yes, these kisses—these kisses are what have been bought by my shame."[130]

This passage revolves around the heartbreaking relationship between Anna and her lover. Here Anna is outraged and cannot even speak. She feels guilty, vulnerable, and unfortunate. He does as well. This is one of the most intense passages of Tolstoy's novel because it sets the stage, the atmosphere of what is going to happen in the story. This is how the lovers feel after their relationship has lasted a year.

Tolstoy's work is aloof; this is why the author does not describe the first year of the relationship. There is a gap, a void that does not allow the reader to imagine a relationship that is passionate; rather, the reader sees a relationship that is frustrated.

In *Anna in the Tropics*, the playwright goes a step further when he portrays the passion that exists between the two lovers, and that is what makes it radically different: Anna is not a frustrated failure, but, rather, an Anna who is full of life, just as tropical fruits are. The second act opens with the two lovers making love in the cigar factory. The stage directions read as follows: "Juan Julian and Conchita are at the factory making love. She is lying on top of a table, half naked, her skirt tucked up. He is there between her legs, shirtless and full of sweat. They have transgressed the limits of their bodies, and he now kisses her gently" (47). In Scene Two, when Palomo confronts his wife and questions her about her lover, she confesses to him that Juan Julián tells her lovingly and tenderly that she "taste[s] sweet and mysterious, like the water hidden inside fruits" and that their "love will be white and pure like tobacco flowers. And it will grow at night, the same way that tobacco plants grow at night" (63). With those loving words, her lover fills the void that her married life causes her to feel.

In Tolstoy's *Anna Karenina*, the consummation of love between Anna and her lover almost goes unnoticed. Between chapters X and XI of part II there is an ellipsis that replaces the description of the lovers' passion. A year passes in that void or omission, but the details of the relationship do not exist. It is as if they are condemned. Anna loves Vronsky, and vice versa, but readers cannot feel the passion that exists between them. The ellipsis is a manifestation of a punishing void.

In *Anna in the Tropics*, there is no sense of the coldness or guilt that the characters in Tolstoy's novel feel. This is evident when Conchita confesses to her husband that her lover is able to fill the void she feels because her husband no longer loves her. Conchita's lover satisfies her as much as her husband once did, and this is one of the fundamental differences between the Russian novel and the play. The allusion to the sexual act and the satisfaction Conchita feels is exactly what Anna Karenina lacks. Anna always tries to be herself, and she lets herself be carried away by her conviction and her instincts. But society condemns her and does not allow her to find the happiness she has always sought. In contrast, in *Anna in the Tropics*, Conchita achieves satisfaction and happiness.

The antagonist is Cheché. He represents a threat to the *lector*, not only because he wants to kill him from the start, but also because he wants to bring cigar-rolling machines into the factory. In this way, it would be easy to get rid of the *lector*, because it would be practically impossible for him to keep his job, because of the decrease in the number of workers and the noise generated by the machinery.

Thus, Nilo Cruz's play shows what was really happening in Tampa around 1930. In 1930 and 1931, at the foot of all the pages of *La Gaceta* there was a statement that read: "Machine-made cigars harm cigar rollers, business, and the community. The cigar industry, like others of its ilk, calls for clever and intelligent publicity in order to maintain and develop production. If manufacturers do not promote their cigars, who will promote them on their behalf?"[131] During the 1920s, cigars became very popular, and, to be able to compete, many factory owners opted to buy machines to produce them quickly. In 1919, 2.5 percent of tobacco products were machine manufactured; by 1925, the figure had increased to 15 percent, and by 1929, the number had reached 35 percent (by 1938, more than 80 percent of all U.S. cigar production was done by machine).[132] That directly affected the cigar rollers, because suddenly their work was no longer necessary. Also, a large number of factories were transplanted to the northern part of the United States, where priority was given to machine-made cigars and cigarettes.

Anna in the Tropics raises this issue. In the play, Cheché, who, incidentally, is from the northern United States, is the one who wants to bring machinery into the factory, but he fails because all the employees vote to continue making cigars by hand. In the play, tradition wins out, and the fact that the new brand of cigar is called Anna Karenina shows how important literature was in the cultural universe of the cigar workers. But in the context of Tampa in the 1930s, the introduction of cigar-rolling machinery was a real threat to cigar workers and *lectores*.

At the end of *Anna in the Tropics*, Cheché kills the cigar factory *lector* because the reading of *Anna Karenina* is destroying him psychologically. But what is intriguing is that he murders the *lector* before he has finished reading the novel aloud. Cheché interrupts the reading without knowing how *Anna Karenina* ends, without knowing that Tolstoy's novel ends tragically when Anna takes her own life. The reading of *Anna Karenina* affects Cheché more than anyone else, because he experiences firsthand the "danger" of literature. Thus, he decides to kill and flee.

But his escape is symbolic of his own failure because, when he sees he has no choice but to run away, he fails to put the machinery into use in the factory. His vision of progress is a failure, just as the train in Tolstoy's novel is a symbol of progress that turns out to be a disappointment. In *Anna Karenina*, nearly all references to trains are negative: at the train station, Anna meets her lover when he is beginning to seduce her; at a train station, Anna witnesses the death of a laborer; and Anna commits suicide by throwing herself in front of a train. "Lord, forgive me all!" Anna cries when the train strikes her: "A peasant muttering something was working at the iron above her. And the light by which she had read the book filled with troubles, falsehoods, sorrow, and evil, flared up more brightly than ever before, lighted up for her all that had been in darkness, flickered, began to grow dim, and was quenched forever."[133]

The train is a metaphor for Anna's failure as well. The train that kills her carries away her whole life as well as the life she throws away at the moment she starts her illicit affair. And in a parallel way, as a symbol of progress, the train is an agent of corruption.

In *Anna in the Tropics*, machinery as a symbol of progress is threatening but does not manage to dominate the scene. Likewise, the death of the *lector* does not signify the suspension of reading aloud in the factory in Ybor City. In anguish over the death of the *lector* and the silence in the workshop, the cigar workers decide to keep reading *Anna Karenina*. Palomo, Conchita's husband, picks up the book and continues to read part III of the work. The fact that Palomo has taken the place of the *lector*, his wife's former lover, shows how far he is willing to go to forgive her and continue the tradition of reading in the workshop.

Anna in the Tropics is an optimistic work that brilliantly shows the way a text is received and how it is capable of transforming its listeners. It also portrays the struggle between tradition and progress, but more important is the allusion to the death of the *lector*. In Tampa at the end of the 1920s, the hunger brought on by the Great Depression and the unemployment generated by the use of machinery made the cigar workers more vulnerable. Once again, the platform of the *lector* was in jeopardy. This time, *lectores* were accused of spreading Communist doctrine in the factories. In November of 1931, a number of cigar workers asked permission to have a parade on the fourteenth anniversary of the Russian Revolution, and the price they had to pay for their request was very steep.[134] Seventeen workers were sent to jail. They wrote a moving letter from jail:

All of us, the imprisoned coworkers, are ill because of the horrible dampness that exists in the cell they've had us locked up in since last Sunday, "as punishment." The cell is the most indecent that exists in the whole jail; there is no light, and it is full of lice and vermin, the toilets are not in working order. . . . Rheumatism is making us all ill, no one can eat the food. We would like the Comité Pro Presos [Prisoners' Advocate Committee] to circulate a petition demanding that we be let out of the cell we are in. All workshops should send a complaint to the mayor or the warden making this request.[135]

The cigar workers at several factories went on strike in support of the prisoners. The owners felt threatened by the public disturbances and accused the *lectores* of reading Communist propaganda. According to the *Tampa Daily Times*: "Originally the practice was a beneficial and instructive one, the readers sitting all day in the factories and reading aloud newspapers, novels and instructive works. The result was that the Tampa cigarmaker was probably better posted on current events than the average American workman in any other industry. But in recent months the readers have turned to the reading of red-hot radical publications and anarchistic propaganda, with the result that widespread unrest developed among the cigar workers."[136]

As a result of the strike, on November 26, 1931, the factory owners decided to rid themselves of what they considered their biggest enemy: the *lector*. The owners declared, as a group, that, "in the past, manufacturers had entered into an agreement with workers, allowing the reading of educational or instructional information, articles, or books, but the abuse of this privilege, through anarchist propaganda, has forced the manufacturers to immediately withdraw the privilege, and starting this morning, reading aloud is eliminated."[137] As a consequence, "the manufacturers will not allow readers to read anything in the factories, and no collections will be permitted in the factories."[138]

Their decision could not have been more definitive, since the following morning, when the cigar workers returned to work, the platforms for the *lectores* had been demolished. That was the real end of reading aloud in the cigar factories in Tampa.

That being the case, the play *Anna in the Tropics* is optimistic, because reading aloud in the workshop continues in spite of the *lector*'s having died. But in reality, reading aloud was banned once and for all in Tampa.

The protests over the elimination of reading aloud were evident, since all of Tampa was once again paralyzed. There were massive demonstrations, and cigar production came to a halt; almost all other businesses also closed their doors.[139] *La Gaceta* said the following on its editorial page:

We used to think that the manufacturers of cigars made by hand were
authentic democrats, of the ilk that defend complete freedom of speech
and of the press, but since this morning, we have changed our opinion. The
manufacturers, who were not the ones who paid the *lector*, have taken reading aloud away and put upwards of seventy or eighty men out of a job. . . . We
object, as the citizens of this free republic that we are, to the dictatorship of
the manufacturers over reading aloud. Abolishing reading aloud in factories
and causing to be unemployed a group of men worthy of a better fate does
not speak well of the manufacturers. Dictatorship, whether it be red or black,
communist or fascist, is always detestable.[140]

Some workers were so outraged that they took drastic steps. For example, at the Morgan Factory, the cigar workers agreed to pay the *lector* a
weekly salary until reading aloud was reestablished.[141] But their efforts were
in vain. Victoriano Manteiga wrote an open letter to the president of La
Unión de Fabricantes de Tabacos [Cigar Makers' Union]:

From the platforms, the cigar workers have read articles praising all the
tyrants on earth, and they have also read journalistic reports and books
extolling the virtues of all men on earth who have taken an interest in the
betterment and happiness of the meek. . . . In Cuba, where a dictatorship [of
Gerardo Machado] exists at present, communist, anarchist, unionist, conservative, and even anti-Machado articles are read in factories every day. The
cigar workers hear the best thinkers of all political leanings, and they accept
the ideas that they see fit. . . . It has not occurred even to Machado himself
to eliminate the platforms in factories, even knowing that articles critical of
him have been read. Why don't you imitate in this sense your counterparts in
Havana, as well as Gerardo Machado? . . . Also, if you don't pay for the reading, if the *lector* is at the service of the cigar workers, why resort to violence
against an innocent man, who merely follows the recommendations of the
reading president?[142]

This letter was read in public before a crowd that was protesting the abo-
lition of reading aloud. But reading aloud was banned permanently. The
cultural practice that enriched the universe of thousands of immigrants
came to an end.

"The strike left a psychological scar on me. I was in junior high school. . . .
My mother was in the strike. . . . The 1931 strike was openly radical. By then,
there was a Communist Party in Ybor City. Leaflets would be distributed

by people whom you knew. . . . The strike was a ghastly one. When the factories opened, they cut off many workers," said José Yglesias, a writer from Tampa.[143] According to Abelardo Gutiérrez Díaz, a *lector* who lost his job,

> because we read and disseminated the labor press, we incurred the hostility of the factory owners. We were accused of making communist propaganda. That simply was not true. The cigar workers paid, and one had to read precisely what the cigar workers wanted. Management did not approve of this system. It was at the height of one of these controversies that they abolished the *lectura*. They [the owners] removed the platform on which we sat. At this point, the workers took to the streets. . . . The *lectura* ended in 1931. After the strike, many *lectores* returned to the factories as cigar workers. And I, with a compatriot, opened a little café in Ybor.[144]

"It would be awful if people thought my father was a political agitator. He was just charismatic, kind, and had a great sense of humor," said Gloria M. de la Llana Deese, the daughter of Joaquín de la Llana, a *lector* whose nickname was "the Count of West Tampa."[145] Anyone who has read Alexandre Dumas' *The Count of Monte Cristo* would agree with those who gave him this nickname. It shows how deeply ingrained the reading aloud of the classics was in the cigar workers.

De la Llana, born in Pravia, Spain, could not have had a more fitting sobriquet. He was always impeccably dressed in a tuxedo or tailored suit (sometimes with a cape), collared, long-sleeved dress shirt with starched cuffs, necktie, top hat, and slip-on shoes or half-boots. When he came to Tampa he was a cigar worker, but later he became a *lector* at the Cuesta Rey and Martínez Ibor factories. "My father always liked literature and reading aloud. He was an impeccable, educated person. When the strike started in 1931, and reading aloud was banned, he had no choice but to start selling ice. Those were hard times. The depression had ruined everything, and my dad lost all the money he had in the bank," added Ms. de la Llana Deese. After having worked selling ice, de la Llana sold coffee beans for the rest of his life. "He wasn't the best salesman in the world, but people idolized him. He would sit down and tell incredible stories to people, and they'd sit there to listen to him. He was a wonderful storyteller and everybody loved him. He was fascinated by literature," his daughter told me wistfully. The ban on reading aloud forced the *lectores* to take different paths, and, to a certain extent, as was the case with the Count of West Tampa, a real human talent capable of reading to and culturally enriching a whole world of workers went to waste.

Manuel Aparicio, one of the most beloved *lectores* in Tampa, had to find full-time employment in the theater and on the radio when reading aloud was banned in the factories. Aparicio was a Spaniard. He was a polyglot and gifted theater actor who ran the theater division of El Centro Asturiano, the headquarters of one of the most innovative programs in American cultural history: the New Deal's Federal Theatre Project, whose theater company was the only one that presented works solely in Spanish. Aparicio wrote several plays, but the most successful was *El mundo en la mano*, which he also directed, and which consisted of stories and characters from Spain, Cuba, and Italy.[146] He brought to the radio his experience as a *lector* and founded a program titled *Momentos Latinos*, which was broadcast on WDAE.[147] His radio show was nothing short of an extension of his work as a cigar factory *lector*. As his daughter, Mary Fontanills stated:

> On the radio he did the same thing he did as a reader. He read. He was so— his ideal was so high. He would pick up the [*Tampa*] *Tribune* in the morning, put it under his arm, go to the radio station, pick up the *Tribune*, and start reading in Spanish. I mean, he could translate instantly. He would read the news right off the cover. Then he would read the *novelas*. He only had a half-hour program. And when he read them he would always leave them hanging just like they do with *Dallas* and all that. And even my own mother could not get him to reveal what would happen next. They would have to wait until the next day. He had a half-hour program five days a week. And that is how, . . . he worked on that for many years.[148]

The popularity of *Momentos Latinos* and the way in which the readings were done over the radio demonstrates how deep-rooted reading aloud was in Tampa society. Domenico Giunta, an Italian immigrant who, like almost everyone else, had learned Spanish to be able to socialize and to understand the reading, said:

> What happened in my family happened in every other family and that was the members of the family had heard these novels, went home and made known what the day's reading consisted of and there were always items of great social value that we appreciated back in those days. Love of family, thrift, education, children, nature, and love of nature. And each evening my sister used to come home and give us, verbally, the episode that took place. That must have [lasted] about seven years in my family up to the time that I became then a teenager. . . . I did not have time to stick around the family table after supper, but earlier, we stuck around the family table . . . thirty

minutes or so after supper to listen to my sister give us the episode of the day, and the news she had heard from the *lector*.[149]

Sadly, the radio gradually replaced the *lector*. Thus, it is not surprising that some *lectores* started to work full time in radio, as was the case with Alfredo Montoto.

Mr. Montoto had been a baseball player, cigar worker, and *lector*—a little of everything. When reading aloud was banned, he began to work full time in journalism and radio. "He used to write chronicles about baseball, in-depth articles, telegrams, and he read into a microphone at a local radio station, . . . he managed the weekly *Información*, and specialized in issues related to La Liga Intersocial [Intersocial League]."[150]

In the 1930s and 1940s, sportscasts were not done in Spanish; rather, the announcer first listened to the program in English and then retransmitted it in Spanish. At least two bilingual announcers alternated with each other, interpreting and transmitting simultaneously.[151] Mateo Rodríguez was also a *lector* who later worked in radio. Rodríguez was born in Cuba at the end of the nineteenth century. He studied acting and played roles in classical Spanish-language plays. When he lost his job as a *lector*, he became an announcer, and, like all other Hispanic announcers, he took English-language newspapers and translated them orally into Spanish. In the 1930s, he went to New York for a time, and there he worked dubbing films into Spanish. He worked the rest of his life in radio and died in the 1970s, up until which time he was still reading the news (this time, directly in Spanish) and recording an advice column for radio station ESOL-AM 1300.[152]

In Tampa at the end of the 1930s, the few factories that remained started to broadcast, with strict limitations, music and radio programs at certain times of day. Starting in 1946, workers were allowed to bring their own radios to the factories during the World Series. That same year, Matías Corcés, a *lector* who had lost his job in 1931 and had to work making cigars on a machine, stated: "The younger generation does not miss us." He added: "Some of them even would have a hard time understanding us, now that they can speak English better than Spanish . . . to the older ones the factories have never been the same since, and they still want us."[153] A petition was circulated in 1944 asking for reading aloud to be resumed in factories, but the Cigar Makers International Union rejected the proposal.[154]

The ban on reading aloud also signaled the end of generations of *lectores*. That is, there were entire families that worked as *lectores*, as was the case with Wilfredo Rodríguez (El Mexicanito), his brother, and his father,

Francisco Rodríguez (El Mexicano). None of the three was Mexican. The father was born in Santiago de Cuba, and his sons were born in Havana. Francisco Rodríguez, who had been a *lector* in the Henry Clay and Partagás factories in Havana, came to Tampa in 1906. He continued reading there and taught his children the profession of *lector*. "Well, he [read] before a piece of paper or book or something and I [tried] to imitate him while he [did] it," said Wilfredo Rodríguez.[155] "If he [my father] read from a newspaper a politician's comments, he would read as if he were talking to the people in a speech."[156] Tone, volume, and enunciation were always important: "It was exactly like the theater, . . . when we were reading a novel we were to make . . . as though we were a character who was talking—whether it was a woman or a child, an old man or an old lady. Not everybody could do that."[157]

Wilfredo Rodríguez' favorite novel was nothing short of *Don Quixote*. "I tried to read that book [as] best [I could], too. But I was never as good as my father," Wilfredo stated.[158]

But what is most intriguing is that *Don Quixote* was also the favorite novel of *lectores* Honorato Henry Domínguez and his father, Honorato W. Domínguez. "We were more than *lectores*. We made the characters come alive," said Honorato Henry Domínguez.[159] Few *lectores* admitted that *Don Quixote* was their favorite novel except those two generations of *lectores*. Without a doubt, those dynasties could tell of a true family literary tradition.

The life of reading aloud in Tampa was nearly unbelievable. It was always under threat because, to many people, it represented an ever-present threat. Reading aloud caused struggles, rebellions, and strikes and ended up making reality more fictional than fiction itself, as was the case with the duel to the death between Jesús Fernández from Asturias, Spain, and Enrique Velázquez from Mexico that December 22, 1903, at the Restaurante Lorenzana. Literature was so taken to heart that it caused killings. The press provoked hatred or bitterness, and there were even kidnappings, such as happened to Francisco Milián.

Reading in cigar factories was never as vulnerable anywhere as it was in Tampa. But this vulnerability motivated the great *lectores* to make decisions that would shape the future of Tampa and of Cuba. Thanks to the *lectores*, José Martí set foot in Tampa, and the support of all the cigar workers was largely instrumental in making possible the Spanish-American War for Cuba's independence. Also, thanks to the work of the *lectores*, it was possible to maintain the Spanish language and a great deal of the Hispanic culture in the United States.

The tradition of reading aloud in Tampa's cigar factories is presented in an extraordinary way in works of fiction such as Nilo Cruz's *Anna in the Tropics*. Likewise, a novel by Cuban author Pablo Medina, *The Cigar Roller* (2005), introduces us to Chano, a cigar factory *lector* in Tampa in the nineteenth century. Medina's novel is interesting because the *lector* is seen and remembered from the point of view of the main character, Amadeo Terra, a Cuban cigar worker who came to Tampa with the first immigrants from Cuba. In the same vein, the novel *A Wake in Ybor City* (written in 1963), by José Yglesias, also recovers the tradition of reading aloud when three of the characters, Robert, Mina, and Dolores, discuss the moral and religious content of the novel *Gloria*, by Benito Pérez Galdós. "I heard that novel read in the cigar factory several times in the days when every factory had a reader," Mina says, right on point.[160]

But the nostalgia for the *lector* is portrayed brilliantly in the musical *The Cigar Box Revue* (1976), written by Phyllis and Norman Zeno. The *lector* is an elderly gentleman who appears in the upper-right portion of the set, sitting in a balcony. He is seen faintly in a dim light. He acts as master of ceremonies throughout the play. With a Cuban accent, he says:

> Good afternoon. May I introduce myself? I am El Lector . . . an anachronism in these days of radio and television, but once . . . ah, yes, once it was my voice and my words that molded the thoughts of men. From early morning to late evening, seated on just such a balcony as this, . . . in those days, as befits a man of some importance, I was paid well . . . greeted with respect as I walked the streets . . . toasted in the cafes. I was El Lector . . . [a] man of learning . . . [a] molder of opinion . . . [a] man of position and influence.[161]

Toward the end of the musical, the *lector* speaks again and talks of the history of Tampa from its early days, starting with the yellow fever epidemic of 1887 and through the First World War, the Communists, Al López, the strikes, and so on. Symbolically, the *lector* has seen it all and has read it all. The musical ends with the *lector* saying: "It is 1976 . . . El Lector is an offstage voice with the volume turned off."[162] In short, it is impossible to study the cultural history of Tampa without learning about the history of cigar factory *lectores*.

FIVE

Luisa Capetillo

Lectora *in Puerto Rico, Tampa, and New York*

⸻•═▪═•⸻

Beautiful Borinquen
Cuba has marked the way
Your brave sons will follow;
They wish to join the fray.

I

On July 24, 1915, Luisa Capetillo got dressed as she always did: she put on her shirt, her necktie, her trousers, her jacket, and her narrow-brimmed hat.[1] Dressed that way, she stepped out onto the streets of Havana, but she was quickly arrested on Neptuno Street by an officer who told her it was immoral for her to dress as a man and that her attire was causing a scene.[2]

Months earlier, Pres. Mario García Menocal had ordered her deportation because he considered her to be a dangerous foreigner. Luisa, originally from Arecibo, Puerto Rico, lived in Cuba for only a year, but from her arrival, the Cuban government viewed her with suspicion because she had contact with cigar makers and leaders of the anarchist movement. In 1915, when a sugarcane workers' strike broke out on the island, Luisa associated with sugarcane workers and anarchists, who criticized the oppressive attitude of the government through protests and demonstrations.

We do not know whether the order of deportation issued by the president was carried out, but when she was arrested for wearing trousers, she defended herself to the judge, arguing that there was no law on the books that banned women from wearing trousers. The judge was speechless and set her free.

It was not the first time Luisa had been persecuted. In her native Puerto Rico, she had been investigated by the authorities, and that had forced her to flee into exile and to take refuge in the United States. During her extensive travels as an exile, she visited Cuba, and being deported, exiled once again, was the destiny that she found for herself and that befell her in life. Luisa was a worker, writer, leader of a number of labor movements, and, most important for this study, a cigar factory *lectora* in Puerto Rico, Tampa, and New York at a time when reading aloud was almost exclusively a man's profession.

It is unknown exactly when reading aloud began in Puerto Rico, but the practice was brought there from Cuba at the end of the nineteenth century. In Puerto Rico, laws that favored the right of free association went into effect in 1873, and starting at that time, cigar workers began to form labor guilds, study groups, and, later, labor unions.[3] Just as in Havana, *La Aurora*, a newspaper for cigar workers, was first published in 1865 in Puerto Rico, and *El Artesano* was launched in 1874. As I have mentioned, the reading aloud of newspapers was the way in which less-privileged classes had access to culture.

Arecibo, where Luisa was raised, was the Puerto Rican hub of radical labor culture at the turn of the century. The rate of illiteracy among the general population was 77 percent; within the cigar sector, it was 40 percent.[4] It was against this backdrop in 1906 that Luisa worked as a cigar factory *lectora*. Before she became a *lectora*, she contributed to some of the newspapers in Arecibo in 1904, and she also worked as a seamstress from her home, embroidering and sewing handkerchiefs and blouses.[5]

Having been a cigar worker and a writer, Luisa certainly understood the importance of the role of reading aloud in the workplace. At that time, the education of women was nearly prohibited, and there were few educational centers, although it must be said that Luisa received a good education both at home and in a school. As she later wrote: "My father had the blessed patience to teach me reading, writing, and the four rules of arithmetic. Later, I went to a school, the principal of which was a teacher from this island, María Sierra de Soler, at whose school I was awarded several certificates, for the examinations in the subjects of grammar, religious history, geography, reading, etc. etc."[6]

Education was Luisa's first priority, but it did not have to adhere to a strict academic curriculum. She used to say: "I speak about everything with a perfect comprehension of what I am saying, with a deep intuition that guides me; but I have not been able to study according to the precepts of schools, lecture halls, or institutions of higher learning, as I was never sent there."[7] Thus, study, whether formal or not, was her priority and, to her mind, a privilege to which everyone ought to have access. Her reading aloud in factories was a means by which to teach thousands of workers.

In the factories where Luisa read, some of the cigar workers supported both anarchist and socialist ideologies. That is, those cigar workers and even workers from other fields were part of the liberal-thinking movement that struggled to provide instruction for workers. It was even the case that, in 1902, four years before Luisa entered the profession of *lectora*, a school was founded for workers in Arecibo, and a group of volunteer teachers was created to provide basic instruction at the workers' local union headquarters.[8]

As a result, Luisa was reading in factories at the time when the Puerto Rican workers were beginning to develop class consciousness. The ideals of the international labor movement reached Puerto Rico through pamphlets, books, and magazines that came from Latin America and Europe. To those workers, the doctrines of Mikhail Bakunin, who proposed libertarian socialism or anarchy, seemed very appealing because he stressed the need and the right to education for the masses, and especially education for women.

As far as Luisa was concerned, literature was more interesting and emotional than politics: "I am irresistibly drawn to literature. To me, writing is the most pleasant and choice occupation, that which most entertains me, which is most suited to my temperament; thus, I feel disposed to cultivate that art and perfect my skills in it, not out of ambition for glory, nor for renown, nor to make my fortune, nor to draw distinctions; my only intent, the only incentive that has motivated me to write, aside from the delight it brings me, has been to tell the truth.[9]"

Still, in spite of the innate passion she had for literature, she felt the need to struggle for better working conditions and education for employees; the platform in the cigar factory was where she could reconcile her liberal views and her predilection for literature. Her vast cultural background is reflected in the written texts she left behind: manifestos, fragments, letters, stories, and plays.

The newspapers that were read in the cigar factories of Arecibo were *Porvenir del Trabajo, Unión Obrera, Revista Blanca, El Socialismo, Tierra* (which was imported from Cuba), and *Motín* (from Madrid). While Luisa played the role of *lectora*, she also took on the task of writing her first book, *Ensayos libertarios*, which was published in 1907.[10] What is essential to know is that before publishing it in book form, the young *lectora* and writer had her writings heard by a wide audience. The style of those essays shows that they were written to be read aloud, and their content, as the title suggests, stresses progressive ideology. In one of them, she says: "Education is the foundation of happiness among people. Teach under the canopy of truth; slash open the veil of ignorance, by showing the true light of progress, free of rites and dogmas. . . . Ignorance is the cause of the greatest crimes and injustices."[11]

In another essay, she attacks religious institutions, emphasizing that "their preaching is trickery, hypocrisy, and they are only concerned with what serves their own holdings and not those of others."[12] She proposes that, if the church were to share its wealth, "poor mothers (since there would be none) would not have to take their young children out of school to send them to work in order to be able to afford their clothing. Thus there would be no illiteracy, no injustice, no envy nor bitterness."[13]

On one occasion, she wrote to the workers in order to talk to them about poverty, stealing, and the law: "Is their any just or educational point to taking a poor wretch to jail for making off with a few plantains or sweet potatoes, or a piece of bread, without asking him if he has a family and if he has found work?"[14] The theme of *Les Misérables* could not be more palpable, especially when she proposes that "better they should build industrial-education institutions and tear down the prisons, or, rather, substitute one for the other. Education and work are the salvation of mankind."[15] Just as Victor Hugo denounced social injustice in the story of Jean Valjean, of his descent into social hell and his moral redemption, Luisa proposes that more justice be done so that everyone might work, be educated, and live in harmony. In *Ensayos libertarios*, Luisa supports the ideology of classical anarchists and proposes that a fair, egalitarian society should exist. Thus, she suggests reading the works of Peter Kropotkin, such as *The Conquest of Bread,* and *Fields, Factories and Workshops Tomorrow*, which she no doubt read aloud as well.[16]

But what else was read aloud in Puerto Rico? The intertexts in Luisa Capetillo's writing suggest that she read not only the work of anarchists, such as *Anarquía*, by Errico Malatesta, and *Federalismo y socialismo*, the classic work by Bakunin, but also philosophical essays by John Stuart Mill and free thinker Camille Flamarion. Needless to say, in the literary terrain, she read Victor Hugo, Émile Zola, George Sand, Eduardo Zamacois, and, especially, Ivan Turgenev and Leo Tolstoy.

Besides reading aloud in workshops, Luisa, as a union representative and propagandist, read in public squares a number of pamphlets and speeches written by her comrades. Although she was a cigar factory *lectora* in Arecibo for only a year, she made sure her complete works were read aloud in the workplace, as she indicates in this description of a trip she took all over the island:

When I reached San Juan, I had the intention of staying, in a well-placed position, or in any manner. I felt obliged to print another edition of my first pamphlet [*Ensayos libertarios*] and to determine the best way to disseminate the literature in the factories. I also felt it necessary to go to Caguas and to Juncos, since La Cruzada Ideal [a march across Puerto Rico to organize and educate workers], led by J. B. Delgado and J. Ferrer y Ferrer, begun by La Federación Libre [Free Federation of Workers], was still in progress. There I had the opportunity to attend and make the humble contribution of my assistance at the workers' conferences in Caguas, Juncos, and Gurabo. And when I returned to San Juan, I went to Arecibo to help distribute written materials for the cigar workers.[17]

When Luisa left her position as *lectora*, she devoted her time, apart from leadership, to distributing newspapers and magazines and to selling her own pamphlets. In 1909, she began to help promote the distribution of *Unión Obrera*, for which she also wrote, and published a magazine that was no doubt read avidly in the workshops: *La Mujer*. A year later, she published *La humanidad en el futuro*, a utopian tale with a general strike as its subject matter, a theme that is explored repeatedly in anarchist literature. Her book *Mi opinión sobre las libertades, derechos y deberes de la mujer como compañera, madre y ser independiente*, published in 1911, was also eagerly listened to all over the island. The text includes essays about women's history in primitive times, marriage, sex education, and women's and men's rights.

In essence, Luisa Capetillo literally wrote to be heard. As we will see later, her most important book was written in Tampa, where she no doubt enjoyed a large listening audience.

II

In 1913, Luisa went to Ybor City and immediately started to do what she knew best: reading aloud and writing. During the summer of that year, she worked as a cigar factory *lectora*, an unusual profession for a woman in Florida.[18] She read the local and international press in the cigar factories, but she also read her own work there. In fact, her book *Mi opinión sobre las libertades*, published in Puerto Rico in 1911, was reprinted in a revised edition in Ybor City and was exhibited in local libraries and clubs.

Surrounded by cigar workers and *lectores* who came from all parts and in the heart of a cosmopolitan center, Luisa devoted her time, apart from reading, to writing her most important book, *Influencia de las ideas modernas*, published in 1916. What is most significant about this book is its inclusion of several plays, stories, and scenes of life in Ybor City. In Florida she was able to devote her time to what she enjoyed most: "I am irresistibly drawn to literature, writing to me is the most pleasant occupation."[19]

Luisa had a large listening audience that no doubt fed her need to write and be heard at the same time. For that reason, it is not surprising that her best theatrical work, *Influencia de las ideas modernas*, which shares a title with the book of the same name, should have the central theme of the struggles of a cigar industry town for its workers' rights. Her political leanings and intellectual makeup become crystallized in this work.

In the text, the main character, Angelina, the daughter of a wealthy cigar factory owner, voraciously reads the works of Leo Tolstoy, Émile Zola, Peter Kropotkin, and Errico Malatesta. Her reading of romantic, realist, and anarchist authors causes her to want to share her wealth with the poor, and she convinces her father to cede part of his holdings to the cigar workers. As for the cigar workers, who had already been protesting for their rights, they receive money in abundance and build houses, day and night schools, theaters, and public reading rooms where readings, especially of the arts, philosophy, sociology, and even psychology take place.[20] In short, in the play, a society is formed that is both utopian and egalitarian, in which everyone has the right to an education, where there are no salaries or money in circulation, and where everyone enjoys a happy life.

Another theatrical work she wrote in Ybor City is *La corrupción de los ricos y la de los pobres o Cómo se prostituye una rica y una pobre*. It focuses on the story of a young woman whose father, with the idea of making money and being able to call his daughter a marchioness, wants her to marry a marquess. She accepts the proposition but regrets it in the end and runs away with a young man, the true love of her life, taking with her an inheritance to which she is entitled.

Another piece, *Cómo se prostituyen las pobres*, concerns the life of a prostitute who cannot work in a workshop because she has not learned any trade at all. Also, in the factories she would be as poorly paid as in the brothel. Obviously, the only difference is that, in the brothel, her customers beat her and insult her.

Two very interesting stories Luisa wrote and read aloud in Ybor City are "El cajero" and another, untitled one the central theme of which is common-law marriage. "El cajero" tells the story of Ramón, a poor boy, who, thanks to his godfather, manages to study and become a cashier in a business, but he is exploited by the rich. One day he decides to run away, taking with him a million dollars in stolen money as well as his girlfriend. The two escape to New York and board a steamship that takes them to St. Petersburg (Russia, not Florida). From there they go to Italy, later to Paris, and end up in

Granada, Spain, where they have a son. What is interesting about this tale is that it combines the Russian atmosphere with an experience in the United States, as does *Anna in the Tropics*, a work I address in Chapter 4.

Luisa's untitled story is a highly stylized text that could very well have been adapted for the stage. The action takes place in Ybor City and is about Elena and Andrés, who meet in front of El Círculo Cubano, a Cuban social center in the city. He invites her to his home, situated on the outskirts of Tampa, and, after a brief courtship, they decide to live together in a common-law marriage outside the bonds of matrimony, and they have three children.

To summarize, in Ybor City, Luisa Capetillo gave her imagination free rein, she wrote her best literature, and she read it aloud during an era when it was not easy to enjoy freedom of expression, much less read texts with anarchist leanings. As Julio Ramos notes, Luisa lived in Ybor City just two years after Juan Vilar, an educated cigar worker born in Caguas, Puerto Rico, was put in jail because he was accused of associating with V. Grillo, an anarchist who murdered one of the heads of the West Indies Trading Company. The detective who brought charges against Juan Vilar based his accusation on the literature he found in the library of the educational center of which the cigar worker was in charge.[21]

As I have emphasized, in most cases, it was the cigar workers who chose the reading material, but in Luisa's case, as she was the author, the cigar workers no doubt listened to her with curiosity, attention, interest, and respect. Perhaps it is due to this dynamic that she produced her best work in Ybor City. The only thing Luisa wrote about her experience as a *lectora* in Florida is expressed in a single phrase of a fragment in which she alludes to time: "I can hear the clock in an Ybor City factory slowly striking twelve."[22]

III

At the beginning of 1919, New York's newspapers were talking about the hunger and terrible conditions suffered by farmworkers and cigar workers in Puerto Rico. Those workers were constantly on strike and calling work stoppages. The daily *La Prensa* tried to take up a collection to help the Puerto Rican workers, but the reading public showed very little interest.

That year, Luisa Capetillo was living in New York, and, in response to what was taking place in Puerto Rico, she publicly denounced the government of the island because of the deplorable conditions in which the workers were living.[23]

Her denunciation started a great debate between Puerto Ricans and mainland U.S. politicians who had an interest in the present and future of

Puerto Rico. At that time, according to the testimony of Bernardo Vega, a Puerto Rican cigar roller who immigrated to New York in 1916, Luisa Capetillo was a cigar factory *lectora* there. In addition to reading aloud, Luisa ran a boardinghouse on Twenty-second Street, near Eighth Avenue.[24] In 1913, Luisa was living in New York, where she made a name for herself as a journalist by contributing to the newspapers *Cultura Obrera*, *Brazo y Cerebro*, and *Fuerza Consciente*. Most of her articles dealt with women's liberation, and these writings were no doubt heard in the cigar factories of the big city.[25] What is known about reading aloud in New York in 1919, that is, in the context in which Luisa distinguished herself as a *lectora*, we know thanks to the *Memorias* written by Bernardo Vega.[26]

Reading aloud was slowly introduced to New York's cigar factories at the end of the nineteenth century, after most of the large factories had moved to Key West or Tampa. In fact, the only account about reading in New York City in the nineteenth century was written by Samuel Gompers, an English cigar roller who immigrated to the United States when he was thirteen years old, in 1863. Years later, in 1886, Gompers became the president of the American Federation of Labor. According to his autobiography, reading aloud took place in the prestigious David Hirsch & Company Factory in 1873, where he was a cigar roller.[27]

For his part, at the beginning of the twentieth century, Bernardo Vega was a good listener who was endowed with varied culture, thanks to the readings and talks that took place in El Morito Factory, where he became a cigar roller when he arrived in Manhattan in 1916.[28] At the cigar factory he struck up a friendship with two Cuban men: Juan Bonilla, a friend of José Martí's; and J. de Castro Palomino, a very educated man. There he also met Maximiliano Olay, who had been a *lector* in Tampa and later wrote *Mirando al mundo*.[29] In 1916, reading aloud had already become standardized in factories where Spanish speakers worked, as most of them had a regular *lector* who read twice a day: the news for an hour in the morning; and in the afternoon, also for an hour, literary, political, and philosophical works in alternation.

But the *lector* was not necessarily a political agitator, as was the consensus; rather, it was his listening audience that insisted on what he should read to them: "At first, the factory *lector*, on his own, chose the works. At that time, literature that was purely entertaining predominated: novels by Pérez Esrich, Luis Val, etc. But as the cigar workers evolved politically, they started to have a say in the selection of reading material. They asserted their preference for social doctrine. They read Gustave Le Bon, Ludwig Buchner, Darwin, Marx, Engels, Bakunin. . . . It's a fact that no cigar worker fell asleep."[30] Later, in New York, there was also a Reading Commission that suggested works to the cigar workers and "chose from among the works of Émile Zola, Alexandre Dumas, Victor Hugo, Gustave Flaubert, Jules Verne, Pierre Loti, José María Vargas Vila, Pérez Galdós, Palacio Valdés, Dostoyevsky, Gogol, Gorky, Tolstoy. . . . All those authors were well known by the cigar workers of the day."[31]

It was the workers who bought the books, and after they were read aloud in the cigar factories, they were usually circulated among the workers or donated to El Círculo de Trabajadores de Brooklyn (Workers' Society of Brooklyn, where most of the members were cigar workers) or to La Escuela Francisco Ferrer y Guardia [Francisco Ferrer y Guardia School]. The books that were not bought were borrowed from individuals' libraries. The newspapers that were read the most were *El Comercio, Cultura Proletaria, El Heraldo, Las Novedades,* and, most of all, *La Prensa.*[32]

As we have seen, reading aloud in factories when Luisa Capetillo was a *lectora* in New York was not very different from that in Tampa or Cuba. The arguments about the reading of any text were also similar. Bernardo Vega recalls a great debate that broke out at El Morito Factory after the Spanish translation of the work *La hyène enragée* (published in Spanish as *La hiena enfurecida*), by Pierre Loti, was read, and even more about *El fuego* (published in English translation from the French as *Under Fire: The Story of a Squad* [*Le feu*]), by Henri Barbusse. The latter is a novel that tells the story of a brigade of soldiers in the trenches who reflect on the future of humanity during the First World War. The plot of Barbusse's work was enough to bring about altercations between cigar workers with varying ideologies. Strangely enough, they had a system that went into effect when arguments occurred:

> At El Morito, as in all the other factories, it was as silent as a church during the reading. At the end of the reading shifts, arguments would start about what had been read. The person at one workbench would talk to the one at the next, without work interruptions. Although no one was formally leading the discussion, people took turns. If the controversy persisted and the contenders continued to insist on their points of view, one of the more educated workers would intervene as a referee. When information or issues of fact provoked arguments, there was never a lack of someone to consult the *mataburros* . . . that's what we called reference books.[33]

Some of the cigar workers had encyclopedic dictionaries on their workbenches to consult after the reading. When there were arguments and the referees were incapable of resolving the dispute, they turned to reference books.

On the workbenches, one could find not only the *chaveta*, the wrapper, and the tobacco leaf, but also, literally, the leaf of paper. As José Martí said metaphorically when he spoke of reading aloud and its corollary, while some "write on the leaf, others roll it." And "On one table, ink, on the other, filler and wrappers. All that is left behind by the cigar is the virtue of he who crafts it."[34]

Conversely, Bernardo Vega tells us, not everything was so drastic or serious, since happiness often reigned. Note the harmony between the playful and the poetic parts of his description: "It was not unusual that, after a tempestuous argument, someone would get all fired up and start telling another story. Heated emotions would cool down, laughter rang out throughout the workshop, and a wave of *choteo* would bounce from workbench to workbench."[35]

The factory's culture also extended into the cafés and social centers, especially El Círculo de Trabajadores, where the cigar workers met in groups and sat around tables to converse or to play Chinese checkers, dominoes, or chess. There they talked about the works that were being read in the factories, about the current news, about history, or about any other topic. What is interesting is that this social practice reflected the worries of the educated cigar workers. Bernardo Vega recalls that, on an ordinary night, one could hear a bit of everything: a group talking about Martí and his death in Dos Ríos; another about the current situation in Mexico (in 1918); others talking about literature; and, finally, those who were discussing theatrical works that were to open in New York—*Tierra baja* (published in translation as *Marta of the Lowlands* [*Terra baixa*]: a play in three acts); *In the World*, by Gorky; and *Uncle Vanya*, by Chekhov.[36] Parties and artistic and literary conferences were also held at El Círculo.

The year 1919, when Luisa Capetillo was a *lectora* in New York, was notable for a financial crisis. Large cigar companies started to acquire machinery to produce cigars, because there was great demand for cheaper cigars. Thousands of cigar rollers were fired, and several factories moved to New Jersey and Pennsylvania. Some cigar workers opted to stay in New York and established small *chinchales* to survive.

Without a doubt, that crisis affected reading aloud in factories, and, thus, a short time later, reading aloud ceased to exist in that part of the United States. Bernardo Vega recalls that, in 1919, the crisis affected Luisa Capetillo (who no doubt lost her job as a *lectora*), whose living situation was precarious: "And since that noble Puerto Rican woman never worried a great deal about money, anyone who arrived hungry slept there [in her boardinghouse], whether he had any way to pay or not. Naturally, her 'business' was in a constant state of crisis, and she often found herself in a tight spot in terms of how to pay the rent on the apartment."[37]

Despite her impoverished state, Luisa fought for the establishment of a school in Puerto Rico for orphaned children, where they could be taught to read. To that end, she asked Samuel Gompers, then president of the American Federation of Labor, for help. She got the money, but in Puerto Rico her project was banned because it was thought that the funds should come from the Puerto Rican people and not from the U.S. mainland.[38] Disillusioned, the *lectora* returned to Puerto Rico, where she died two years later.

Bernardo Vega, who, thanks to reading aloud in factories and the support of his fellow cigar workers, managed to get a solid education, at that time possessed a library of more than six hundred volumes. Toward the end of his life, when he moved away from New York to live in the country, he indicated that, "in the back of the house, in the yard, I built a wooden structure and in it I installed my two most treasured possessions: my books and my *chinchal*."[39] But after a trip to Puerto Rico, he pointed out that, "when I returned to the country house, I discovered an irreparable loss: water had flooded 'my library,' which, as I indicated, was also my *chinchal*, and I lost my books and papers, which were important to me."[40]

We can only imagine the leaves of paper of his books and the leaves of tobacco, shipwrecked under his workbench and his desk, crumpling, tearing, dissolving. This catastrophic scene is nothing short of a metaphor for the disappearance of reading aloud in the cigar factories of New York.

ENTREGA 29.ª   TOMO I.

LA AURORA.

PERIODICO SEMANAL DEDICADO A LOS ARTESANOS.

REDACCION Y ADMINISTRACION:
Calle de la Reina núm. 6.

DOMINGO 6 DE MAYO DE 1866.

SUSCRICION.
un real sencillo la entrega.

EL PORVENIR LITERARIO EN CUBA.

Cuantas veces un recuerdo sirve de alivio á nuestras penas, y mucho mas cuando él nos trae á la memoria los dias felices que brillaron en bien de nuestra literatura. El Liceo de Guanabacoa dejó grabado para siempre en el corazon de todo cubano amante á su pais, los recuerdos mas agradables; jamás podrán borrarse de nosotros aquellas noches felices, aquellas noches deliciosas que invadia sus espaciosos salones la juventud estudiosa y entusiasta por el porvenir glorioso de las letras en Cuba. Aun parece dibujarse en nuestra mente aquella modesta tribuna desproveida de todo adorno de urbanidad, engalanada alguna que otra vez con hermosas guirnaldas de flores naturales, símbolo del amor, como queriendo significarnos el amor al estudio, mas glorioso aun cuando esa tribuna se levantaba en medio del salon aristocrático de las noches de baile.

Esa modesta tribuna era la señal de civilizacion que daba Cuba á sus adversarios, á los que creen que es el baile y la orgia lo que nos entusiasma, los que creen que son un mal al pais las bibliotecas, las lecturas en los talleres, las escuelas en el campo, en fin de todo lo que sea progreso. Esa tribuna era el monumento que presentaba el pais en presencia de sus hijos como para atestiguar los hechos pasados y protestar contra el atraso de la inteligen-

cia: el pueblo así lo comprendió y supo dar pruebas de aprobacion en entusiastas aplausos.

En esa tribuna se le tributaron brillantes aplausos á los eminentes literatos Jorrin, Azcárate, Riesgo, Escobar, Rodriguez, Céspedes y otros que supieron con sus inteligencias vencer á los que desde un principio lucharon por derribar tan sublime institucion. Allí aplaudimos por primera vez las hermosas composiciones de nuestro celebrado poeta Saturnino Martinez, y pudimos aplaudir de cerca los heróicos versos del cantor de Cuba José Fornáris. Tambien nuestras paisanas dieron vida con sus talentos al Liceo; mas de una vez el público que concurria á esos salones victorió á las distinguidas poetisas Merced Valdes Mendoza y María de Santa Cruz, aun resuenan en nuestros oidos aquellos deliciosos versos dedicados al primer aniversario del instituto querido.

Al Liceo de Guanabacoa se debió el primer periódico que circuló por la villa; á él tambien le cabe la honra del establecimiento de la imprenta. Guanabacoa se vió dignamente representada en su querido periódico «El Progreso,» verdadero intérprete de la civilizacion y cultura de los pueblos.

Podemos decir que desde esa época trabaja Cuba por el adelanto de sus hijos, á pesar de los inseparables obstáculos que encuentran á su paso, barreras que nunca le han faltado desde su conquista á la fecha;

Lecturas que entusiasman.

Lectura que aprovecha.

Drawings by Víctor Patricio Landaluze, "Readings That Everyone Enjoys"
and "Useful Reading," *Don Junípero*, May 6, 1866
(Courtesy of Biblioteca Nacional José Martí and Joan Casanovas)

Club San Carlos, Key West, 1960s
(Courtesy of Monroe County May Hill Russell Library)

Postcard of the Havana American Cigar Factory, Key West, 1896
(Courtesy of Monroe County May Hill Russell Library)

The Vicente Martínez Ybor Cigar Factory, Ybor City (Tampa), 1887
(*Courtesy of the University of South Florida Libraries Special Collections*)

The Corner of 7th Avenue and 16th Street, Ybor City, circa 1927
(*Courtesy of the University of South Florida Libraries Special Collections*)

Luisa Capetillo, *lectora* in Puerto Rico, Tampa, and New York, Havana, 1915 *(Courtesy of Laboratorio Fotográfico, Sistema de Bibliotecas, Universidad de Puerto Rico)*

Lector Joaquín de la Llana, known as "el Conde" (the Count), Tampa, early 1920s *(Courtesy of Gloria M. de la Llana Deese)*

Lector—upper right—at the Corral-Wodiska Factory, Tampa, 1929
(Courtesy of the University of South Florida Libraries Special Collections)

Ybor City residents listening to a World Series game broadcast in Spanish and sponsored by *La Traducción*, one of the local newspapers, 1930s
(Courtesy of the University of South Florida Libraries Special Collections)

Staff of *La Traducción*, the Ybor City newspaper
founded by *lector* Ramón Valdespino, Tampa, 1936
(Courtesy of the University of South Florida Libraries Special Collections)

Victoriano Manteiga, *lector* and founder
of the newspaper *La Gaceta*, 1939
(Courtesy of *La Gaceta*)

Lector in a Havana cigar factory, 1933
(Photograph by Ewing Galloway. Courtesy of Ramiro Fernández Collection)

La Caridad Leaf-stripping Plant, San Juan y Martínez, 2003
(Photograph by Araceli Tinajero)

Lector Santos Segundo Domínguez
Mena, San Juan y Martínez, 2003
(Photograph by Araceli Tinajero)

Partagás Cigar Factory, Havana, 2001
(Photograph by Araceli Tinajero)

Lector Ángel Borges reading at La Caridad Leaf-stripping Plant,
San Juan y Martínez, 2003
(Photograph by Araceli Tinajero)

Lector Bernardo Campos reading without a microphone
at El Corojo Plantation Selection Facility, Pinar del Río, 2003
(Photograph by Araceli Tinajero)

Lectora Odalys Lara Reyes, La Corona Cigar Factory, Havana, 2003
(Photograph by Araceli Tinajero)

María Caridad González Martínez, writer, tobacco worker, and former *lectora*, at
the entrance of the Niñita Valdés Leaf-stripping Plant, Pinar del Río, 2003
(Photograph by Araceli Tinajero)

Tobacco workers at the Manicaragua Cigar Factory
listening to the *lectora*, Irenia Morales, Las Villas, 2003
(Photograph by Araceli Tinajero)

Lectora Magalys Torres Iglesias next to her minilibrary
and behind her reading (and reception) desk at the entrance
to the VD-2 Leaf-stripping Plant, Vivero, Pinar del Río, 2003
(Photograph by Araceli Tinajero)

Lector Francisco Águila Medina, LV-9 Cigar Factory, Santa Clara, 2003
(Photograph by Araceli Tinajero)

Lector Jesús Pereira Caballero reading at the Partagás Cigar Factory, Havana, 2003
(Photograph by Araceli Tinajero)

Lector William Pichardo reading at the cigar factory museum
located on the grounds of La Aurora–León Jiménez Cigar Factory,
Santiago, Dominican Republic, 2004
(Photograph by Araceli Tinajero)

PART THREE

CIGAR FACTORY *LECTORES* IN CUBA, MEXICO, AND THE DOMINICAN REPUBLIC 1902–2005

PREVIOUS PAGE: *Lector* Bernardo Campos reading without a microphone
at El Corojo Plantation Selection Facility, Pinar del Río, 2003
(Photograph by Araceli Tinajero)

SIX

Cuba, 1902–1959

———+∎∎+———

In 1903, at the dawn of the twentieth century, Cuba was born as an independent nation, and reading aloud in cigar factories resumed. Víctor Muñoz, El Abogadito [the lawyer], was not an attorney, but, rather, one of the most dynamic and sophisticated *lectores* of his day. During Cuba's war for independence from Spain, he worked as a *lector* in Tampa, and once the new century was under way and independence won, he was back in Havana, reading in one of the leading factories. Cuban historian and novelist Wenceslao Gálvez y Delmonte describes him as "tall and thin, with a very nice vocal quality, and that's one of the things he's very successful at; his voice perfectly fills the largest *galera*, pleasantly striking one's eardrums. Accustomed to reading, he no more than glances at a whole paragraph and recites it while looking around at everyone in the factory, and they are astonished, and admire the retention abilities of this prodigy."[1]

One of the first accounts from the turn of the century indicates that reading was already well established, at least in Havana, by 1905. *Lectores* read for approximately three hours per day. One and one-half hours were devoted to newspapers, and one and one-half hours to poetry or novels. A more intricate system than that in Tampa was instituted, since in Havana, the cigar workers elected a president, a secretary, and a treasurer. Each cigar worker paid the treasurer fifteen cents a week. The fee was mandatory, and if a cigar worker did not pay, the *lector* would not read until he or she did. If more than a day later the cigar worker still had not fulfilled his or her obligation, the foreman had the right to suspend the employee. The cigar workers created this strict system, which shows how seriously the role of the *lector* was taken starting in the twentieth century.[2]

The funds that were collected went toward the salary of the *lector* and the cost of buying newspapers and books. The cigar workers chose the newspapers they wanted to have read to them, but before the *lector* read them, the reading president and reading secretary reviewed the text and marked the parts that the *lector* was to read. The selection of novels was much more complicated: a dozen titles could be submitted to a vote, but, generally, only four novels were seriously considered. The cigar workers simply voted, and thus the work was selected.

If the selection of the novel was very contentious, or if the cigar workers did not know which to vote for, they asked the *lector* to help them choose. The *lector* was always an educated person with whom the cigar workers could consult about any question. James H. Collins, who visited the Cabañas Factory, wrote that the British novels that had been read in translation in that factory were *Vanity Fair, Oliver Twist,* and *A Tale of Two Cities,* as well as works by Shakespeare and poems by Lord Byron. The only American novel that had been read twice was *Uncle Tom's Cabin.* Still, that factory's favorite authors were Cervantes, Benito Pérez Galdós, and Victor Hugo.[3] The cigar workers could buy the novels and newspapers at half price once they had been read; consequently, no library was maintained.

Workers selected the *lector* with great care. The reading president usually chose a novel and marked the passages that the candidate was to read. Then the applicants for the position had to read the passages chosen in the factory one hour a day for a full week, at the end of which the cigar workers voted and chose the new *lector.*

Conversely, when the cigar workers were not happy with a *lector,* ten signatures on a petition submitted to the reading president were sufficient for the president to ask for the resignation of the *lector.*

In 1905, Víctor Muñoz, El Abogadito, was the *lector* at the Cabañas Factory and one of the editors of the Havana newspaper *El Mundo.*[4] What was striking about him was that in Havana he continued the practice of some *lectores* in Tampa and Key West: he orally translated English-language newspapers, although in Havana he mainly read Spanish-language newspapers published in Cuba. Gálvez y Delmonte says: "[El Abogadito] translates [orally] from English with such ease that it seems he is reading in Spanish, without stammering or hesitating, and he presents the translated sentences in the most polished, correct Spanish."[5] In addition, Muñoz introduced Mother's Day to Cuba, a custom that was already celebrated in the United States.[6] For that reason and many others, El Abogadito was without a doubt the most sought after *lector* in Cuban factories (as he had been in Tampa's factories) at the end of the nineteenth and beginning of the twentieth centuries. Gálvez y Delmonte says of his manner of reading:

> [He must be] very intelligent in order to be able to interpret the different authors whose works he reads, in the style of the great artists; he knows how

far he should take the recitation. . . . He does not stoop to the level of others who have, unfortunately, become famous *lectores*, overacting by playing the comedian on the platform, by reading with a nasal old woman's voice when the book calls for it, or with an Argentinian child's accent. He does not bark like a *rooster*, or crow like a *dog*, or work any of those wonders for which those who find them necessary are famous. He does not need to. On the contrary, he knows the value of reading and he stays in his place, protecting it. He does not allow reading to be prostituted. . . . He is in control of the factory and the reading; he knows he need not run into difficulties in the course of it, and with a complete mastery of its worth, he reads with the self-confidence and aplomb with which things are done when one clearly demonstrates that he knows how to do them. He is not afraid of being surprised by unusual words, or that he will stutter when he comes across some extraordinary term, since he has such a complete grasp of Spanish that he could recite *Don Quixote*.[7]

Apart from the allusions to Víctor Muñoz and his reading aloud, the *lector* is rarely mentioned in twentieth-century Cuban cultural history.

Since Cuba gained its independence from Spain in 1902, brilliant studies have been published in Cuba about tobacco, its history, culture, and literature, beginning with Fernando Ortiz's monumental essay, *Cuban Counterpoint: Tobacco and Sugar* (1940—first published in English in 1947). However, with regard to reading aloud in cigar factories, apart from the groundbreaking historical monograph written by José Rivero Muñiz in 1942 ("La lectura en las tabaquerías")—but not published until 1951—and *Biografía del tabaco habano* (1959), by Jorge García Galló (who bases his work on Rivero Muñiz's sources), the *lector* appears only occasionally, as if he were merely a figure from yesteryear.[8] Nevertheless, it is appropriate to examine the works in which the *lector* does appear, directly or indirectly, in order to see what traces this profession has left on Cuba's literature and how this reflects and sometimes shapes its history.

In the Cuban film *El romance del Palmar*, directed by Ramón Peón, noteworthy actor Rolando Ochoa plays the part of a *lector*. His role is brief, but the movie shows the impact of reading aloud in a selection and leaf-stripping plant in the valley of Vuelta Abajo. In the film, a man from Havana (Alberto) travels to Vuelta Abajo and discovers a selector who is a great singer. He tries to seduce her, but she does not reciprocate until Alberto sends for a novel from Havana. The *lector* in the factory where she works reads the novel, and she listens to it. She identifies with the main character and changes her mind. She decides to go to Havana to sing at the Palmar Cabaret de Luxe. There she realizes she has been tricked by Alberto but also meets the true love of her life, Uvaldo, with whom she returns to Vuelta Abajo to get married and live happily ever after.[9] In literature, as I have noted, the play *Anna in the Tropics* recovers the tradition of reading in Tampa; nevertheless, apart from that play, few literary texts allude to cigar factory *lectores*.[10]

In the novel *The Agüero Sisters* (1997), by Cristina García, the little that is known about Reinaldo Agüero, the grandfather of the two sisters who are the main characters, is found in the final letter his son Ignacio wrote and which is buried in a copper coffer on an old ranch near Camagüey. The novel tells the story of Constancia and Reina, whose mother was murdered when they were children. Two years later, their father commits suicide.

Over the course of the story, Constancia immigrates to the United States in 1959, and Reina stays in Cuba until 1990, when she decides to leave the island and reunite with her sister. Constancia returns to Cuba clandestinely to dig up the coffer and read the letter her father wrote. In it, she discovers the enigma of her mother, Blanca's, murder. Ignacio, the sisters' father, murdered her.

What is of interest to us here is the story of Reinaldo, the sisters' grandfather, a Galician who arrived in Cuba one year after the country won its independence from Spain. He was an educated man, a musician by trade. When he arrived on the island, he played the violin on the street until someone suggested he become a cigar factory *lector* because he had a "grandiloquent voice," and that is what he did. He was a *lector* for the rest of his life in El Cid Cigar Factory in Pinar del Río. The novel points out a tangible historical fact, since it is true that, in order to become a cigar factory *lector*, even these days, the most important thing is a good voice, although, as we have seen, aptitude and experience in the art of recitation are important, too.

By way of this episode, one notes an insistence on going back in time in order to research family origins. In the first place, the fact that Reinaldo was Galician is a source of pride to his granddaughters, especially Constancia, who boasts that it "made them true *criollos*."[11] In addition, the birth of a nation is described, since Reinaldo arrives in Cuba just a year after it gained independence, and his son is born in 1904, when the first president of the Republic of Cuba, Tomás Estrada Palma, visits Pinar del Río.

On another level, it is important to note a sort of literary genesis. That is to say, it is not incidental that the factory where Reinaldo worked as a *lector* is called El Cid, the name of which takes us back to the origins of Spanish literature and to the time when all texts were read aloud. On his first day as a *lector*, the first line Reinaldo reads is "In a village of La Mancha."[12] The fact that he reads *Don Quixote*, not another text, relates to, once again, the insistence on wanting to go back or begin the literary canon from the "Archive," as Roberto González Echevarría would say.[13] Let us not forget that Reinaldo's story is written in a letter that comes out of a coffer, a detail that has an implicit connection with *The Tale of Inappropriate Curiosity*, the eight hand-written pages that are taken out of the case in *Don Quixote* and are read aloud.

The *lector* in *The Agüero Sisters* reads Dickens and Victor Hugo, but the interesting fact here is that the cigar workers "more often than not left the choice [about what to read] to him," and he was always "revered for his . . . splendid renditions of the works."[14] We see that his enjoyment of classic Spanish, British, and French works gradually becomes a sort of library that reflects his refined taste, since he is also an avid admirer of the Greek and Roman philosophers Plato, Epictetus, and especially Marcus Aurelius, although his favorites also include Unamuno and Darío.[15] Taken together, these texts are indicative of a historical framework that spans the beginning of the tradition of reading aloud to the era in which the practice started to disappear.

García's novel illustrates how the enjoyment and practice of reading aloud has been gradually lost through the years. For example, Reinaldo is diagnosed with throat cancer, and his son drops out of school in order to be able to take care of him and to read his whole library to him "day after day, tome after tome."[16] His illness of the throat can be interpreted as the threat of the disappearance of the profession of *lector* and, by extension, of the cultural practice of reading aloud, which has taken place outside cigar factories and in other social circles for a long time.

Garcia also mentions the microphone and radio as possible replacements for the practice and as its primary enemies. For this reason, the *lector* is portrayed as a legendary figure, tied to yesteryear, when a group of people used to happily gather around an individual: "In the afternoons, when he customarily read from novels, townspeople gathered outside the factory with their rocking chairs and their embroidery in order to listen to the intriguing tales that drifted through the open windows."[17] This scene harkens back to the past, and therefore to the preindustrial era, when people gathered to listen while they did some kind of handiwork. Nevertheless, this nostalgic era disappears when Reinaldo dies, the cancer having spread to his mouth and jaw.

Reinaldo's death signifies the decline of reading aloud, because the *lectores* who follow him lack his brilliance, and because they begin to use microphones. His son Ignacio proudly turns down the position his father held for so much of his life.

On other levels, we can see that future generations lose the enjoyment of reading as well. For example, Reina, Ignacio's daughter, recalls her happiest years as those when her father used to read her grandfather's favorite texts and others to her: *The Meditations of Marcus Aurelius*, "classics of zoogeography, nineteenth-century French and Russian literature, histories of the Greeks, the Romans, and the Mongol invaders."[18] On the other hand, Reina's daughter Dulce breaks with this tradition. For instance, when her mother, who is sick in bed, asks her daughter to read to her, Dulce "ruins a sentence's melody, skips words she doesn't understand," and abruptly stops reading to announce that she is leaving Cuba. What is most revealing is that she interrupts her reading in the middle of a passage of *The Meditations of Marcus Aurelius*, the exact book that her great-grandfather, her grandfather, and her mother treasured most. This constitutes a rupture in the practice of reading in society and its waning in cigar factories.

Ultimately, what Ignacio has written in his final letter turns out to be symbolic: "I have often wondered why someone of Papá's talent never sought to make a larger impression on the world."[19] This comment may be read as a reflection of the absence of the *lector* in Cuba's cultural and literary history, since the *lector* is a character that has barely left a mark, someone who "remembers the strict minimum, reads aloud, like the *lector* at a cigar factory, and misunderstands everything, or rather gets everything all mixed up," just like the main character's mother in *Yocandra in the Paradise of Nada*, by Zoé Valdés.[20]

During the first three decades of the twentieth century, the *lector* sat at a kind of pulpit about four yards high, with no rail or canopy, located in the center of the room, next to the workbenches, so that everyone could see and hear him. At the beginning of the 1920s, the platform of the *lector* began to undergo a transformation due to the arrival of radio. As in Tampa, the radio debuted in Havana in 1923, at the Cabañas y Carbajal Cigar Factory. A radio was brought into the factory, and the *lector* put on headphones so that he could transmit the news he heard. As in Tampa, the radio was installed so that the cigar workers could stay up to date on the news of the World Series.[21]

"The radio is making another conquest," wrote the Havana correspondent for the *Sun* in 1930.[22] That year, more than a dozen Havana factories (at that time, there were thirty-four) had a radio installed, but the platform of the *lector* remained untouched. "The radio is only turned on in the afternoon," explained the foreman of the Henry Clay Factory.[23] In the morning, as always, the *lector* came to the cigar factory and read the newspaper and magazines from the platform, but in the afternoon, music began to be substituted for the voice of the *lector*. "Many of the older workers are loyal to the Readers, but the younger element is keen for the radio, and the radio may win complete favor in time,' the foreman added."

In fact, as Cristina García proposes in *The Agüero Sisters*, in the 1920s and 1930s, the radio started to represent a true threat to reading aloud. Of the thirty-four Havana factories, however, more than half refused to have a radio installed because the cigar workers preferred to listen to the *lector*. However, this was not all: the factories that already had a radio installed were American owned. Conversely, the oldest cigar factories, such as the Partagás Factory, which was not financed by American capital, prohibited the installation of a radio due to the factory's enthusiastic and proud tradition of reading aloud. The heads of the American factories thought about the subject this way:

> When the Reader climbs down for a respite the workmen begin talking to one another, and their production slows up. Hence the manufacturers' coddling attentions to their Readers. But the radio does not require coddling and it never has to take time to rest. Its drone need never cease, and it can keep a roomful of workers amused every minute of every shift, and this point in its favor is being grasped by some of the manufacturers. They like the radio, even though they have to pay for its installation, whereas the workers themselves pay the Readers.[24]

This way of thinking was overly simplistic. In any case, debates over the installation of radios continued, and to a certain extent, the device did become a threat to the *lector*. Although the radio never replaced the *lector* completely, it did come to represent a certain degree of competition, because, in some cases, the amount of reading had to be decreased. At that time, the *lectores* in large Havana factories earned the equivalent of twenty cents per worker per week, which was quite a generous amount, because there were hundreds of employees in each factory. Without a doubt, the reduction in reading time affected the pay of the *lector*. But finances aside, the debut of the radio affected the reading of literature the most, because in factories such as Henry Clay, as we have seen, literature simply became outdated.

"The disappearance of the factory *lector* won't last," decreed a journalist at the beginning of the 1950s.[25] Obviously, the airing of novels on the radio was also a threat to reading aloud. The journalist continued: "One spin of the dial is all you need to find out the day's news, or to enjoy a dramatized fictional tale; the vibration of cylinders and pistons affords the audience neither continuity of hearing nor the ability to delve into the meaning of the literary work."

Likewise, the microphone definitively transformed reading. As we see in *The Agüero Sisters*, the *lector* refused to use a microphone. His son wrote: "Papá had a deep, sonorous voice, cured to huskiness over the years by the sheer volume of smoke he inhaled. Although he nursed his throat regularly with honey and lemon, he refused to yield to the temptations of the microphone, which, he was convinced, distorted the robust timbre of his voice."[26]

At the beginning, not only did some *lectores* refuse to utilize the microphone, but also more than anyone else did, the cigar workers rejected it, as was the case in Tampa. The amplifier was more than a sieve through which the voice of the *lector* was "filtered"; rather, it ushered in the transformation of the platform. In other words, the *lector* had always sat up high so that the reading could reach everyone, and the use of the microphone suggested that the platform should not and did not need to be so high. The *lector* had to move down literally and symbolically, since it was no longer necessary for him to read from high up on his "throne," as an American journalist put it.[27]

On the other hand, the use of the microphone, although it involved a drastic adjustment, made the work of the *lector* easier and changed the physical layout of the platforms. Over time, the sort of pulpit was transformed into a wooden platform, like a stage approximately five yards long by five yards wide, on which a type of lectern with a seat or a writing desk was placed. The *lector* read from there with either a hanging or a tabletop microphone.

Gaspar Jorge García Galló, cigar worker, teacher, attorney, as well as PhD in literature, wrote that "guidelines have been established for radio transmissions. Mechanical progress has reached the *lector*, who currently reads into a microphone that carries his amplified voice throughout the whole main workshop. He does not have to exert himself as he did before, but it has, in a way, caused him to lose his personality. Now it's easier to be a *lector*."[28] His account is one of the few that exist about reading aloud in Cuba in the 1940s and 1950s.[29]

Although reading aloud never became uniform, that is, not all factories had the same reading schedule or read the same texts, García Galló indicates that, at that time, in spite of the radio, there were three reading shifts: one in the morning and two in the afternoon. In the morning, print media were read for forty-five minutes. Usually the *lector* started by reading the international news; later, he would read in-depth articles or editorials, and he would finish with predetermined sections. In the afternoon, the first shift was designated for reading the popular press, and the second for reading literary works. García Galló indicates that listeners in all the factories enjoyed the works of Vargas Vila, Ricardo León, and Guido de Varona because they were "resonant and harmonious." He continues:

Those [literary works] that are read in cigar factories, leaf-stripping plants, and selection facilities vary widely in content and quality. They include everything from erotic novels such as those of El Caballero Audaz, Pedro Mata, and Eduardo Zamacois, to didactic novels, such as *El abuelo, Los miserables, Fecundidad, El culpable*, etc. [We also listened to] works about local customs and manners, historical novels, adventure stories, science-themed novels, philosophical texts . . . from Jules Verne and H. G. Wells to Miguel de Unamuno and Maxim Gorky. From *Cecilia Valdés*, to *Don Segundo Sombra, Doña Bárbara*, or *La vorágine*, to *Así hablaba Zarathustra*, and *El anticristo*. Everything goes into that literary *ajiaco* [stew] or jumble: insignificant novels with no depth or form whatsoever to profound historical or philosophical books. The industry's workers are always hunting for the latest literary novelty to hit the market.[30]

Therefore, in spite of the platform's transformation and competition from the radio, the reading of literature aloud continued.

In addition to reading, the *lectores* promoted cultural events in the factories; therefore, they became cultural facilitators who were crucial in fostering these events.[31] El Teatro Popular, created by Francisco (Paco) Alfonso in the 1940s, rapidly became of service to the labor movement. El Teatro Popular created a mobile, collapsible structure, but, symbolically, it was in the Sindicato de Torcedores de Cuba where the company staged its productions. The members paid dues of thirty cents per month. Lázaro Peña, an occasional cigar factory *lector* who at that time was the general secretary of the CTC (Confederación de Trabajadores de Cuba—now known as Central de Trabajadores de Cuba—the official labor union), opened the season. Works written by Martí, Luaces, Avellaneda, Guillén, Pichardo Moya, José Luis de la Torre, Óscar Valdés, Félix Pita Rodríguez, José Montes López, Luis Felipe Rodríguez, Diego Vicente Tejera, and Paco Alfonso himself were staged. Actors also performed works by foreign playwrights such as Lorca, O'Neill, Molière, Calderón, and especially the Soviet authors Gorky, Leonid Leonov, and Constantin Simonov.[32] In the factories, *lectores* were the ones in charge of promoting artistic performances. Therefore, their role was not limited to reading aloud, but, rather, included cultural and social promotion of dances and events that took place outside the factory. Since many people liked sports, especially baseball, cigar facilities formed their own teams. In fact, there had been teams of cigar makers since the nineteenth century. The *lector* became the team's announcer and promoter. The responsibilities of the *lector* were gradually increasing.

SEVEN

Cuba, 1959–2005

———┤▬▬├———

Santos Segundo Domínguez Mena, who was a *lector* for sixty-five years, said the following about reading aloud before 1959:

> First I was a *lector* in the selection facility, and later in cigar factories. There was a sort of contract. I got paid five cents per person per week. So I had to look for a selection facility or a cigar factory that had enough people, because it wasn't the same thing to read in a place that had twenty people as in one that had eighty.
>
> Before Fidel Castro came to power, there was a kind of give-and-take. It was sort of an agreement. After Castro came to power, the salary was set at 138 pesos a month. That's exactly what I earned until 1984.
>
> After Castro came to power, the factory gradually got bigger. The reading schedule stayed more or less the same. I would read print media for forty-five minutes in the morning, and whatever work the workers themselves chose for forty-five minutes in the afternoon. Traditionally in this country, the cigar worker has been a person with a certain amount of education and who has had a desire to become even more educated.
>
> The only change that took place after Castro came to power was that people were even more educated. Culture was always brought into the factory, before and after. There were never any problems about what was being read. There were a few altercations between the workers and the owners, but that didn't have anything to do with the reading. Reading aloud was never intended to bother the owners or the government. I don't miss reading to others, because what I don't have now, I just don't have anymore.[1]

As Domínguez Mena states, starting in 1959, the *lector* began to have a standard salary and became a government employee. A fixed work schedule was also set for him: usually from 7:00 A.M. to 4:00 P.M., and two Saturdays per month from 7:00 A.M. to 1:00 P.M. Although there was little variation in reading schedules, as we will see later, the *lector* gained more responsibilities.

There was also a change in the workforce. Gradually, more women were recruited as cigar makers, where previously it was a job done almost exclusively by men. Both male and female cigar makers continued to be paid as pieceworkers. The same change took place with the *lectores*, as gradually female *lectoras* started to occupy the platform. In fact, there are now more female *lectoras* than male *lectores*: of the more than 230 cigar factory, leaf-stripping plant, and selection-facility *lectores* in Cuba in 2005, 137 were women and 97 were men. Likewise, the proportion of male to female *lectores* is a reflection of the percentages of male and female personnel in the factories. More than 50 percent of the workers were women in 2005. The listening audience is made up of approximately 25,000 people. But who were the female and male *lectores* in 2005?

Just as was true in the past, to become a *lector*, the candidate need only have a good voice. Further, just as it was before Castro came to power, today's *lectores* come from a variety of sectors, but most were previously employed in education or communications. There is no, nor has there ever been, set training for the *lector*. Reading aloud has always been a self-taught, innate discipline, but becoming a *lector* has never been easy. It is important to recall what Domínguez Mena said:

> When I became a cigar factory *lector* for the first time, it was because I already liked it. Ever since elementary school, whenever parties were planned and something had to be read aloud, it was given to me. I soon grew accustomed to it. I had a better reading voice than other children. The others spoke too softly. I was the one who was chosen for parties. Besides that, I did recitations, and I read at any little party that was held at school. But in those days [the 1920s and 1930s], *lectores* promoted themselves, since they went from factory to factory to show what they knew about reading by reading novels aloud, and that was done in a place where there were a lot of people, so that there would be a lot of coins. Also, *lectores* had competition, because other *lectores* came from other parts of the province of Pinar del Río and even from Havana. It wasn't easy.

Odalys Lara, who has been a *lectora* at the La Corona Factory in Havana for fourteen years, recalled in an interview:

> When I lived in the city of Cárdenas, I worked at the radio station, at Radio Ciudad Bandera de Matanzas, and I started doing a program playing the music of rural Cuba. I worked there until we moved to Havana. Then I

started to work at Radio Enciclopedia, on a program called *Cita en la Enciclopedia*, which airs every day from 10:00 to 11:00 A.M. The program covers all kinds of cultural topics, especially the lives of famous artists who play musical instruments, and also many other items of general interest. That's where I aired the "appointments" [*citas*] and I was there for a while, until I decided to go to a meeting for *lectores* in this factory.[2]

Not all *lectores* have had experience reading to an audience before they go before the workers, since often it is the cigar makers themselves who apply for the position of *lector*. Carmen Rodríguez Pérez, who has been a *lectora* in the El Surco Factory in Camagüey for thirty-five years, says:

I worked here; first I was a leaf stripper. I started when I was fourteen, because I worked in the *chinchales*, in the small private factories. At that time, there was a little factory across the street from my house, and that's where I started to work, from the time I was a little girl, since I was ten. When the intervention took place, I started here, at fourteen. They used to pay us a small salary until we reached working age at seventeen. When I was the youth leader, I used to read, and I was in my element when I was reading. I liked it. One day, a coworker said to me: "Why don't you try out as *lectora*?" Then all my coworkers really helped and supported me. That's how I became a *lectora*.[3]

It happened in much the same manner for Olga Lidia Véliz, who was a *lectora* at the VD-31 Leaf-stripping Plant in Viñales, Pinar del Río, in the early 1990s:

My mom worked as a leaf stripper and she suffered a lot during the pre-Castro era. She didn't earn much and she worked very hard. She wasn't allowed to leave the factory even though her breasts were overflowing with milk. They wouldn't let her go nurse us. That really stuck with me. In my mom's day, there was no reading aloud in the factory, but when I started to work as a leaf stripper, there was, and that's how I became a *lectora*. Ever since I was a little girl I have read a lot, lots of books. We don't have professional credentials, but we've always read a lot.[4]

In several cases, *lectores* used to work in education. Grycel Valdés Lombillo Pérez, who has been a *lectora* at the H. Upmann Factory in Havana since 1992, says:[5]

I was a high school teacher, a teacher of ancient history. I took a crash course. There was a Call to Revolution, because that was when a lot of teachers left, and in the basic secondary schools there was a huge number of students and no teachers for them. So I took a crash course and then I started to go further in my studies. Every week I studied more, and then I went to college. I taught for twenty-four years, and once, by chance, I ran into an acquaintance who said, "Since you like activity and being with groups of kids so much, wouldn't you like to be a *lectora* in a cigar factory?" And that's how I came to be in this factory.

Bernardo Campos Iglesias, who has been a *lector* in the V13 Selection Facility in El Corojo, Pinar del Río, since 1999, says:

I was a teacher for thirty-six years. I have a bachelor's degree in philosophy. I spent my early years going to school in the Soviet Union. I became a translator there.

When I retired from education, I started to work as a *lector* in a cigar factory. But I remember that, when I was a child, I used to read aloud in a leaf-selection facility. I was sent there to read because I was a good *lector*. I used to read in a selection facility owned by the Padrón family. They used to tell me what I was supposed to do. At that time I didn't have a vision, but I knew how to read well because I had read a lot. . . . I knew how to express myself.

In those days, that is, before Castro came to power, a man used to come in to read novels aloud: that was all he did. I only read the newspaper. During the first years of the Revolution, they employed me as a *lector*. At one time, I was in a combat battalion. When the Bay of Pigs conflict took place, they needed someone to read aloud from among those who were not high ranking. And since I was a good *lector*, I read them the newspaper every day. I was given two newspapers a day.

Now I'm a *lector* again. I read without a microphone, but it's okay. I've always read viva voce.[6]

Zaida Valdés, who was a *lectora* in El Laguito Factory from 1998 to 2005, says: "I was an economics teacher all my life, and I retired at age fifty-five, but I didn't know what to do with my time and energy. That is, until one day, someone told me about a position as *lectora*. I was really excited, because devoting myself to reading meant I would keep on learning and keep on teaching at the same time."[7]

The cigar makers have always selected the *lector,* before and after 1959 (when Pres. Fulgencio Batista left power and Pres. Fidel Castro took charge of the government). When people apply for the position of *lector*, they are usually asked to read a newspaper article or a passage from a novel. The cigar makers listen intently. The applicant who receives the most applause— by way of the *chavetas*—is the one who is hired as the *lector*. Each factory has more or less the same rules, although in some of them, the tryout lasts several weeks. Luis González Artiles, who was a *lector* in two factories for twenty years, one of which was a leaf-stripping plant and the other a selection facility in the town of Cabaiguán, recalls that one of the best experiences in his life was when he was chosen as a *lector*:

> I had always worked at a printing company; I was a typesetter by trade. I knew a lot about grammar, spelling, and the Spanish language. When I lost my job and I went to try out as a *lector*, three people who wanted the job showed up at the factory. We all had to read passages from *Su gran momento*, by Elinor Glyn. The competition was so stiff that the tryout lasted two weeks, and in the end, a referendum had to be submitted to the leaf strippers, and I was the winner.[8]

At the Trinidad Cigar Factory, Marcela Montero Gutiérrez, who was a *lectora* for fifteen years, pointed out that her tryout to become the *lectora* lasted a month: "I was a disciple of Armando Juvier, a former *lector*—a real *lector* through and through, one of the good *lectores* who expressed himself very well. He was the one who gave me the confidence to take the microphone, and he got me to lose my fear of public speaking. But even so, the tryout lasted a month. After that month, I was given a test in a library where I had to read several texts and answer questions."

In general, however, because reading aloud is a tradition and the workers are used to listening, the tryout for becoming a *lector* is brief, since the audience immediately chooses the applicant they like.

The platform for the *lector* evolved because of the radio and microphone. Where they used to stand behind a kind of pulpit, *lectores* began to read aloud at a writing desk and, eventually, a sort of presiding bench or press box with space for several individuals and a tabletop or hanging microphone. *Lectores* now read from a platform with a proscenium yards away from the workers. Some platforms have a control panel with a small, integrated transmitter and a type of control screen.

In the large Havana factories, the platform measures up to ten yards long by five yards wide and is elevated one and a half to three feet high. An extremely old platform, which, although it is worn, stands out for its splendor and magnificence, is that of the Romeo y Julieta Factory. The platform is one yard high and is rectangular with a fine mahogany finish. Along the edges are pine inlays that adorn the sort of stage. On top in the center is a small writing desk. As the table is small, there is a space measuring yards in front and in back of it, which gives one the feeling of being before a proscenium. Behind the table are two worn leather chairs, and at the back looms an old black upright piano, which gives the platform an appearance of majesty and grandeur. To the left of the platform there are ten rows of *vapores* side by side, and across from it there are at least two dozen more, and ten more to the right. The factory looks like a theater in which the platform is the stage and the workbenches are the spectators' seats. This platform recalls what the platforms were like years ago. The piano has not been played in decades, but its presence shows that the platforms were not meant exclusively for reading.

One of the most spacious platforms, and perhaps the most practical, is that of La Corona Factory. The desk is an eight yard–long presiding bench with room for nine people. Although its proscenium cannot compare with that of the Romeo y Julieta Factory, its sheer size is imposing, because at the back is a wall with immense paintings of Lázaro Peña, Fidel Castro, and Camilo Cienfuegos. To one side, the Cuban flag on a flagpole adorns the platform, giving it a presidential and patriotic feel. Behind the platform is a sign that reads: "At La Corona We Can Get the Job Done," and beneath it the succinct phrase: "Our Goal is 171 Million Cigars." From there, the *lectora* reads to three hundred workers who sit directly in front of the platform in rows.

Two other well-cared-for platforms are worth mentioning for their magnificence and elegance. The first, with its distinctive pine finish, is that of the Partagás Factory. Five wood and leather chairs are placed at the table, and the *lector* sits in the middle one. Dozens of visitors and tourists file across this platform every day.

Since the nineteenth century, it has been a common practice to allow visitors into some factories. Therefore, the factories are like museums, and what is exhibited and how it is exhibited become very important. The platform in El Laguito Factory is even more magnificent than the one in the Partagás Factory. It is truly a factory/museum and destination for celebrities or people with special passes, such as diplomats or heads of state. The platform is finished with the finest mahogany; it is five yards long, with at least four fine ceremonial wooden steps leading to it. Integrated audio equipment sits atop the desk on the right-hand side. No one can be seen from this platform, as it is situated across from a corridor that leads to a patio and, beyond it, a garden.

In several factories, the platforms do not face the workers. One such example is the VD-2 Leaf-stripping Plant in Vivero, Pinar del Río. The *lectora* sits at the reception desk looking over the street. Across the way are a tobacco plantation and a *guarapera* (a stand selling sugarcane juice). She reads from there, unable to see the faces of the hundreds of leaf strippers working behind her.

Another platform from which the *lectora* cannot see the leaf strippers is in the VD-31 Leaf-stripping Plant in Viñales. Although previously the *lectora* there sat before the workers, it was decided to give her a small, separate room with a desk and chair so she could spread her materials out.

At the Manicaragua Factory, the platform used to be up high, approximately four yards tall and across from the rows of workbenches, so the cigar makers could see the *lectora* directly. This platform was built on the second floor with eleven steps leading to it. That space was converted into office space, and the reading now takes place downstairs at a small desk, where the *lectora* faces the street. A wall to the right blocks the audience from the *lectora*'s view.

In many cases, the *lector* reads from a booth with a sort of control panel that allows him to see the workers. Outside the booth, there is a cement or wooden platform with a writing desk and chairs, although, as a rule, there are never more than five. Thus, there is a separation between the booth and main platform. In this case, the *lector* uses the platform to carry out a variety of cultural and artistic activities, and the booth to undertake reading. In any case, the platform's extension reflects the diverse responsibilities of the *lector*, which have certainly increased throughout the years.

All factories have a specific reading schedule that everyone abides by and respects. Nevertheless, along with reading aloud, cigar makers are also exposed to a variety of radio programs or informative or cultural activities. For example, the LV-9 Factory follows the schedule outlined in Table 1.

As is evident in the schedule, workers listen to the radio much more than they do to reading. Nonetheless, there are factories in which there are two reading shifts: from 8:30 to 9:15 A.M., the *lector* reads the newspaper, and from 1:30 to 2:15 P.M., a novel or other fictional work. In La Corona Factory, there are three shifts. From 8:00 to 8:45 A.M. the *lector* reads a little of everything: quotations, information about important events that took place that day in history, and articles on a variety of topics. These readings come from magazines, books, pamphlets, and encyclopedias. During the second shift, the *lector* reads the newspaper, and during the third shift, from 1:30 to 2:15 P.M., the *lector* reads literature. Different schedules have been established according to the agreements between the workers and the administrators of each factory.

TABLE 1. LV-9 FACTORY READING SCHEDULE

Program	Schedule	Minutes
News overview	7:45–8:15 A.M.	30
Planned reading: magazine articles; thoughts; poems	9:00–9:30 A.M.	30
Music	9:30–10:00 A.M.	30
Radio soap opera	10:00–10:20 A.M.	20
Morning meeting (factory production is discussed)	10:20–10:30 A.M.	10
Music	10:30–11:15 A.M.	45
Radio program	12:00–12:40 P.M.	40
National news: radio	1:00–1:30 P.M.	30
Reading of novel	2:00–2:30 P.M.	30
Final bulletin (open topic)	2:45–3:00 P.M.	15

SOURCE: Francisco Águila Medina, 2003.

Works of fiction are chosen by way of a rigorous voting process. In general, the reading committee presents five works. The *lector* reads the summaries of the texts and then goes around to the workbenches to collect the ballots. The work that receives the most votes is the one the *lector* reads. Occasionally, the selection process is a little more complicated, as Francisco Águila Medina explains:

I have my own technique. Each *lector* has his own technique. In my case, I have a group of contributing coworkers to whom I distribute different works. There are about fifteen contributors. They're the employees who like to read, and they read fast. So I take advantage of the opportunity and give them books so that they will give me their opinions about them. I give them a variety of genres. After each one of them reads the book, they give me their evaluations: "I recommend it," or "I don't recommend it." Well, they are familiar with my style; the work should have appropriate language, it should have a positive message, a good topic, it should be stimulating. There are so many requirements to keep in mind in selecting a work!

After the contributors give me their proposal I take five or six books to the president of the reading committee, but we always end up presenting three works. We always try to maintain balance. For example, we present a love story, a crime novel, and a historical novel, but I absolutely have to include a love story in each proposal.

I ask the contributors about the plot, and then I write a synopsis. When I present the work, I also present the author's background information and a portion of the book. Making the proposal is like making a commercial. I read them the review and a passage so that they get an idea of what the work is about. Then I go from workbench to workbench and collect the ballots. It's very interesting. Some say: "I vote for the first one, the second one, or the third one." They do that because they don't want to be interrupted. There are others who say: "I vote for the crime novel, the one about espionage, or the love story." That's where you can see their tastes according to genre. And there are some who explain their vote according to nationality: "I vote for the Cuban one, the Spanish one, or the British one." Others vote according to the prominence of the author, that is to say, Victor Hugo, etc. But there always has to be a negotiation, because sometimes the workers complain and protest: "Hey, you didn't propose a crime story," or "When are you going to do one about swashbucklers?" They themselves ask for what they want.

The reading president has to sign the document that indicates which work has won the majority of the vote. I can't start reading without her signature. It's ceremonial, but without her signature, it's not valid.[9]

In 2000, the education level of the workers in the factory where Francisco Águila Medina read was as follows: 4 had gone to school as far as the sixth grade, 34 as far as ninth grade, 163 to basic secondary school, 140 to high school, and 21 to higher education. And, in a 2001 survey about preferences of literary works, 144 women said they preferred love stories, 7 said adventure, 6 said science fiction, 4 said novels about local customs and manners, 7 said espionage, 2 said historical novels, 7 said mysteries, 21 said crime novels, 13 said suspense, and 2 said testimonial novels. On their own behalf, 21 men said they preferred love stories, 32 said adventure, 7 said fiction, 2 said novels about local customs and manners, 8 said historical novels, 3 said mystery, 28 said crime, 13 said suspense, and 7 said testimonial novels.[10]

Books that are submitted to a vote are on loan from public or private libraries. If *lectores* have books they think the cigar makers might enjoy, they usually share them and submit them to a vote. On many occasions, the cigar makers have brought in their own books for consideration. Private libraries have played an extremely important role. Sometimes certain employees have abundant libraries bequeathed to them by relatives that they make available to the *lectores*; people outside the cigar culture also make their libraries available. This was the case in Cabaiguán, where for two decades Luis González Artiles made use of the private library of Ms. Dulce Obregón, who lent him volumes from her collection of more than six hundred books. Sometimes texts appear randomly, especially in recent times, when *lectores* have had contact with foreign tourists who come to the factory and leave them books.

When I went to El Laguito Factory, one of the first factories I visited in 2001, I asked *lectora* Zaida Valdés where she got the books she read, or whether she had a library someplace. We were sitting at her modest desk, which was separated from the platform and had three drawers on the right and three on the left, as well as a table lamp atop it. She told me there had never been a library in the factory. Slightly embarrassed, she turned around and slowly opened a bookcase behind her desk. She took her own books from it, in the following order: *La prisión fecunda*, by Mario Mencía; *El corazón de un cazador solitario*, by Carson McCullers; *Ernesto Che Guevara: Escritos y discursos*, by Ernesto Guevara; *Esto le zumba: Cuentos humorísticos*, by Héctor Zumbado; *Asesinato en el Nilo*, by Agatha Christie; *Aventuras de Sherlock Holmes*, by Sir Arthur Conan Doyle; *Mientras agonizo*, by William Faulkner; *El valle de los relámpagos*, by Eduardo Barredo; *Fiesta*, by Ernest Hemingway; *La barraca*, by Vicente Blasco Ibáñez; *La familia de León Roch*, by Benito Pérez Galdós; *La serpiente de oro*, by Ciro Alegría; *Detectives en acción*, edited by Agenor Martí; *La cueva del muerto*, by Marta Rojas; *Los bandidos de Río Frío*, by Manuel Payno; and *Parte de mi alma*, by Winnie Mandela. All these books had been read aloud.

Zaida Valdés was the only *lectora* who possessed her own library (albeit limited) in the factory. Factories have never maintained libraries, with very few exceptions. Ms. Valdés also recalled having read *La madre*, by Maxim Gorki; *Doña Bárbara*, by Rómulo Gallegos; short stories by Edgar Allan Poe; as well as short stories by Onelio Jorge Cardoso and several works by José Lezama Lima.

I also found a library in the VD-2 Leaf-stripping Plant in Vivero, near San Juan y Martínez, Pinar del Río. Ironically, in San Juan y Martínez there was no public library for years, because the building that had housed it was in danger of collapsing. Since there was no public building, the librarians assigned themselves the task of going out to promote reading. To this end, they set up fifteen circulating minilibraries that moved from place to place, such as the cigar facility, the Municipal Committee headquarters, the fire department, the senior citizens' center, and the Revolutionary Defense Committee headquarters.[11]

Thus, it became customary to have a library at the cigar facility, even though it was a revolving one. It must be made clear that Cuban libraries have always been available to the cigar facilities, and that mobile libraries are brought to the cigar facilities once or twice a month, depending on arrangements that have been made. However, what I found interesting was that, in this case, the mobile library stayed at the factories for a while. Magalys Torres Iglesias, the *lectora* at the VD-2 Leaf-stripping Plant, showed me the library and pointed out that it served two purposes: the first was, obviously, to allow the *lectora* to choose from it the texts that she would read to the cigar makers; the second was so that the workers could borrow books to read at home.[12] Therefore, the *lectora* also functions as a liaison between the public library and the workers.

The VD-2 Leaf-stripping Plant had the following books: *La vorágine*, by José Eustasio Rivera; *Don Segundo Sombra*, by Ricardo Güiraldes; *Noche de espadas*, by Saúl Ibargoyen; *Nueve cuentos*, by J. D. Salinger; *La isla en peso*, by Virgilio Piñera; *Ciclones con nombres tiernos*, by Bogomil Rainov; *El corsario negro*, by Emilio Salgari; *Narraciones*, by Mark Twain; and *Crónicas para caminantes*, by Ángel Tomás.

At the Pedro Larrea Factory in Sancti Spíritus, *lectora* Ana María Valdivia noted that "novels are boring for the workers," and, therefore, they do not want to hear literature.[13] Unconvinced, she kept a small library in the factory and pointed out to me that, occasionally, she read passages from novels or poems, although short ones. She had the following titles on the shelf: *Antología de décimas: Canarias—Cuba*, by Marlene García Pérez; *Visión íntima: Cartas escogidas de José Martí*, edited by Daisy Cué and Ibrahím Hidalgo Paz; *La familia Unzúazu*, by Martín Morúa Delgado; *El sol en la ventana* (a collection of short stories), by Carlos Alé Mauri; *El grillo del hogar*, by Charles Dickens; *Cuentos de la Alhambra*, by Washington Irving; *Adiós Hemingway* and *La cola de la serpiente*, by Leonardo Padura Fuentes; *Un caso difícil*, by Arnaldo Correa; and *Dos mujeres*, by Gertrudis Gómez de Avellaneda. "I personally prefer Gertrudis Gómez de Avellaneda," she stated.

Because there is no official system that keeps track of which books have been read more than once (with a few exceptions that I will address later), the only records that exist are the accounts of *lectores* and cigar makers. In this sense, we are dealing with itinerant, wandering libraries, because they are recorded only in the memories of those who read or heard them.

As I indicate in the Introduction, Santos Segundo Domínguez Mena recalled that he read aloud all the works of Victor Hugo and Alexandre Dumas that he could get his hands on, but his most pleasant memories were of reading *Los miserables*. He also recalls having read *Cecilia Valdés*, by Cirilo Villaverde, and *El puente de los suspiros*, a novel by Michel Zévaco. Strangely enough, he said, "I never got to read Miguel de Cervantes, since I had to read the work that got the most votes."[14]

Nicolás Chavollera, who was a *lector* from 1970 to 1984 in the city of Santa Clara, indicated that he recalled reading *Los miserables*; *Las impuras* and *Las honradas*, by Miguel de Carreón; as well as *Juan Criollo* and *Generales y doctores*, by Carlos Loveira. Luis González Artiles, *lector* from Cabaiguán, recalled that some of the best-loved novels he read were *Rebeca, una mujer inolvidable*, by Daphne DuMaurier; *Primavera en otoño*, by Franz Werfel; *El Conde de Montecristo*, by Alexandre Dumas; and *Gaspar Pérez de Muela Quieta*, by Gustavo Egurén.

"For twenty-eight years I made the mistake of not keeping a list of what I read," stated Carmen Rodríguez Pérez, of the El Surco Factory. When I interviewed her in 2003, she was reading *A solas con el enemigo*, by Iurii Dol'd-Mikhailik, and a few days earlier, she had finished reading *Y si muero mañana*, by Luis Rogelio Nogueras. She recalled having read *Los miserables* and *El jorobado de Nuestra Señora de París*, by Victor Hugo; *Por quien doblan las campanas*, by Ernest Hemingway; *Un hombre de verdad* by Boris Polevoi; *La guerra y la paz*, by Leo Tolstoy; *Nadie es soldado al nacer*, by Konstantin M. Simonov; *Don Quijote*, by Cervantes; *Biografía de un cimarrón*, by Miguel Barnet; *El siglo de las luces*, by Alejo Carpentier; *Vindicación de Cuba* (a compilation of texts by José Martí), *El árabe*, and *El hijo del árabe*, by Edith Maude Hull; a variety of works by Raúl González de Cascorro, such as *Aquí se habla de combatientes y de bandidos*; and several books by Nicolás Guillén.

Jesús Pereira Caballero recalled having read *Don Quixote*, by Miguel de Cervantes; *La pasión turca*, by Antonio Gala; several works by Stephen King; *Como agua para chocolate*, by Laura Esquivel; *Cuando amanezca*, by Fran Daurel; and *Vidas cruzadas*, by Isabel Letelier. *Papillón*, by Henri Charrière; *El Conde de Montecristo*, by Alexandre Dumas; and *El perfume*, by Patrick Süskind were read more than once. He did not finish reading *El juez de Egipto*, by French novelist Christian Jacq. Mr. Pereira Caballero explained with some melancholy:

Unfortunately I didn't get to finish that novel. That book really made an impression on the cigar makers. Really, it was too much. It was a shame that the friend who lent it to me asked for it back when I was halfway through it. I've done all I can to find it. I've moved heaven and earth to find it, but I can't. And it's one of the works that affected people the most, because it shows a lot of human emotion. On the other hand, I did get to read Alejo Carpentier, but they didn't like it much, because his style is very complicated and difficult.[15]

Odalys Lara indicated:

I prefer Cuban literature to be predominant. That's very important. I know that you have to cover everything, but I'm more interested in reading Cuban works. There are also other authors whom we are all interested in, such as García Márquez, Shakespeare, Agatha Christie, and poets Neruda, Paz, Storni, and Benedetti, but the Cuban writers we like most are Leonardo Padura, Amir Valle Ojeda, Daniel Chavarría, Cirilo Villaverde, Alejo Carpentier, Nicolás Guillén, and José María de Heredia.

Boccacio's *El decamerón* was a work that was being reread in the H. Upmann Factory when I interviewed *lectora* Grycel Valdés Lombillo Pérez in 2001. She had read *Veinte mil leguas de viaje submarino*, by Jules Verne; *Preludio en la noche*, by Javier Morán; *La venganza del muerto*, by Rubén Vázquez; *El conde Lucanor* and *El libro de los sabios*, by Don Juan Manuel; *Doña Perfecta*, by Benito Pérez Galdós; *Diario del Che* and *Crónica de una muerte anunciada*, by Gabriel García Márquez; *Martín Fierro*, by José Hernández; and *El huésped de Job*, by José Cardoso Pires.

One of the few *lectores* who kept a record of works read was Francisco Águila Medina.[16] The following are some of the works that he read from 2000 through 2003: *Cecilia después*, by F. Mond; *101 cuentos clásicos de la India*, edited by Ramiro Calle; *Diario de la guerra*, by Alfonso Rojo; *Secretos de generales*, by Luis Báez; *Los que se quedaron* (conversations with Luis Báez about interviews in Cuba in 1959); *Diario del Che en Bolivia*, by Ernesto Guevara; *El coche número 13*, by Rafael Calleja; *Las apariencias no engañan*, by Juan Madrid; *La isla de los delfines azules*, by Antonio Morales Rivera; *El último de los mohicanos*, by James Fenimore Cooper; *Hombres sin mujer*, by Carlos Montenegro; *Enigma para un domingo*, by Ignacio Cárdenas Acuña; *Este es mi tutor*, by Corín Tellado; *Pacto de sangre*, by James M. Cain; *El capitán tormenta*, by Emilio Salgari; *Mi verdad*, by Vitali Borovnikov; *El príncipe de la niebla*, by Carlos Ruiz; *El Capitán Blood*, by Rafael Sabatini; *Miguel Strogoff*, by Jules Verne; *La mansión de los abismos*, by Joan Manuel Gisbert; *Lazos de sangre*, by Sidney Sheldon; *El retrato de Dorian Gray*, by Oscar Wilde; *El árabe*, by Edith Maude Hull; *La mitología griega*, by Pierre Grimal; *El asesinato de Rogelio Ackroyd*, by Agatha Christie; *Los centinelas de la aurora*, by Arnoldo López Tauler; *La venganza*, by Emilio Salgari;

Tiburón, by Peter Benchley; *Una virgen llama a tu puerta*, by Ramón José Sender; *El rosario*, by Florence Barclay; and *Leonela*, by Nicolás Heredia.

In Trinidad, Lázara Cantero Marino told me that she did not recall many of the texts she had read, but that she had loved *Biografía de un cimarrón*, *Cecilia Valdés*, and the poems of Virgilio Piñera, Nicolás Guillén, and Dulce María Loynaz.[17]

In Pinar del Río, Yuneimis Miló González of the Francisco Donatién Factory told me that the cigar makers enjoyed the romance novels of Corín Tellado, such as *No sufras por mi traición* and *No olvidaré tu traición*, although she also read *Sab*, *Veinte mil leguas de viaje submarino*, *El Conde de Montecristo*, *Los miserables*, *Las honradas*, *Las impuras*, *Biografía de un cimarrón*, and *Gigante moral* (an essay about Che Guevara), by Adys Cupull and Froilán González.[18]

Irenia Morales Reyes, one of the youngest *lectoras* in Cuba, who read at the Manicaragua Factory, told me that she had read *El monte de las cien caballerías*, by Efraín Reyes Morciego; *Donde cae la luna*, by Noel Navarro; *Fabriles*, by Reinaldo Montero; and *El Martí que yo conocí*, by Blanche Zacharie de Baralt.[19]

At the Manicaragua Leaf-stripping Plant, *lectora* Marta Valle Rodríguez had read several Cuban works, including *El último ángel de la memoria*, by Rubén Wong Subirat; *Nuevos cuentistas cubanos*, edited by Eduardo Heras León; *El camafeo negro*, by María del Carmen Muzio; *Jugar al silencio*, by Rafael Morejón Valdés; *Biografía de un cimarrón*, by Miguel Barnet; *La noche del aguafiestas*, by Antón Arrufat; *Subir al cielo y otras equivocaciones*, by Rogelio Riverón Morales; and *Reflexiones en torno al espiritualismo de José Martí*, by Alexis Jardines.[20]

In some factories in Las Villas, *lectores* began to keep records in 2001 of what was read. The following is an overview of what was read from 2001 through 2002.[21] At the Esperanza Factory they read *Del amor y otros demonios*, by Gabriel García Márquez, *Aventura sin fin*, by Metsy Hingle, and *Dos mujeres*, by Gertrudis Gómez de Avellaneda. At the Santo Domingo Factory, they read *El club de los martes*, by Agatha Christie; *Aletas de tiburón*, by Enrique Serpa; *Religión y transculturación: El aporte aborigen*, by María Daysi Fariñas Gutiérrez; *Los aztecas*, by Victor Wolfgang Von Hagen; *Soñando contigo*, by Lynda Sandoval; and *Biografía de un cimarrón*, by Miguel Barnet. At the Ranchuelo Factory, they read *Jane Eyre*, by Charlotte Brönte; *El corsario negro*, by Emilio Salgari; and *La máscara*, by Leonardo Padura. At the Falcón Factory, they read *Pusimos la bomba—¿y qué?* by Alicia Herrera; *Ramona*, by Helen Hunt Jackson; and *Fidel y la religión: Conversaciones con Frei Betto*, by Fidel Castro. At the Placetas Factory, they read *La República: Dependencia y revolución,* by Julio LeRiverend; *La contrarevolución cubana,* by Jesús Arboleya Cervera; *El amante de Lady Chatterley,* by D. H. Lawrence; *El sombrero de tres picos,* by Pedro Antonio de Alarcón; *Cumbres borrascosas,* by Emily Brönte; *Doña Perfecta,* by Benito Pérez Galdós; *Del amor y otros demonios,* by Gabriel García Márquez; *Las impuras,* by Miguel de Carreón; *Juanita la larga,* by Juan Valera; and *La sierra,* by Juan Almeida Bosque.

In certain places, in almost all cases in which a literary text is read, reading aloud is kept to a minimum, that is, a short story or poem. There are several reasons for this: people are not used to having literature read to them because it has not happened for years; workers prefer radio soap operas; or working conditions do not permit the *lectores* to do their job. When I went to La Caridad Leaf-stripping Plant in San Juan y Martínez, *lector* Ángel Borges was explaining the content of *Ismaelillo,* by José Martí. Later he pointed out the following:

> Tomorrow is the International Day of the Child, and to raise awareness about it, it occurred to me to bring in a work by Martí, so that the workers could learn how much he loved children. I'm interested in showing how Martí's way of thinking applies to today, and how we can help children; that's really what I'm after. That's why I told the leaf strippers that, if we love our children unconditionally, this must be how their personalities are reflected in Martí's texts: they're mischievous, quick, loving little kids, and, ultimately, they all have different personalities. I'd like to awaken their interest, so that if they want to give a child a gift, they give him that book.
>
> My job is to introduce books to them, to encourage interest in reading. That's why sometimes I read compositions by a variety of poets. I read to them about writers and titles with the hope that they'll buy books in order to read them to their families. Books in our country are very expensive. We're used to having a lot of books. It used to be that it was unusual to see a book that cost more than three pesos, but in recent times, the prices of books have changed. That's why, in order to promote reading, what I do is buy magazines and sell them to them, especially when they come with inserts. There is a publication called *Universidad para Todos.* I buy it, and I've sold a lot of copies of it. We've thought about creating a minilibrary here. I have a few books. Not that many. I also like to ask the leaf strippers to bring in books if they want to. And I went to the school and talked to the Pioneer Leader, and we talked about some books that aren't available in their library. Those books are going to be brought here. I don't read a lot of literature, but my job is to awaken interest in it.[22]

Of the 230 *lectores* in the cigar facilities of Cuba in 2005, only 118 had a radio, of which only 89 worked. As a result, there are dozens of *lectores* who have to do their job without a radio or microphone. I visited the José González Trecha Factory in the tiny village of Guayos in Sancti Spíritus in 2003. The *lectora*, Josefa Mustelier, read novels for only ten minutes a day because she had no microphone. The factory had a cement platform with a booth for reading, but she could not do her job from there because no one would be able to hear her. She had to go up on the platform and read standing up, but since the platform was not as elevated as those from years ago, reading time was kept to a minimum.[23]

Likewise, Bernardo Campos, *lector* at the El Corojo Plantation Selection Facility in Pinar del Río, read without a microphone. In that facility there was neither a microphone nor a platform. Therefore, the *lector* had to stand in the middle of the large room so that most of the workers could hear him. Under these conditions, the reading shifts and their content varied. Bernardo Campos pointed out the following:

I work all morning. I should work three shifts: two in the morning and one in the afternoon, but since conditions don't permit that, I work all morning. Since the selection facility is very large, and I don't have audio equipment, I work all morning, and in the afternoon I get ready for the next day. I read for twenty minutes in one place and then I go to another for twenty minutes. And it's rare that I get to read, and that's why I speak to them with pauses. This is a very big place with three floors, and I go to talk to the workers on each floor. I prepare ahead of time, and I tell them about all national and international events. Sometimes I bring them poems: I tell them anecdotes, and I get to read them a short passage of something. I also talk to them about baseball and boxing. This is most important when the National Series is being played. I talk to them about softball and about the anniversaries of important events, about Castro's speeches, the situation in Iraq, a little of everything. Sometimes I recite poetry that I have memorized. For example, "La despedida":

Though perhaps I still love you I say good-bye
I don't know if you loved me, or if I
loved you, or maybe we both loved to excess.
This affection, sad, impassioned, reasonless,
I planted in my heart so I could love you.
I don't know if I loved too much, too little,

but I will never love again like that, it's true.
Your sleeping smile still stays
in my memory and my heart says
that I will not forget you—but here alone
knowing I am losing you
perhaps I feel for you a love I've never known.

They like those poems. Maybe they do some good for people who've been through something like that. I listen to the news, and I watch *Mesas Redondas*, [which is] shown on television every day, and I summarize what happened at each table, what was discussed, who was on, etc.

There are people here who don't have a radio or television at home. Or if they have a television, they don't have a radio, or neither of the two, because they're broken. So the next day they ask me what the news was, what was mentioned, what was said. I don't have time to read novels, so that's why I just talk about them.

As we have seen, the work conditions of the *lector* have changed the dynamics of reading aloud, since there is more of a tendency to comment on and summarize texts than to read them, and speeches and recitation are preferred over reading. In order to get an idea of what is spoken about on a typical day, let us look at the way *lector* Bernardo Campos Iglesias discussed the news on May 29, 2003:

Good morning. As you know, today is a very important day in the lives of all of our country's workers. It is the birthday of the leader of the working class, Lázaro Peña.

Everybody knows that Lázaro Peña was born on a day like today, but the year was 1911. He was born to a poor family. As a child he went to school for only a short time, because you know that children who were born when this country was capitalist had to help their families.

Unfortunately, his father died long before Lázaro Peña grew up. That means that starting at a certain age, when he was a teenager, Lázaro Peña went to work to help his mother, who brought him into the world. His mother, who was a leaf stripper, brought him into this world.

Lázaro was a mason, a carpenter, and, occasionally, a *lector*; that is, life took him down those paths. He was growing up, and life was his teacher. He saw how the proletariat classes were exploited, how the working class was exploited, and this touched his soul, and he dedicated himself to fighting for the defense and triumphs of the labor movement on a national level. . . .

In 1974, Lázaro Peña died, and Castro bid farewell to the hero. In homage to Lázaro Peña, we can tell you that today a group of workers from this center is at the main ceremony for the Day of the Cigar Industry, which is being celebrated in the province of Pinar del Río—that is, they're in Pinar del Río because they deserved it, because of the work that was done after coming through the storm, the right to celebrate the Day of the Cigar Worker was won.

With regard to the *Mesas Redondas* that was on yesterday, I'm not going to talk much about it, because they discussed Europe. But what did they discuss and analyze about Europe? They analyzed the economy, they analyzed politics, and they analyzed social issues. The Cuban panelists did an analysis of Germany, France, and England, and what the European Union entails, and its future. They discussed what was happening with the dollar, and they discussed several economic phenomena. When socialism crumbled, many countries became part of the European Union. Let's see what contradictions may exist between members of that entity.

We also want to explain and let you know that, unfortunately, there has been another earthquake, the third one, in Algeria. I had spoken with you previously about a group of Cuban doctors who were serving in Algeria, and that our country had sent thirty doctors and over ten tons of medicine; that is, the solidarity that our people feel is brought to bear with friendly countries, and with countries that are our enemies. But we are friends of the people.

Sometimes we're not friendly with some governments, but we help them anyway, as was the case with the government of Uruguay. We've sent them vaccines in the past to save their children. . . .

Now I'm going to read you a blurb about this book that many coworkers have asked me to read.

Reading time is minimal, limited to a few minutes. As we have seen, the *lector* does a summary and mixes his review with a speech. This does not occur when the *lector* has a microphone, because the listening audience expects a reading directly from a text.

The reading methods that are utilized in each factory depend not only on intuition, preparation, and the *lector*'s selection of intertexts, but also on reader reception codes that the audience transmits. Each factory is a small world unto itself with a unique relationship between the *lector* and the audience. For example, it is essential to take into account the physical space that separates the transmitter from the receiver, and to what extent the audience can see the *lector*. Along the same vein, it is crucial that *lectores* be able to see and hear the listening audience's reaction. As I have mentioned, in most cases the *lector* sits before the *galera*, or main part of the factory, and reads to at least a hundred workers. Nevertheless, there are instances in which the *lectores* are unable to see the workers face to face, but, rather, only out of the corner of their eye, because the platform or writing desk faces a wall or a side of the factory. Some desks are in a type of booth, and the glass window that separates the *lector* from the audience interferes with the communication between them. There are also platforms that are completely separated from the main part of the factory, in a separate room from which the *lector* cannot see anyone.

In the case of the VD-2 Leaf-stripping Plant, the *lectora*, Magalys Torres Iglesias, sat at the reception desk at the factory's entrance, across from a tobacco plantation and a *guarapera*. As she faced outside, she did not have the opportunity to see her audience; therefore, while she was in the process of reading, the forewoman was the liaison between the *lectora* and her audience, as she gradually let the *lectora* know what was going on in the main work space. Because only a wall separated them, the leaf strippers called out from the other side of it: "We can't understand you," or "Read that again, please."

This is one example of the importance of the space in which reading takes place, and to what extent the *lector* can communicate directly with the audience. The ability to see the listeners' faces or not is quite significant to the *lector*, because that implicitly or explicitly influences the dynamics in play during the reading process and the strategies used to keep the audience's attention.

Given the tradition of reading, *lectores* always face a very demanding audience that insists on a clear, pleasant reading. As Francisco Águila indicated to me: "The job of a cigar maker is very personal, and at the same time, it's a craft that requires a lot of concentration. Inside every one of them is an artist, a specialized artist, because they don't all make the same product; there is differentiation, a variety of kinds of cigars, and each kind of cigar has its own specific secrets. So you're working for artists who are plying their trade, and as *lector*, you should have an artistic sensibility."

But in spite of their working for artists who feel emotions very profoundly, each factory operates according to certain codes that favor or create obstacles for the task of the *lector*. Therefore, the reading methods utilized by each of them are intimately related to those rules. There are at present more women than men working in the cigar industry. In fact, in cigar factories, approximately 60 percent of the workers are women, and in leaf-stripping plants, approximately 90 percent are women. Also, audiences are not uniform, because there are those who have worked there for decades, and there are also many young people who have just started. The older generation is used to listening to reading every day, while the younger one is not. For her part, Zaida Valdés emphasizes the following:

> The only problem is that the younger generation has a lot of trouble getting used to the reading. There is a very young aspect here in this factory. At least the older people have reading ingrained in them. They're used to listening, and daily reading is part of their lives. Young folks want to listen to music. They pay less attention, because they're just not used to it. We *lectores* have to make the cigar makers happy. We have to give them what they ask us for, and that's where the generation gap comes into play.

Likewise, one must take into account to what extent reading has been part of the life of a factory or workshop, since, in certain cases, whether it be due to financial or political difficulties, the presence of *lectores* has been sporadic, and the practice of reading has been lost for five or ten years at a time. As a result, the audience is not used to listening.

Conversely, there are places in which the opposite has occurred, as is the case at El Surco Factory, where reading has been under way without interruption since the 1970s. There the cigar makers simply do not know how to do their jobs without listening to the voice of the *lectora*, Carmen Rodríguez. When she is absent, the next day the cigar makers tell her: "Oh, honey, you didn't come in yesterday and I forgot what I was doing."

One of the ways the *lector* is aware of whether the audience is interested and understanding what he says is by way of the silence that is generated. As Jesús Pereira Caballero says:

> According to how quiet the workers keep, I realize what kind of job I'm doing, and I gauge whether I'm reaching them or not. This is the parameter that the *lector* really uses to know whether he's working efficiently. Total or near-total silence, which is not easy to achieve before two hundred and some cigar makers. Your voice must be assertive; well, not so much your voice as a fluent reading, with good, clear diction that reaches people. But if the *lector* doesn't achieve silence in the *galera* when he's reading, he hasn't achieved his goal. He must read perfectly, or almost perfectly.

On the other hand, silence does not necessarily represent the listeners' acceptance of a good reading, but, rather, may be a negative reaction to the content of what is being read, and not how it is being read. *Lectores* are always under pressure to make themselves heard and hopeful that their listeners are enjoying the content of what they are reading, which is where *lectores* must negotiate or intuit their selection of articles from print media. Also, silence tends to be broken depending on how much the cigar makers are enjoying the reading, which is shown by way of laughter and applause, or by banging their *chavetas* against their workbenches. Conversely, silence can also be broken by shouts and comments of disapproval of the content. According to Grycel Valdés Lombillo Pérez:

> They can boo and hiss, and that's okay, because I get carried away by what I am doing, since I do it more than anything so that they have a good time while they're learning something. Sometimes they don't like something and they start yelling, and I tell them: "I'm going to wait until you quiet down, because, just like I like to hear what you have to say, I also like to be heard." Sometimes when I'm reading, they start to complain. When they stop, I start again. They complain again, and I start over until they finally let me continue.

The irony of her situation lies in the fact that, although on one hand, she must make her listeners happy, on the other, she can never be certain whether they will like what she plans to read to them, especially when it is the newspaper, because, with regard to fictional works, as I have mentioned, the cigar makers themselves do the choosing.

Independently from reading before an audience that is either used to listening or is not, there is a symbiotic relationship that exists between reading time and production time. That is to say, the cigar worker measures reading time not by a digital or analog clock, but, rather, by the number of cigars rolled, by the number of leaves stripped, by the number of bands put on, by the number of boxes varnished, and so on. Francisco Águila emphasized that the process of measuring time for cigar workers involved "unbelievable magic." He told me that, "during the time I'm reading, they keep track of a certain amount of production. They take the time that I'm reading to roll a certain number of cigars. If I speed up or slow down by two minutes, afterward, they know it when they count their cigars, even if they don't have watches. This carries with it an inherent sense of magic that you can see only in here."

As we have seen, each factory operates according to its own codes. At El Surco Factory, the so-called codes of conduct are much stricter. Therefore, whether cigar makers like the text or not, no one should or may speak out loud during the reading. It is strictly forbidden to raise one's voice. Even when the foreman goes around reviewing each worker's production and has a question or comment, he speaks very quietly. When someone coughs, he does so discreetly to avoid breaking anyone's concentration. Once the reading has started, no one has the right to interrupt, not even the reading president. One must wonder to what extent the fact that reading has been a strict, uninterrupted tradition has to do with the adherence to such rigid rules, which are more like the rules of monastic behavior with which I deal in Part I.

As I have indicated, newspapers are usually read during one or two forty-five-minute shifts. Currently, very few newspapers are published in Cuba; therefore, the ones that are almost always read are those that have national circulation, such as *Granma*, *Juventud Rebelde*, and *Trabajadores*. *Lectores* also read local papers, but this is rare, since they circulate only sporadically. For example, in Havana, *El Habanero* or *Prensa Latina* is read; in Holguín, *Ahora*; in the Province of Granma, *La Demajuaga*; in Pinar del Río, *Guerrillero*; in Ciego de Ávila, *Invasor*; in Santiago, *Sierra Maestra*; in the Province of Sancti Spíritus, *El Escambray*; in Santa Clara, *Vanguardia*; and in Guantánamo, *Venceremos*.

All the newspapers that are currently read aloud are six to eight pages long, which obviously limits the *lectores*. But if we stop to think of the number of newspapers that flourished before Castro came to power, and even up until the end of the 1960s, the question that must be asked is which newspapers were bought during that time and why. Also, as there was a far wider selection of newspapers available then, another critical question is which specific sections of the newspaper *lectores* chose to read. Santos Segundo Domínguez Mena recalled that among the many newspapers he used to read were the Cuban papers *El País* and *El Mundo*. In the past there was a wide array of publications, and, consequently, it must have been a great challenge to select a specific newspaper and the specific sections of it, due to the size of the newspaper. Before examining the order in which the newspaper is read, we must focus a bit on the preparation methods of the *lector*.

The preparation time each *lector* requires is inextricably tied to his or her experience and philosophy. There are *lectores* who give the newspaper a cursory review and get only an idea of what they will cover that day. There are those who are much more methodical, who mark the text, highlight the most important parts, and look up vocabulary that is unfamiliar. Conversely, there are those who believe the news should be fresh and new, both for the *lector* and the listener, with the goal that both should enjoy the novel feeling of the media. Odalys Lara stated that she believed in this latter strategy: "I feel more self-assured reading the news for the first time. I like news best at first glance. I like to confront the text and give it the right tone, guided by pauses, commas, periods, and dashes. I always feel most comfortable at first glance." Carmen Rodríguez indicated to me:

With my experience, I sit down ten minutes before I'm scheduled to read and go over the news. Part of my preparation is listening to and reading a lot of news. This is something that teaches the *lector* a lot. The newscast is an intricate part of the *lector*. It's not the same thing to see a written word as to hear it pronounced. When you read, you should take care to notice whether you're dealing with a question, a dressing-down, or praise. You have to adapt so the workers can interpret what you're reading.

And Nicolás Chavollera, who was very meticulous and always reviewed the newspaper with rigorous care during his years as a *lector*, pointed out that

I was always thinking, studying, and analyzing. As a presenter, I always had to be prepared, and that's exactly what I used to demand of myself when I was a *lector*. I utilized a presenter's sensibilities, but I never talked to the cigar makers as such. News for someone who is working has to be read slowly, with a really clear voice. Often, the listeners don't understand a certain word, and you have to substitute a different one, a synonym, so that it will be something they know. That's why it's so important to prepare.

Olga Lidia Véliz recalled: "I always read to myself before reading aloud. I always checked when there was something I didn't understand. I always looked things up because you also have to make use of the dictionary. There are words I don't understand. If there was a word in English, a language I haven't mastered, I always tried to find someone who could tell me how to pronounce it and what it meant. As a *lector* you must be prepared, because if you're not, you'll never reach the worker." However, due to the demands and ephemeral nature of time, especially early in the morning, when the first reading shift starts and the *lector* has just gotten his or her hands on the newspaper, preparation is not, nor is it expected to be, as rigorous as it is during later shifts.

Because all current *lectores* read *Granma* since its circulation is the most consistent, the first question that arises is which sections of the newspaper are read first and which are left for last. Without a doubt, the order of reading is guided by at least two objectives. The first has to do with the tactics that are used to capture the listeners' attention. The second revolves around the philosophy of the *lector*, since selecting one section first and not another already implies, in itself, an ideological and personal agenda. In some factories, the reading president marks the sections that must be read first. The other sections and the order in which they are read are left to the discretion of the *lector*. Zaida Valdés told me: "When I read in the morning, I try to awaken the cigar makers' interest. That's why on Mondays I read topics such as news from the capital, openings, politics, social events, the economy, and culture." Odalys Lara devotes fifteen minutes to national news, fifteen to international news, and the rest of the time to cultural news, sports, and television schedules.

There are other *lectores* who are stricter with regard to reading time for certain articles, such as Francisco Águila, who explains: "I read segments, I read two to three columns that don't take more than ten minutes, because with this type of topic, if I go longer than ten minutes, it tires or saturates the listener, and as a result provokes rejection. The newspaper takes up a lot of their space and attention, and they need to have a rested mind for it." In general, and based on the accounts of the *lectores* whom I interviewed, cultural news and sports are what generate the most interest, which is why they are left for last.

On August 14, 2001, I had the opportunity to see and hear Francisco Águila read the newspaper at 9:15 A.M. during the second reading shift. As we will see later, the method he utilizes is guided by pauses and short introductions before he reads a specific article. Also, this *lector* takes the time to describe the photos that appear in the newspaper and to mention the authors' names:

All right, let's continue with our reading schedule. Now we're going to move on to the news overview. The first thing you notice when you pick up today's edition, on the first page, is the presence of three of the great leaders of our continent: Fidel, Hugo Chávez, and Fernando Henrique Cardoso. In a column, our special envoy tells us the following. . . .

Now let's review other parts of the world—events that happen around the world. Specifically, let's go to the Middle East and the conflict in that area. Let's listen . . .

I'll continue with coverage of these topics, but first, there are important topics that may have the attention of the media. . . .

Now I'll read another newsworthy item, "Peace Accord Signed in Macedonia." Let's listen . . . We'll continue with coverage of this later.

Now let's cover the proceedings of the World Festival of Youth and Students. We'll continue with coverage of what's going on at the festival.

Now let's go to the sports page. . . .

Now let's talk about what has been written about the report sent to us by the Center of Information, Promotion, and Analysis of the Cuban Book Institute. Today they are introducing us to a creative artist, Reina María

Rodríguez, who was born in Havana in 1952. . . .
    Finally, an interesting note about virginity.

Analysis of the order in which he reads reveals that, first, the reading flows, because the *lector* is certain to make transitions between articles, or between sections, so that the listener does not get confused. He gradually guides the listeners so they know he has gone on to a different section, and he intervenes when he introduces different sections and articles: "Now let's review other parts of the world. . . . Specifically, let's go to the Middle East and the conflict in that area."

Second, he uses key words—"Let's listen"—to announce that he is going to start to read the article. The *lector* endeavors to separate from the text, as if he has gathered his group of listeners to *listen* to the written word. This strategy creates a harmonious atmosphere for the community of listeners and recalls the nostalgia of times past, when groups of people gathered in a circle to listen to a *lector*.

Third, note how subtly he interrupted the news he was reading to say: "We'll continue with coverage of this later." Why interrupt a news item? Here we should consider several issues: time limits; the news item is not generating audience interest and is left for last in case there is extra time; or the news is very good and is interrupted to maintain interest. The most essential reason, however, is that the *lector* does not just read, he also summarizes the news that he has before him, as is the case with the item about the Information Center. The *lector* is not reading, but, rather, summarizing, to create a more dynamic presentation. He leaves cultural news and sports for last and closes on an interesting note that he knows will generate interest: virginity.

Lectores must be quick thinking, eager, and sure to cover everything while they keep the audience's attention. This difficult process was lucidly described by Odalys Lara, who pointed out that one also needs to proceed with caution:

When there is a variety of news, you insert items according to how the atmosphere feels. When you feel like a topic is provoking a lot of interest, then you change to a topic that is more calming, that makes them think, that makes them reflect. This is especially true of topics such as psychology, human relations, the nature of friendship, parent-child relationships, marriage. Well, you vary the reading and insert things that keep the temperature from rising too much, so that the workers feel energetic and so that they don't talk a lot, so that they don't interrupt.

Thus, a piece of news that provokes a great deal of attention can function as a double-edged sword. *Lectores* must be clever, because they have to be able to think on their feet.

Zaida Valdés was very selective in her reading, because she took the time to reflect on the articles she had read immediately after reading them: "I only choose a few news items from the media. I don't like to pile it all on. For example, I choose a piece of news about Latin America. After I finish reading it, I start to make comments about the item. I go into depth, I give examples, I offer explanations, I share anecdotes that are related to the topic. I take my time." As a result, the reading process is accompanied by opinions, comments, and critical analysis. This is a characteristic with which the *lectora* contributed to the reading process and benefited the workers, because they were not just passive listeners hearing the news; they learned about part of the cultural knowledge of their *lectora*, as they would in a classroom.

Occasionally, *lectores* reflect on an article they have read or discuss it in depth, depending on their style. Other times, they choose a quotation, give it a close reading, and ask everyone's opinion. Using the quotation as a starting point, the workers start to reflect and even debate. Conversely, on occasion, it is the audience that decides to speak up about a specific issue. In this case, cigar workers take the microphone and give their opinion or reflections about the quotation, and coworkers get to go up on the platform to give their point of view. The platform becomes a forum in which everyone may participate. Therefore, reading aloud does not travel only in one direction, but also becomes an exercise in dialogue, almost like a classroom in which everyone listens, talks, participates, and teaches.

Reading works of fiction is a true art. *Lectores* must "measure" the text they are going to read so that it coincides with the time allotted for reading. This requires preparation before undertaking the reading. As I mention in Part I, in the past, written works were meant to be read aloud; therefore, the author wrote chapters that were not too long, so that people could listen to a section in one sitting without interruption. This tactic was utilized until the nineteenth century, when novels began to be published in installments. The great works of the nineteenth century—*The Count of Monte Cristo, Madame Bovary, Anna Karenina, El periquillo sarniento,* and many more—were published in newspapers, in which case the author had to end each chapter at a suspenseful moment.

Since novels are no longer written or published in this manner, *lectores* confront a challenge. Francisco Águila explained: "Novels are not read by the chapter, because the chapter created by the author doesn't coincide with the time you have; so you have to adapt the reading to your own set of rules. I read and abbreviate, although my reading time doesn't coincide with the way the author has structured the work. The one who's writing isn't thinking that, later, his work will be adapted for a film, or television, or radio, or a cigar factory *lector*." Jesús Pereira Caballero added: "I read for exactly forty-five minutes. And there have been cases in which the novel is so interesting that they want me to keep reading, and well, I usually stop at a key moment while they're interested. Sometimes they ask me to read for fifteen more minutes, and, well, I oblige." It is strictly forbidden to say what is going to happen later in the work, and neither the *lector* nor anyone who has read the novel may skip ahead. When the workers are enjoying the reading, and the *lector* is able to generate suspense, production increases, because the cigar makers are not absent from work. As Grycel Valdés Lombillo Pérez emphasized: "People aren't absent because they don't want to miss the reading. It's as if they were watching a soap opera on television; they can't miss work because they can't miss what is going to happen tomorrow. There are carts in the factory that are used to move material. When I'm reading, those carts aren't allowed to come through because they make noise. People are very attentive when the novel reading shift is coming to an end."

Jesús Pereira Caballero recalled: "Sometimes the cigar makers tell me their ideas of what might happen in the next chapter: 'So-and-so is going to do this, such-and-such is going to happen,' but I can't say anything. There are a few workers here and there who get annoyed because they really want me to tell them, but I can't; I have to keep it a secret. Well, that gives me an idea of how interested they are in what I'm reading. I'm a professional."

On the contrary, whenever Luis González Artiles was coming to the end of a work he was reading, he used to feel like the text was missing something: "So I'd add something; I'd add hugs and kisses to spice up the story, especially at the very end. Authors go into a lot of detail, and then at the end, they don't embellish, they're stingy, that's why I'd add a little something at the end."

The case of María Caridad González Martínez, who was a *lectora* at the Niñita Valdés Leaf-stripping Plant, is unique. She wrote twenty-one novels so she could read them to her audience. None of them are published. Some of the titles include *Oscuridad y destino, Secretos, Corazones de piedra*, and *Tallando sueños*. What is interesting about her experience is that she wrote according to the audience's taste:

> Well, I used to write novels in notebooks, on sheets of bond paper, on stationery, on whatever kind of paper I could get my hands on, because sometimes

there is a paper shortage, too. So I wrote them in longhand. Sometimes
before I finished a novel I started to read it. It had [a sense of] immediacy
about it. Sometimes I made corrections while I was reading. When I had
time to finish them before I read them, I did make revisions. But I was
always pressed for time, and I had to read things I hadn't finished yet. I didn't
know yet how it would end; depending on what people thought of it and
what they suggested. . . . I would manipulate the plot. Sometimes I'd write
an ending I knew they'd like. Other times I surprised them and wrote something they didn't like. But, well, I tried to even things out more or less.[24]

Modulation of the voice and dramatization are key when one is reading
a literary work. *Lectora* María Caridad González Martínez indicated the
following:

When you put emotion into what you're reading, it's because you like what
you're reading. That being the case, the listener is also enjoying it. If people
like it, that's exciting, and you try to put more passion into what you're reading. When it's something you've written yourself, you know why you wrote
what you did, and you know what every word means. In that case, emotions
are more intense.

That's why people liked me to read to them so much, because I read what
I had written, I knew what my purpose was in reading, and people got emotional: they'd cry, they'd laugh, and everything. That was really something, but
it was because I knew what I was reading and why I was reading it.

Sometimes when you read something by someone else [another author],
it has its own metaphors and double entendres, and you don't get it. You don't
realize it at the time. Sometimes, the second time you read a book, you catch
on to what you didn't the first time. When you read something for the first
time, it hasn't made an impression on you yet, and you don't give it the tone
that you could have. But when it's your own text, you are familiar with everything from the start, how it's going to turn out and what's coming up, so you
give it a tone that lets people know what's in store. People liked that a lot.

I have to acknowledge that the other authors are real writers, and the workers liked that, too. I used to improvise because, for example, I read Leonardo
Padura, who is a very Cuban writer who uses very colloquial vocabulary with
a lot of obscene words, but he knows how to use them in his own way, and
they don't seem obscene when you read them. You read here, and you can hear
it in houses across the street because of the factory's microphone, and sometimes there were words I'd have to work with in my own way because they
were obscene. If those words are left out, the reading loses its charm.

But the best experiences were when I read things I had written. Everybody who writes likes to be heard.

There are *lectores* who dramatize works and those who do not. Carmen Rodríguez Pérez did not dramatize what she read, but she "got into" the reading:

The *lector* really has to like his job, because his message has to reach the audience. We're not talking about reading for the sake of reading; you have to get into what you're reading. I become the character I'm reading about. For example, when I read *The Hunchback of Notre Dame*, the workers brought to my attention that I took four days to finish the novel. When they hang the gypsy woman in the novel, I started to cry. I stopped reading the first day. I came back to it the second day and started to cry again. . . . I was imagining the troubles she had gone through. This happens to me with a number of books. I can't take it, I get too emotional. When you read, you should be careful to see if you're dealing with a question, a dressing-down, or praise. You have to adapt so the workers can interpret what you're reading.

Another *lectora*, Odalys Lara, explained:

I give emphasis to the reading, but I don't do the voices of different characters. Why don't I do voices? Because I think it's easier for a man to simulate a woman's voice than for a woman to simulate a man's voice. What I try to do with my reading is to make people feel good, to get them to learn something, to enjoy it, to be transported by their imagination to where the action is occurring, but I'm not a comedian. I want the audience to understand and identify with the characters' tone, with what they talk about, with the plot, but not necessarily because I use a less-serious voice or make noises.

None of that, according to Francisco Águila: "I only dramatize now and then. I try to find texts that are written in the third person so that I feel more comfortable, but the cigar workers like the books to be in first person. When I read *Cecilia después*, a humorous version of *Cecilia Valdés*, I had to imitate a robot's voice, as if I were computerized. They really liked that." Conversely, as we will see later, there are *lectores* who dramatize works in an extraordinary way.

"Honey, you read so badly . . . don't you feel what you're reading?" Jesús Pereira Caballero, the *lector* at the Partagás Factory said to Grycel Valdés

Lombillo Pérez, the *lectora* at H. Upmann. Jesús advised her that, to a certain extent, *lectores* essentially have to dramatize everything:

> You have to put your whole heart into what you're reading, even if it's the news. If you're talking about Palestine, you can't say there were so many dead and so many wounded and leave the information at that. No, no, no, no. You start to dramatize: a child died, you say how he died, with the feeling you have to put into it, with your voice cracking, not with the same voice as always. Now, if you're talking about sports, you can't talk the same way as always. You have to say, with the emphasis of a sportscaster, Cuba won three to two!

Grycel learned from Jesús, who simply believed that "every novel should be dramatized": "When I read *El juez de Egipto*, I really got into it. The cigar workers really liked it, because I had to make many different animal sounds, such as gorillas, dogs, etc. It was a big hit." Later he added: "I think every *lector* has his own specific style, a personal style. The *lector* is made over time, and he needs a few years to become what he will be. When I was in school, I liked to read a lot, and I saw a lot of movies. I like dramatization, so I incorporate it in my vocation as a *lector*. This really helps me. When I'm reading, some people think the radio is on."

With regard to the radio, not only do some *lectores* dramatize, they also learn the special effects that are used on radio soap operas, as was the case with Luis González Artiles:

> My experience started when I caught a soap opera on the radio. I would listen to it closely, and that's how I learned, by repeating what they did. I would give a woman's voice a twist.
>
> First, I used to prepare my reading, just as athletes do; I would concentrate. That's how I established dialogues between different voices. I did the same thing with sound effects: I would produce the sound of water with an x-ray film, I did the wind with my mouth, a horse with coconut shells, and so on. I imitated a hurricane using a box of matches. It was like a radio soap opera. I had no preparation or technique. Whatever I did, I did spontaneously.

There are *lectores* who simply do not read novels (although they do read short stories and poems), as was the case with Ángel Borges:

> I haven't enjoyed reading novels, because in the morning we listen to two soap operas on the radio, and a social guidance program with a variety of

topics: health, science, family problems, etc. And then a romantic radio soap opera. In the afternoon, at 2:00, a universal literature novel is played, and at 3:00 another soap opera. That's why I feel like they wouldn't absorb it if I picked up and read them another novel. When you listen to soap operas on the radio, you hear the studio effects, the radio effects, and the sound effects. Everything is very specific, even how much time the *lector* and the host have. So it's very difficult for me to bring the novel's message to life. To me, it's hard to compete with the radio.

As we have seen, the way in which novels are read varies according to the philosophy and training of each *lector*. Nevertheless, in all cases, the most important thing is the listening public's reaction and demands.

In the process of reading works of fiction, mainly novels, short stories, and poetry, and especially at the end of the reading of a text, the audience actively participates. In general, if someone wishes to give an opinion about the text that is being read, the microphone on the platform is yielded to him so that he can express himself. Jesús Pereira Caballero indicated:

> Sometimes workers try to say what they think of the text in their own words. They come in and state their viewpoints. For example, sometimes they talk about what they think Guillén's poems mean. They have their own opinions. Most of them have an opinion. Since they've gone to school, they are really drawn to poetry. Occasionally, I take a verse and ask them what it means. Then they come back with an answer. This takes up a bit of time, because they stop working. But it doesn't matter, because their cultural awareness increases.

Odalys Lara indicated: "A lot of times, they have questions when I read something very specialized, something very interesting, and especially when there's something in the plot they don't like. In that case, a debate takes place and several of them participate."

Francisco Águila said: "Even when I read short stories, the workers make comments. So it's not just reading, but also following a model in which everyone participates. It's important to get the listener to become an active being. Sometimes workers come up on the platform and are very oppositional, they come up to say something, to reflect on literature, and to debate."

Nicolás Chavollera pointed out: "I always talked to the workers before and after reading. Whenever I finished a novel, I devoted at least a day to reflecting on what had happened in the work. That reflection was a priority, and the workers always came up to the platform. The cigar workers never had to buy the books that were read to them. We listened to the texts right there and we discussed them. The workers were experts in the art of listening. They were scholars by ear."

Lectores are in charge of a countless number of activities. In the first place, they are the ones who turn the platform into a kind of stage. The *lector* coordinates what takes place in that space. He is in charge of announcing the workers' birthdays. With that in mind, one or another of the cigar workers composes a poem or a ten-line stanza, which is read by either the author or the *lector*. On occasion, *lectores* produce compositions for the cigar workers, as is the case with Olga Lidia Véliz Callazo, who composed the following for the birthday of a leaf stripper (Caridad Díaz) at the VD-31 Leaf-stripping Plant:

Remember, Caridad, do you?
the time we talked
you said that I lost it
but none of that is true.
A little contrariness
came over me then
I could not believe
that you had retired
And to Pablo you had denied
all your love, woman.
Caridad, the guilty one
only accuses himself, woman
and you made me read
something you liked indeed
and at your age it's true
you can't satisfy
or give pleasure to
a man in fine fettle
But Pablo will settle
for very little woman.
Today, when home you go
take an early bath
and with your own hand
start to knead the dough
in a little bowl
add a little rum

then see how full of fun
your old man will become
when he sees the little bud
he will hit a home run.
Caridad, Pablo says
that you are everything to him
that you mean a lot,
that he really loves you
and that there is no need
for you to sacrifice
you should control that vice
that everything is through
and that I should let you know
your mind is going to go.

In most cases, *lectores* function as masters of ceremonies and announcers. Luis González Artiles, former *lector* at a leaf-stripping plant in Cabaiguán, recalled in our interview that in the workshop there were activities known as "sparks," which took place for an hour three times per week. He was in charge of decorating the platform so that the leaf strippers could come up and sing, recite poetry, or present dramatic works as a group. They also played the radio and had dance contests. The platform therefore functioned as a stage on which a variety of artistic demonstrations unfolded.

Lectores keep up to date with regard to the anniversaries of important events, and usually before they start reading, they announce dates of important national and international events that occurred that day in history. For example, they announce February 14 (Valentine's Day), May 1 (May Day), March 8 (International Day of the Woman), May 10 (Mother's Day in Cuba), November 20 (Universal Children's Day), and June 5 (World Environment Day). They also remind the workers about important dates for the country, such as the birthdays or deaths of national heroes, for example, Antonio Maceo, José Martí, or Ignacio Agramonte, as well as July 26, the anniversary of the attack on the Moncada military base, and even August 13, Fidel Castro's birthday. In order to commemorate these events, the cigar workers participate by singing, writing speeches, or reading messages or poems that they have composed themselves.

May 29 is the Day of the Cigar Worker. Without a doubt, the coordination of events to take place both inside and outside the factory falls to the *lector*. On that day, he is in charge of encouraging participation in special events. There are recitations and dancing, instruments are played, and messages are read on the platform. There is a special lunch that day, and usually work ends early so that everyone can dance to the beat of the music that reverberates throughout the factory. In coordination with the trade union or outside organizations, the *lector* encourages the workers to participate, whether it be in speechmaking contests or recitation.

The *lector* is the facilitator of cultural and athletic activities in which the workers participate. These take place outside the factories. There are national poetry contests sponsored by the cigar industry, such as the Carlos Baliño, the Celia Sánchez, or the Rodrigo Jerez. To that end, *lectores* announce contests, promote participation, edit the poems that will be entered into the contest, and send them in. The *lector* also coordinates participation in games such as dominoes, chess, and Chinese checkers.

Baseball is an essential part of the cigar worker's cultural life, and the *lector* has an important role to play as both coordinator and announcer for the games. Most factories or workshops have baseball teams that compete on both the municipal and provincial levels. Since some *lectores* are former radio announcers, they have become very interesting, original *lectores*. For example, in El Surco Factory, cigar makers remember the unforgettable job that Alfredo de Arma did. He was one of the best-loved *lectores* and used to go to the factory teams' baseball games, where he took notes, edited them, and the next day read them as if he were reading a sportscast as a professional announcer on a television or radio sports channel would.

A variety of contests take place in the factories. If there is not a regularly scheduled time for them, *lectores* sporadically and spontaneously create different kinds of games. Ana María Valdivia of the Pedro Larrea Factory in Sancti Spíritus devoted all day Saturday to what she called the "Knowledge of Facts Program," competitions with questions and answers, riddles, oral crossword puzzles, and the identification of different historical and current figures. There are *lectores* who occasionally quiz workers about the capitals of countries, names of presidents, rivers of Latin America or Europe, and so on.

The organization of visual expression also falls to *lectores*. In different parts of the factory, one can often note blackboards with illustrations of historical figures, famous quotations, poems, chronological charts, and drawings that enrich the cultural horizons of the workers. In certain cases, whether on their own initiative or at someone's request, *lectores* put up installations exhibiting letters, photographs, or a book or pamphlet about a historical figure. While the installation is up, the *lector* makes frequent reference to the exhibit, reads passages from or about the work of the person in question, and shares countless anecdotes. Reproductions of paintings by artists such as Wifredo Lam,

Pedro Pablo Oliva, or Manuel Mendive Hoyo are also exhibited so that the cigar workers' vision is broadened as much as their hearing.

Therefore, the factory operates as a type of museum for which the *lector* acts as curator. Ángel Borges of La Caridad Leaf-stripping Plant in San Juan y Martínez has done an extraordinary job in this respect. In 2003, besides selecting and mounting magnificent installations, he was planning an exhibition of books that was part of the Pinar del Río Book Fair, which took place in February 2004. His mission was to disseminate culture by visually displaying a variety of books that had just been published, as well as reviewing them, with the hope of creating interest in his listening audience. The book was an exhibit inside a glass case in a work space and, in combination with the tasks of the *lector*, represented a degree of excellent planning and educational endeavor that was much like one would find in a library.

Lectores bring a world of culture to cigar workers not only through books, but also through their work as liaisons between the world of the factory and the cultural universe that exists outside its doors. Their job is to get in touch with different cultural and academic institutions and act, first, as intermediaries and, later, as presenters, coordinators, panelists, or masters of ceremonies. Extremely important figures from the political, diplomatic, and artistic world have graced the platforms. For example, Fidel Castro, accompanied by politicians or foreign visitors, has visited several platforms. In this case, the *lector* is the one who yields the microphone to these very important people.

Professors, doctors, attorneys, scientists, psychologists, and historians visit from universities to give lectures related to their fields of specialization. For example, doctors give talks about health problems such as AIDS and other more common communicable diseases. Attorneys speak about labor law or specific issues such as divorce or workers' rights. Scientists talk about the environment and tobacco production, and psychologists have occasionally been assigned the task of giving a variety of lectures related to women's self-esteem. Historians discuss topics such as the *orishas* in Cuba, historical monuments, and, in essence, a whole world of culture. On occasion, these activities are repeated on a regular basis; thus, these events operate as seminars.

It is necessary to emphasize that a dynamic dialogue occurs between the lecturer and the audience. It is not a question of just presenting a talk, but, rather, of doing whatever can be done to facilitate a dynamic conversation so that all the cigar workers may be enriched and reap benefits from the conference. This is evidence of the essential nature of the profession of the *lector* as leader and liaison for a wide array of events.

Lectores are constantly in communication with provincial libraries, not only because they borrow books, but also because they invite librarians to visit the factories. The *lector* introduces the visiting officials on the platform, and they review new and old books, bring in encyclopedia volumes and read entries, present magazines, and make announcements about the variety of cultural activities that take place in the library, such as readings for children, conferences, and literary gatherings.

Writers have the privilege of being listened to by a demanding audience. Poets, short-story writers, and novelists visit factories to read passages from their works and to reflect on them, or to discuss the creative process. Not only do they present their own new works, but they also come in to read and discuss specific topics as well as classic and contemporary authors. For example, in the spring of 2003, at the LV-9 Factory, author Arístides Vega Chapú read part of his book *El riesgo de la sabiduría* and shared with the cigar workers the process of creating his poem "Escrito en San José." On some occasions, writers do not read their works, but they do leave a copy in the hope that it will be heard someday, as was the case with Chilean author Patricio Riveros Olavarría, who visited the LV-9 Factory in February 2004. In fact, the *lector* read his novel *La mujer del cura Soto* immediately following the visit.

On November 1, 1979, *Granma* publicized a series of literary readings in cigar factories of books by Cuban authors. Raúl Ferrer, Imeldo Álvarez, and Onelio Jorge Cardoso inaugurated the series. In May 2003, a group of writers from across Cuba met in Santa Clara: among them were Otilio Carvajal, Alberto Sicilia, Jorge Luis Mederos, Amir Valle, Luis Manuel Pérez Boitel, Guillermo Vidal, and Rebeca Murga. All of them went to visit the LV-9 Factory. "We, the authors, are here to participate in several cultural activities in Villa Clara, in celebration of the Second Annual UNEAC [Union of Writers and Artists of Cuba] 'Enrique Labrador Ruiz' Book Award. We hope that our art [literature] blends with the tobacco, but that it never goes up in smoke," detective fiction writer Lorenzo Lunar Cardedo wrote in a factory guest book.

Zaida Valdés recalled a visit to the Laguito Factory from a Brazilian writer who introduced his novel *Corazón salvaje*.[25] She also had pleasant memories of when Alden Knight came in to read his poetry. When it comes to reading poems, sometimes the poet and the *lector* alternate; first one of them reads a poem or a stanza, and the other continues, which makes for a dynamic, soulful reading.

Museums also make their presences known in the factories. Thanks to coordination by the *lectores*, agreements are made with curatorial boards for their members to come into the factories to exhibit cultural artifacts.

For example, they might bring in a mirror, a teapot, a hand fan, a handker-chief, or any other artifact they think will stimulate the workers' interest. For approximately half an hour, the object in question is exhibited on the platform; its creation, what it is made of, and its history are discussed. At the conclusion of the presentation, the workers may ask general or specific questions about the item.

Many television actors have also made appearances on the platforms, especially when the television programs they are on are in vogue. The *lector* contacts television management or the Department of Culture and later plays the role of host.

The same occurs when radio soap opera artists visit factories to discuss their roles on the programs. They are especially welcomed, because radio soap operas are an essential part of what is broadcast in factories. These artists share aspects of their professional lives with fans face to face, and the cigar workers eagerly pose questions about the culture of their jobs, the soap opera's plot, and the special effects they listen to so attentively while they are working.

Theater groups also appear on the platforms, especially since these groups abound in Cuba. Both local and national groups present talks. If space permits, that is, if the stage (or, rather, the platform) is large enough, they perform short skits or parts of recent works, classic works, or a dance. In this sense, the platform becomes a space that is not only educational but also artistic.

Musicians have always played an extremely important part in the cultural universe of the platforms. In fact, as I have indicated elsewhere, they have debuted on them since the nineteenth century. Not by chance, at the Romeo y Julieta Factory, there is still an old piano, a reminder from times past when music was part of the established cultural programming. Currently, and without discrimination, soloists and groups appear to promote their new productions, and groups are hired to celebrate anniversaries of important events. In addition, provincial and national choirs appear, as well as musicians who alternate with comedians, dramatists, people who recite poetry, choirs made up of the elderly who find joy in the faithful audience, and children's choirs that sing, recite, and act. Ultimately, the *lector* orchestrates this musical, harmonious world.

Without the hard work of the *lectores* as public relations coordinators and as liaisons with a variety of institutions, these activities would be practically impossible. One of the greatest challenges is maintaining a dynamic and entertaining atmosphere while creating a cultural, educational environment. This constant struggle is especially difficult when dealing with such a large audience. Although the listeners are in different departments in the factory, and not all of them can see the *lector*, everyone can hear him. The *lector* must always keep track of time and stay in control of what is said and heard, just as a radio or television announcer does.

Now then, with all these activities, anyone might wonder how the cigar workers can do their jobs. What is most surprising is that production does not decrease, since the workers are used to listening. With the exception that, at times, a worker here and there leaves his workstation to participate in an event, production continues without stopping.

There is no doubt that cigar workers in the main part of the factory are the privileged ones, as they have always been, since they have the opportunity to see and hear what is taking place on the platform. This is not the case in other departments, where the workers can only hear what happens on the platform, but this does not create a barrier to the amount of attention they give the reading and the wide variety of cultural activities that take place.

As we have observed, since Fidel Castro came to power, the activities of the *lectores* have increased. Likewise, the reading committees have expanded: there are a president, a vice president, a union and administrative representative, two members-at-large (one a young worker and the other an outstanding worker), and, last but not least, of course, a *lector* or *lectora*. Therefore, the *lector* and his committee are an extremely important part of the work and cultural lives of the cigar workers.

During the summer of 2000, the Museo de Tabaco [Cigar Museum] in Havana held the Cultural Advancement Program for Cigar Industry *Lectores*. This was the first meeting of *lectores* at the national level. The objectives of the program were to teach them about the history of reading aloud in cigar facilities, and they were invited to participate in reading and public-speaking workshops in which oral narration, the news media, dramatization, and reading methodology were discussed.[26] The meeting was a success because, until then, the *lectores* did not know one another. Since that meeting, an effort has been made to train *lectores* by way of courses run by the *lectores* themselves and by volunteers (from the Communist Party's Provincial Schools, the CTC, the José Martí Cultural Society, universities, and radio stations) who are part of the National Technical Advisory Council of *Lectores*. Courses have been taught in the provinces of Pinar del Río, Villa Clara, Sancti Spíritus, and Holguín, and in Havana.

Between April 13 and July 7, 2005, the CAPELET Project, Personalized Training for Cigar Industry *Lectores*, began. Social communication, interpersonal relations, journalism techniques, oral expression, literary

TABLE 2. LECTORES IN FIRST CAPELET PROJECT CLASS, VILLA CLARA, APRIL 13, 2005

Name	Sex	Factory	Work Start Date	Educational Level
Mayelín Bermúdez Martínez	F	Esperanza	June 21, 2001	12th grade
Tatiana León Luques	F	Santo Domingo	August 25, 2001	12th grade
María de las Merces Solís Batista	F	Ranchuelo	May 17, 2004	12th grade
Anita Sánchez Zafra	F	Falcón	November 1, 1999	12th grade
Cristina González Muñoz	F	Placetas	August 10, 1994	12th grade
Francisco Águila Medina	M	Santa Clara	October 1, 1996	BA in history
Yanetsi Martínez Castillo	F	Camajuaní	April 4, 1997	12th grade
Belkis Domínguez Domenech	F	Encrucijada	February 1, 1994	12th grade
Irenia Morales Reyes	F	Manicaragua	January 28, 2003	12th grade
Osmaida Chión Carmona	F	La Moza	December 24, 1984	12th grade
María Cristina Ramos Rivero	F	Remedios	January 1, 2003	12th grade
Medelén Duarte de la Paz	F	Quemado	June 15, 2003	12th grade
María Expósito González Elena	F	Vueltas	May 2, 1982	12th grade
Yuleisy Cabrera Espinosa	F	La Quinta	March 18, 1999	12th grade
Pilar María Susacasa Barroto	F	Cabarién	July 1, 2003	12th grade
Magaly Milián Cortina	F	Jicotea	December 1, 1993	12th grade
Marlén Jiménez Aira	F	Sagua	July 5, 2002	12th grade
Elaine Rodríguez Estévez	F	Camajauní Leaf-stripping Plant	May 1, 2002	12th grade
Marta Madelén Valles Núñez	F	Manicaragua Leaf-stripping Plant	September 25, 1995	12th grade
Luis Vicente Abreus Morell	M	Báez Leaf-stripping Plant	November 22, 1982	12th grade
Luis Vicente Abreus Morell	M	Falcón Leaf-stripping Plant	November 22, 1982	12th grade

SOURCE: Francisco Águila.

appreciation, theater arts, and the history of tobacco are taught (see Table 2 for members of the first class).[27] In these seminars, apart from improving their skills, *lectores* have the opportunity to share experiences, texts, and methodologies. For the first time, the *lector* in Cuba is not alone.

Meetings of *lectores* also set guidelines under which, to a certain extent, some readings and especially titles of literary works have begun to become standardized. Although the *lector* does not choose the texts, his opinion carries a great deal of weight.

In summary, for the first time in the history of reading aloud in cigar facilities, an effort has been made to study and understand more in depth the profession of the *lector*. In most cases, before 2000, the *lector* was known almost exclusively to his listeners in the factory and to those who appeared on the platform. For the first time, there is a growing recognition of the importance of the work done by *lectores* and their significance in Cuba's cultural history.

As we have seen, it has been difficult or nearly impossible to ferret out the lists of texts read aloud throughout the twentieth century, with the exception of the data I have presented here. Also, reading aloud in cigar facilities demonstrates how the practice is not a product of illiteracy. Furthermore, the efforts that are under way to support *lectores* represent an incentive that offers the promise of an even more fruitful tomorrow for the profession.[28] One of the few journalistic articles that have been written about the *lectores* during the 145 years of their existence says: "There will always be a *lector* in cigar facilities" (*Diario Trabajadores*, March 4, 2002). At least there is hope.

Now let us listen to the echoes of the *lectores* in Mexico.

EIGHT

Mexico

The Echoes of Reading

—┤■━■┤——

Leaving furrows of light
Across the frothy sea
At Veracruz port
I arrive happily.
The future mists part
And I know in my mind
That in Mexico I will find
The same protection
Which my production
In Cuba did provide.

Mexico! Your protection
Which to the just you never deny,
My ambition will satisfy
If you grant my petition
And of my production
I will give you the most excellent;
And awaiting now impatient
Your positive reply
You who are an emporium of gold
Will give me gold most brilliant.

ANONYMOUS, *Álbum de la Fábrica*
de Cigarros La Belleza (1892)

Reading aloud in cigar facilities in Mexico began during the Ten Years' War in Cuba between 1868 and 1878. It was brought to Mexico by Cubans and Spaniards who were fleeing the war and who settled in the state of Veracruz.

In addition to its natural beauty, Veracruz enjoys the advantage of fertile land and a climate similar to that of Pinar del Río. Its location favors the growing of tobacco. The most important tobacco region is located in an area called Los Tuxtlas. In the past, there were also factories in the state's major cities, such as Veracruz and Xalapa.

In Banderilla, a small village adjoining the latter city, La Perla Cigar Factory is located.[1] Decades ago, La Perla, established at the end of the nineteenth century, had its years of splendor and glory. In 2005, the factory had dwindled in size to a small workshop with only eight individual workbenches. There were four workbenches in a row on the left-hand side of the workshop, and four on the right, so that the cigar makers faced one another. There were just five women who did the selecting, leaf stripping, cigar rolling, and banding and wrapping. The rest of the room was empty, save for a barrel and a large, wooden, six-yard-long by two-yard-wide table, both in the corner of the shop. In that space nearly trapped in time, reading aloud once took place.

All that is known about the former *lectores* at La Perla comes from the mouths of former cigar makers. Mateo Murrieta Hernández, a veteran cigar maker, recalled:

> When I started working at the factory in 1960, I remember that the cigar makers who had been here longer than I had said there used to be *lectores* here. At that time, the factory was very large; there were over two hundred employees and several different departments. A long time ago, the older people used to tell us that in the past there were *lectores* who used to go up on a platform at the side of the shop and read from there. Of course, there was reading only in the main workshop. I never found out the names of any of the *lectores*, and I never listened to one read, but that was something that once existed here. It must have been very nice.[2]

María de Lourdes Contreras, a cigar maker at La Perla in 2005, remembered the following:

> I started to work as a cigar maker at El Toro Cigar Factory in Xalapa in 1963. At that time, the factory had many employees. There were over a hundred of us. In the big room, there were about forty-five of us cigar makers. The rows each had ten workbenches in them, and we sat side by side. Across from one row was another row, so we could see our coworkers' faces.
>
> In those days, a *lector* used to come in to read to us. His name was Otón. He was a sixty-five-year-old man. He had a full, clear voice. He was a very educated, conscientious person. He used to read to us for an hour every

afternoon. He always brought his own books in and read us brief novels or short stories.

I have a very bad memory, and I don't remember exactly what he read to us. But it was nice that he came into the factory, because we'd be quiet and concentrate on the reading. He used to walk up and down between the workbenches with the book in his hand. And we loved to listen to him! He used to read just as a hobby.

When I started at that factory, he had already been reading there for a few years. I only heard him read from 1963 to 1965, which was how long I stayed at that factory, but he kept reading there for a few more years. Since reading was his pastime, we never had to pay him at all.

But let me tell you that when there wasn't any reading in the factory, there was a lot of racket. A lot of noise. We all talked a lot so we wouldn't get bored. There was a lot of hot air. Since the factory owners never let us listen to the radio, not to music or anything else, well, we kept ourselves entertained by talking. There was really a lot of noise when there was no reading.

When I left El Toro Factory, I really missed the *lector*, because it was always nice to listen to him speaking. Most of the other factories didn't have *lectores*, and the radio was strictly banned. That was really sad. But when I came to work at La Perla, at least here we were allowed to listen to the radio. It was one of the few places where the radio wasn't banned.

But it was true that the foreman was the one who was in charge of controlling the radio. It was a huge, beautiful, ornate radio on four legs. That's where it was, in that corner of the workshop, behind a railing, and the foreman was the only one who was allowed to touch it. He used to decide what we were going to listen to. He always put on music. That's all. At least with music on you're happier and less bored. Well, music is better than nothing.

Just imagine, everything's always been banned here, and not just here, but in other factories, too. Here you can't drink coffee or smoke or bring in food. And fruit—don't even mention it.[3]

The banning of the radio, such a basic, important medium, demonstrates the mentality of the owners and foremen of the 1960s. Because of this, it is not surprising that reading was so short-lived in Mexico; it has always represented a threat.

But not everything was banned. As Mexico is such a religious country, the feast day of the Virgin of Guadalupe or of any saint the cigar workers wish to venerate is observed, as was the case in Spain in the nineteenth century. There are altars with statues, depictions of the Virgin Mary, and crucifixes on those altars in factories. Religious holidays are respected and celebrated fervently. Cigar workers do not listen to the voice of a *lector*, but, symbolically, they feel that they are listening closely to "the Word of the Lord."

The voice of the *lector* exists only in the memories of the few cigar workers who had the privilege of hearing it.[4] Most cigar workers these days listen to the radio and have no idea of the importance of reading aloud in a work setting. "At least here we were allowed to listen to the radio," observed María de Lourdes Contreras.

The ban on reading aloud in Mexico has always been a common practice. That is to say, the practice was introduced by Cubans and Spaniards and quickly caught on in textile factories. There, novels and the newspaper were read, although there was never a specific *lector*. When the working-class press emerged, employees began to read the weeklies aloud during working hours and in small groups during their breaks. But starting in 1872, the owner of one of the factories threatened his employees with a reduction in salary and with being fired if he caught them reading aloud in the factory:

> The administrator of La Fama Factory has justified his actions, as you indicated in your July 7 issue, in a manner befitting a person of his station, by giving an express order to one of the master weavers of the weaving department, where he believes there is the most reading aloud, as there are times when work conditions permit the worker to enjoy a bit of education through readings, whether they be of novels or newspapers. But knowing that some employees were making their own interpretations of their rights and making complaints, as you are aware, he exercised his right to throw out the first ones who spoke up. And now, seeing as how the press is making an effort to help rectify these abuses, he has told his master artisan explicitly to inform his workers that the day he finds anyone reading aloud, that worker will be fined four reales in the first instance, and in the second, he'll be out on his ear.[5]

The ban on reading aloud spread to other factories without exception, and the reading of newspapers, whether working-class press or not, was not allowed. The prohibition of reading aloud was a political measure that expressed paranoia with regard to education and the civic conscience of the workers, although cracking down on discipline in the workplace was used as an excuse. However, as we have seen throughout this book, in most cases, reading aloud did not generate noise, but, rather, discipline. Alberto Leguísano, an artisan who was disappointed by the owners' reaction to reading, wrote the following:

Look at him, today a businessman,
Who yesterday was lucky to sell tins;
Disguised he feels himself a gentleman
Forgetting now his humble origins,
He's a grotesque and ordinary sort,
A carpenter's rough manners does display,
He thinks himself a noble in the court
But barkeep is the image he conveys.
In politics he feels he holds great sway;
He thinks himself a patron of the arts;
He vaunts his decency in every way;
Yet seeing him it's obvious from the start
He's naught but a poor devil; in essence,
A perfect prototype of ignorance.[6]

Struggles over workers' rights (reading aloud, among other things, was considered a right) led to several widespread strikes. Solidarity with cigar workers became apparent in the writings of Mexican intellectuals, not to mention the writings of José Martí.[7] In spite of this, however, reading aloud continued to represent a threat and thus occurred sporadically.

The radio ban in most cigar factories in Veracruz in the 1950s reaffirms or, rather, proves why reading aloud could not proceed successfully. Needless to say, the absence of a radio meant missing not only music, but, by extension, the world of information in the latest news, not to mention the cultural programming disseminated by this means of communication. With its massive coverage area, reaching the farthest corners of Latin America, and its unique programming of soap operas and a variety of music, Mexican radio never wanted for listeners. Nevertheless, ironically, in Mexican cigar facilities, just where it could have reached a dedicated, enthusiastic audience, the radio was banned. Therefore, the world of information and music was compensated for only by the voice of the *lector*, that solitary, volunteer *lector* whose echo has been inscribed only in the far reaches of memory.

The radio is no longer banned. The remaining five employees at La Perla Factory listen to one. They prefer to listen to music and occasionally cultural programs. They do not listen to the news, as they prefer to see and hear it at home on television. Music is a sort of background they listen to at low volume while they converse and work.

There are much bigger factories, such as the Santa Clara, located in San Andrés Tuxtla, and Te-Amo, situated in Sihuapa; both have hundreds of workers. There also, employees only listen to the radio. There is no memory of there having been a *lector* in either factory.

It is doubtful that there has never been reading aloud in the main cigar centers in Mexico. It is more likely a disappearance of memory or the lapse from generation to generation that has muted and omitted the recollection of the *lector*. In the Santa Clara Factory, the cigar worker with the most seniority, Santiago Baxin Fiscal, said:

> There's never been reading here; we just listen to the radio. In the morning, we always put on the news. Later, they put on whatever station you want. We always agree to one, and whoever's in charge of the radio is the only one who changes the station. The person in charge of the sound is not really in charge of it, but, since the sound equipment is near him, in the banding department, he's in charge of it. He also does us a favor by putting on the CDs we bring in: *norteña, ranchera*, ballads, tropical, romantic music, a little bit of everything.[8]

Practically the same holds true at Te-Amo (A. Turrent Cigar Factory). There, in the main workshop where at least 150 employees work, there is a large set of audio equipment located in a corner of the room. In this factory, there is not the same sense of harmony enjoyed at the Santa Clara Factory. Here, the cigar workers who are not in agreement with the choice of radio station being played at any given time take out their own small portable radios, put them on the table, and a dissonant *ajiaco*, as a Cuban would say, ensues, which no one can understand or enjoy.

As we have seen, for generations the radio has definitively replaced reading aloud. But it is not all noise and uproar; there is also a healthy camaraderie, and most of all, in factories, workers listen to "the Word of the Lord."[9]

An interesting activity is celebrated at the Santa Clara Factory on the Feast of Our Lady of Guadalupe (December 12). The most distinctive feature is that, in the corner of the factory where the banding department is located, there is a small altar dedicated to Our Lady of Guadalupe. Two framed images decorated with multicolored lights and paper flowers grace the corner. In preparation for the Feast Day, the cigar workers stop working at noon. They all gather before the altar and take down the larger image. The large group exits the cigar factory and begins a procession to a church located in the center of town. During the procession, on the way to the church, the icon of Our Lady is passed from one participant to another. They meet up with other groups that are doing the same thing.

When they reach the church, they leave the portrait of Our Lady there for several hours and sing "Las mañanitas," "La Guadalupana," and other songs to honor her. Afterward, they process back and return Our Lady to the workshop, where they hang her back on the wall, sing to her, pray to her, and worship her until midnight.

The women are in charge of making tamales, *buñuelos* (fritters), and small sandwiches for everyone. These are accompanied by *atole* (a soft drink made of corn flour), *champurrado* (chocolate *atole*), and rice pudding. Everyone enjoys spending time together among the factory's rows of workbenches, and shortly after 1:00 A.M., they all go home.

María de Lourdes Contreras recalled:

> The only day we can enjoy each other's company at work is May 3, when we worship the cross. That day the cross [a white wooden cross one and one-half feet high] is taken down from the altar. It is cleaned, repainted, decorated, and passed from workbench to workbench, and we all sing to it. This day we stop work early, at noon, and after we sing to the cross, we all eat. That day we bring food in to work, and we all celebrate here, we all sing. It's as if here you could hear the Word of the Lord. But the voice of the *lector* was always very nice.

Reading aloud in Mexico was very short-lived, but this fact is not surprising, because a strict ban was implemented from the beginning. There is an abundance of references to tobacco in Mexican literature. In *Astucia, el jefe de los hermanos de la hoja o Los charros contrabandistas de la rama*, Luis G. Inclán notes how Mexicans and Cubans sold tobacco leaves in Mexico in the nineteenth century. Tobacco is mentioned in many novels and books of poetry, such as *El águila y la serpiente* and *La sombra del Caudillo*, by Martín Luis Guzmán; *Mi general* and *Campamento*, by Gregorio López y Fuentes; *La luciérnaga*, by Mariano Azuela; *Tropa vieja*, by Francisco Urquizo; *Nocturnos*, by Xavier Villaurrutia; *Los signos del zodiaco*, by Sergio Magaña; *Los frutos caídos*, by Luisa Josefina Hernández; *Ojerosa y pintada*, by Agustín Yáñez; *Aura*, by Carlos Fuentes; *El principio del placer*, by José Emilio Pacheco . . . the list is nearly endless. In comparison, the voice of the *lector* was heard very little. Today, all that remains are echoes of the memory of his voice.

NINE

The Dominican Republic

Reading Aloud and the Future

————|▪▪|————

The first time I heard a *lector*, I was hiding under a workbench. When I started to work at the factory, I still wasn't a cigar maker, because at that time they wouldn't take children. I started working when I was thirteen. They gave me a job at the Flor de Licey Factory. I had to hide under a workbench to strip leaves and sort them. When the inspectors came, I would hurry up and sneak out, because they didn't want minors working. That's how I heard the *lector* for the first time. He used to read aloud in a corner of the workshop. The year was 1951.

Thus does José Collado Polanco, a cigar worker from Tamboril, a town situated in the province of Santiago de los Caballeros in the Dominican Republic, remember his time in the cigar factory. The region is noted for its idyllic beauty and because it is the heartland of tobacco.

It is unknown exactly when reading aloud arrived in the Dominican Republic from Cuba, and there are few accounts about *lectores*. But what is most interesting is that there is still an active *lector* in that country. Before we learn more about that *lector*, let us listen a bit to what reading aloud was like in decades past.

José Collado Polanco remembers:

I was a cigar maker from 1951 to 1981, and I recall there were several *lectores*: Antonio Martínez, el "Negro Capellán," César Rodríguez, Virgilio Camejo, Cirilo Évora, and Gregorio Comprés. They were all cigar makers except César Rodríguez. They used to read aloud on a little square platform on the side of the workshop. In the morning, from 8:00 to 9:00, they read the news-paper, and in the afternoon, from 1:00 to 2:00, they'd read a novel.

We cigar makers had to do a "task" in order to pay the *lector*. That is, we had to make fifty cigars among us when he read to us for a shift, and a hun-dred cigars when he read for two shifts. That's how we paid him. There were ninety-nine of us working there. They read *El Caribe, El Listín Diario*, and *El Nacional*. What was read was the news. They read very little or no sports. Many short, very superficial novels were read, short novels that took two weeks to read.

The only novel I really remember is *El derecho de nacer*. I remember that one because it was read several times. I don't remember the other ones. Sometimes there were novels we didn't like, and we'd say: "Stop there. Get another one." They brought in a lot of novels and started them, and if we didn't like them, well . . . let's try the other one.

In those days, we came to an agreement among us cigar makers and honestly said what we liked and what we didn't. When we were listening to a novel, we would always end up commenting on what had happened and what was going to happen later on. We always talked about the novel.

Just imagine: we would get to work at 4:00 A.M., sometimes at 3:00 A.M. We had to work a lot, a whole lot, just to survive. We didn't listen to music, because that drives you crazy. The reading really entertained us. The coffee, soup, oatmeal, and cake they used to sell entertained us, too. But we were always crazy about hearing the *lector*. Nobody gets bored when they're waiting for something. We always liked the reading, but later there weren't any more *lectores*. I don't know why.[1]

Manuel Jaques, a cigar maker who for fifty-nine years worked at La Aurora Factory, one of the oldest in the Dominican Republic, situated in the city of Santiago de los Caballeros, recalled:

The *lectores* always kept the workers well informed. They read aloud from all the newspapers, and they read novels.

Conrado Espertini was a great *lector*. He really liked to read, but he passed away. He was a good cigar maker. He was from the capital. He was a versatile *lector*, and we cigar makers really got used to hearing his voice. People from outside also liked to hear his voice. When they walked down adjoining streets, they'd stop and listen to him. Since he read with a microphone, they could hear him. He read in the morning and in the afternoon.

As far as novels go, I remember he read *Los tres mosqueteros* [The Three Musketeers] and many short novels by women. He also read Vargas Vila. But the one I liked the best was *Miguel Strogoff*. The cigar workers were the ones who brought in the novels, or they borrowed them from La Hermandad Cigarrera, a society that was made up of all the cigar workers in the Cibao region.

There was a library there with a lot of variety. They had many books. That library also lent its books to different individuals to take home.

Every cigar maker rolled three cigars to complete the work of the *lector*, because he stopped earning while he was reading. That's why we cigar makers had to compensate him by each chipping in three or four cigars.

After Conrado Espertini, there were other *lectores*, but, honestly, they were the pits; we didn't like them.

The other factory that used to have a *lector* was La Habanera, our competitor. There was a *lector* there, but not in other factories. It seems to me that reading aloud was copied from Cuba. I don't know. But after that, there were no more *lectores* for years.[2]

In 2004, there was a *lector* at La Aurora Factory, where reading aloud had resumed in 1991.[3] What is surprising about the factory's main workshop is that its rows of workbenches are arranged in a horseshoe, just as the tables in the refectories of Benedictine monasteries are laid out. There are five workbenches in each row, and the rows are aligned in such a way that the employees are able to see each other's faces. There are eighty-five cigar makers in the workshop, and, surprisingly, there is a *lector*, but he has neither a platform nor a desk that is exclusively for reading. The *lector* has to sit at one of the desks in the tobacco dispensary, across from the rows of workbenches. Without a platform, however, it is difficult to see the *lector*.

When I arrived at the factory early in the morning on July 22, 2004, the *lector*, William Pichardo, announced that he would read *El Noticiero La Aurora* as a radio announcer would. His voice sounded like that of an announcer or presenter. He immediately picked up *Hoy* and began to read the headlines. Next, he read the news about baseball for twenty minutes or so. After that he read an in-depth article about cell phones, followed by the horoscopes, and he finished by announcing an event that would take place in Santiago de los Caballeros and the town of Licey al Medio.

William Pichardo indicated the following:

By the time I came to the factory, it had been many years since reading aloud had been discontinued here. I got here in 1996. Here they had what they called a "school," where they taught me how to make cigars, but I didn't like it. One day someone came up with the idea, I don't know who, of going back to that culture of reading the newspaper aloud. My supervisor asked me if I liked reading, and I told her I did.

At that time, there were about four guys who wanted to change jobs, and they gave us each a test. They got us a magazine and told us, You choose any passage you want to read to us. We had to read in front of Manuel Jaques, an experienced listener and lifelong cigar maker; Manuel Inoa; Héctor Checo;

and several other supervisors. We each read, and they chose me. They told me, Tomorrow, you're going to read the newspaper for about an hour. Read what's most important, and then later we'll talk about your salary.

I work in the quality-control department. My job is completely separate from reading aloud. Here everything is completely separate. Several years ago, they made me a platform. I used to sit there, and I felt freer, but now I sit at a table in the retail shop. The platform was taken to the factory museum that tourists visit. I'm not happy sitting at the table. On the platform, I felt like I was in control and was the master of all I surveyed. I'd like them to make me a platform so we could go back to the way things used to be, because where I read from now, there are a lot of people walking back and forth.

The reading schedule is usually from 7:30 to 8:15 A.M., but since the newspaper isn't delivered at a specific time, that messes everything up. When it gets here, I pick it up and read. But sometimes the newspaper gets here after 8:00 A.M., and then I don't have time to read anymore, because I have other responsibilities. And if the newspaper doesn't come at all, I don't read.

The only reading shift is in the morning. We get all the national newspapers at the factory. Here we get *Hoy, Listín Diario*, and *Diario Libre*. I always choose *Hoy*, because it's a truly independent newspaper. It's not controlled by government officials, as is the case with certain newspapers that are manipulated and lie to people. I think *Hoy* tells the truth, but there's news that I can't read, because it says something bad about the company. I also can't read news that has to do with sex or news that talks about death or violence. I can't read bad news.

This is a really good company, because they give us classes about the danger of alcoholism and drug abuse. That's why I know what I can and can't read aloud. When I don't read the newspaper, I take it home, read, and explore it. I pick out an article or two and read them aloud the next day. It doesn't matter what day they were published. Either way, I know they didn't read it. They don't have access to print media. They get here at 6:00 A.M. and leave at 5:00 P.M. They don't buy newspapers and they don't watch the news, with all these blackouts we have here. Blackouts here last almost twenty-four hours. That's why it's important to read articles aloud even though they're stale.

When reading aloud was reintroduced, I was told I would be given access to books, poems, and novels, but the workers didn't like them. I started reading a novel or two, but I didn't end up finishing them. They didn't pay attention to the reading. They weren't used to listening to literature. But one time a manager lent me a book for me to read every day; I read it. I did finish that book. There were reflections, readings that nourish the spirit and encourage people who hear the message.

They also like to hear magazine articles. I've read passages and stories here from the magazines *Rumbo, El Ritmo Social, ¡Oh Magazine!* and even *Reader's Digest*. My coworkers also contribute. They bring me all kinds of readings about any phenomenon that has occurred, about things that aren't printed in newspapers, clippings of reflections, and many other things.

As for me, I never rest. I'm always looking for things to tell them about. I always try to read or say something so that they stay with me and really listen. I like to read reflections that lift the spirit, stories that get you right in the heart, stories that lighten the workload, stories that help us forget all the problems we have in this country. It's a shame that we're a country with no real leaders and that we have dysfunctional situations and officials.

I announce all the notices that are posted on the factory walls. I have to keep the employees up to date about all the activities that take place, about training sessions and all sorts of things. I dedicate Mother's Day, Father's Day, Secretary's Day, and all the other days that commemorate someone exclusively to them. I read messages, poems, cards, wishes, and even short compositions that the workers write themselves. I have to read all of that to them. They never take the microphone, maybe because they don't want to lose time from their jobs, or maybe because their supervisor might get after them about it. They sit tight, although, of course, I'm open to dialogue.

The worst thing about my job is the interruptions. Many times, I've lost my concentration, because somebody walks by and yells or says something to me. When I go back to reading, a lot of times I make mistakes, and then they complain. There are several interruptions.

Anyway, I move mountains to do a good job reading all the news, but if something important comes up in the other department I work in, I have to interrupt the reading, and that's as it should be. After all, I read aloud, but I don't work exclusively as a *lector*.

A little over half the employees here are men; the rest are women. When they listen to programming on the radio that's in the retail shop, there are no problems, no disagreements. There's a set schedule for each type of music. In the morning, ballads, boleros, and soft music are played. Starting at 2:00 P.M., we listen to merengue and *bachata* so that people liven up.

When I read aloud, there are disagreements. The girls like you to read them the horoscopes and the latest dirt on celebrities. They also listen very closely to sports, but they aren't that passionate about them.

For the guys, sports are essential. I keep them informed about everything having to do with baseball. I have to give them the statistics from the scheduled games, with each team's pitchers, and I even have to specify if they're left-handed or not. Many times, they want to hear what a certain pitcher's record against another pitcher is. They want to know whether they've batted freely or whether anyone's gotten a run off him so that they can make their own calculations. They're interested in knowing exactly what's going on in the Major Leagues from start to finish.

Baseball is essential, and I'm crazy about it, too. I love to hear what's going on with Pedro Martínez. The cigar makers say that when he wins I get all enthusiastic, and I give details about what happened during the game, but when he loses, they say my attitude changes and I tell them Pedro Martínez lost, and that's it, I don't say anything else. It's a lot of fun. They love to hear my voice. I believe that with all my heart.

As we have seen, reading aloud in the Dominican Republic lacks continuity. According to my informants, reading aloud has never been afforded the space or the discipline it has received in Cuba. As the first interview cited here shows, short novels were read, and if they were not to the audience's taste, they were interrupted immediately. This rarely occurred in Cuba.

Also, the selection of texts has always been in the hands of the *lector* in the Dominican Republic, which suggests not so much a lack of interest as of knowledge on the part of the cigar workers with regard to what is being published around them. Likewise, the lack of enjoyment of novels shows that the audience is not accustomed to listening to a text for a long period. This is not to say that there is no enthusiasm for literature, because, as we have seen, short stories and poems are read aloud. The interruption of reading, or, rather, its lack of continuity and persistence has caused the audience to lose the habit of listening to long books. In the past, however, novels, travel books, history books, and treatises were read. This fact was revealed by a library situated in a hidden corner of the city of Palmar Abajo. Let us visit it.

Palmar Abajo's rolling hills are blanketed in light green grass. Its splendor rivals that of the magical Viñales Valley in Cuba. In the distance, tobacco houses, a type of hut in which the leaves are dried, can be seen. This is the site of one of the oldest factories in the Dominican Republic, the Carbonell Cigar Factory.

Modernity has not made its way to this valley. There are two huts; one is very large and houses the main workshop; a smaller one contains a large wooden table and tobacco presses. There are ten rows of four workbenches each in the main workshop. Very few cigars are rolled; thus, there are no more than ten cigar makers, both men and women. The cigar factory's offices are in a corner of the main workshop, where I found a library. This is the only library that has been preserved in a cigar facility in the Dominican Republic.

"The culture of reading aloud has declined tremendously in this country, especially these days," stated Jorge Carbonell Farina, who has been a cigar maker all his life.[4] His father was one also, from the time he arrived from Spain in 1894. Jorge Carbonell added: "I remember that the best-liked books when there was reading aloud were *El derecho de nacer* and *La madre*.[5] But there hasn't been reading since the 1950s. My father and I used to lend books to the *lectores*. We have a modest library, but it has a variety of books."

In effect, it was a simple library, but it occupied an entire wall. On the shelves I saw entire sets of *Poesías clásicas hispanoamericanas*, *El embrujo de Sevilla*, *Civilización y barbarie*, *Martín Fierro*, volumes of the complete works of José Martí, of Cervantes, of Lope de Vega, Cuban encyclopedias, books by José Asunción Silva, by Rubén Darío, by Santos Chocano, by Andrés Bello, by Hugo and Dumas, books about Simón Bolívar and Benito Juárez, a book of speeches by Joaquín Balaguer, a whole collection of *Historia de la República Dominicana*, *Hostos y Cuba*, the complete works of Pedro Henríquez Ureña, and dozens of titles of topics related to tobacco.

Jorge Carbonell added sadly: "I'm sorry that I never kept a list of what books were read; it was a little of everything. Reading aloud has been lost here and people aren't used to it at all. Nearby, in town, there's a library, but it's practically been destroyed. There are very few books in it. It's open now and then, and people steal the books. They've even stolen books I donated myself."

When I finished my interview, Jorge Carbonell asked me to read "Marcha triunfal," by Rubén Darío, aloud. As I am accustomed to reading viva voce in the classroom, I read with great pleasure. Before I left, he said to me:

You've given me an idea. I'm going to resume reading aloud for the cigar makers to hear. I'm also going to set up a little free school here in the cigar factory. The children can sit at that table in the workshop. Here many poor children don't have a school to go to. They don't even have the means to get to one. At least fifteen of them or more will fit at that table, even if it's a tight squeeze. I'd like to start by reading to them so that they learn.

Astonished, but full of pride and emotion, I asked him: "What are you going to read to them?" Without thinking about it for even two seconds, he answered: "I'm going to start with *La edad de oro*, by José Martí."

I immediately recalled that one of Martí's dreams was that his daughter, María Mantilla, would found a school for girls. He even designed a curriculum for the future school. The Apóstol expressed this in a tender, emotional letter he wrote to her from Cap-Haïtien on April 9, 1895, a month before his death. In the letter, Martí suggests, among other things, that the girls be taught "an explained reading class, by explaining the meaning of words, the Spanish language. No more grammar than that. Children discover grammar through what they read and hear, and that's all that works for them."[6] In that very moment, I realized that my research had concluded.[7]

Epilogue

Over 140 years have passed since reading aloud became an established practice in cigar factories in Cuba. As we have seen, although the practice was banned several times, especially in nineteenth-century colonial Cuba, the institution remains afoot and is currently enjoying great success.

Reading aloud is a traditionally Cuban cultural practice that was exported to Spain, the United States (including Puerto Rico), Mexico, and the Dominican Republic. Thanks to the cigar makers who continued the reading tradition outside of Cuba, thousands of employees have had the opportunity to listen, learn, and delight in the voice of a *lector* who enriched their cultural experience.

In the case of Spain, it is interesting that such a cultural institution was adopted and practiced, especially because it arose in what was then colonial Cuba at a chaotic time in history: just before the Ten Years' War in Cuba and the Glorious Revolution of 1868 in Spain. Reading aloud was very short-lived in Spain because of the early mechanization of the cigar industry at the end of the nineteenth century, labor struggles, and the loss of Cuba at the end of the Spanish-American War in 1898. Nevertheless, although reading aloud was short-lived, as history shows and as has been depicted in fiction, a number of Spaniards made the journey to Cuba and became *lectores*, which demonstrates that the practice enjoyed great support and interest.

In the case of Mexico, reading aloud was instituted successfully in the nineteenth century, but it was banned because it was considered a threat to the owners. Despite the ban and lack of continuity, volunteer *lectores* came forward to go to the factories to read to cigar workers.

In Puerto Rico, there were *lectores* or, rather, *lectoras* of the caliber of Luisa Capetillo, who was a labor leader, writer, and *lectora* not only in her hometown of Arecibo, but also in Florida and New York. However, reading aloud took place in Puerto Rico only during the last decade of the nineteenth century and the first decade of the twentieth.

In Key West and Tampa, reading aloud grew to vast proportions, because it was instituted and continued almost without interruption from the time Cubans first set foot there in 1868 until it was permanently banned in 1931. What is most revealing about the practice in the United States is that the work of the *lectores* allowed cigar makers to have books and newspapers read to them in their own language, and thus they were able to keep their native tongue alive in a foreign land. In addition, and especially due to the reading, several Spanish-language newspapers proliferated, which enriched the United States' cultural life.

In the Dominican Republic, reading aloud was instituted in the Cibao region, but it underwent a series of interruptions. It is the only place outside of Cuba, however, where the practice continues.

Those who established reading aloud in factories for the first time in Havana did so to further an educational agenda: they wanted the cigar workers to learn something while they did manual labor. They had the idea and philosophy of using entertainment to teach, which is why it is not surprising to learn that the first workers' publications in Cuba dealt mostly with literary texts.

What they had in mind was to create the habit of reading. On one hand, the cigar workers were encouraged to read to themselves in the library or any other private place; and on the other hand, an effort was made to keep the audience in the habit of listening to a *lector* reading aloud. When reading aloud was introduced in the workshops, people were more accustomed to listening to someone reading aloud for many reasons: the only texts they could get were newspapers, and the custom of reading aloud at home was firmly ingrained in them. Therefore, people read that way at home or met in public places to hear someone read serialized novels or the latest news.

As I have mentioned, when reading aloud was instituted in Cuba, the level of illiteracy in the tobacco sector was minimal compared with that in other sectors. In addition, cigar makers in Spain, Mexico, Puerto Rico, and the Dominican Republic were exposed much less frequently to culture than were Cuban cigar makers. Thus, it would be erroneous to believe that reading aloud was instituted in cigar facilities simply because people did not know how to read.

Also, the fact that the cigar makers themselves paid for the reading transformed them, to paraphrase French sociologist Pierre Bourdieu, into "agents of their own cultural capital."[1] With literacy campaigns undertaken at the beginning of the 1960s in Cuba, it is easy to show once again that reading aloud is not a direct result of illiteracy.

In fact, as I have demonstrated throughout this study, reading aloud is

EPILOGUE

an activity that is and has always been practiced in educated circles. Consider the current popularity of book clubs in which members choose a book and meet periodically to discuss the text in question. Their activity is sociable and productive, but very little reading aloud is done. The text is merely discussed. Reading aloud continues to take place when authors present their books or other writings at clubs, institutions, or bookstores, where audiences, usually educated, are eager to listen.

In educational settings, such as classrooms, the time devoted to reading aloud has decreased drastically over the years. Reading to oneself has also decreased, because people read electronic fragments, not complete texts, on their computers. Therefore, the reading aloud that takes place in Cuban cigar facilities not only continues a tradition that has been in effect since time immemorial, but also entertains and teaches a huge segment of society, which, it goes without saying, is well read, writes well, and listens well.

Through the years, the profession of *lector* has changed. In the beginning, *lectores* were cigar makers who took turns reading to their coworkers. Later, the profession of *lector* was established—that is, the person who read aloud was from outside the cigar facility and came in exclusively to read. Most of those *lectores* were journalists, educators, and even politicians, as was the case with a *lector* in the United States. Almost all practiced their profession as *lector* part time. A few were full-time *lectores*, usually reading aloud at a number of factories.

As I have mentioned, the *lector* was always compensated by way of the fee the cigar makers paid him, whether directly in cash or by way of producing extra cigars to make up the salary for the one who did the reading. When radio came on the scene, it was thought that it would be the end of the profession of *lector*, but such was not the case. Rather, a rivalry began between the radio and the human voice.

After Fidel Castro came to power in 1959, the *lector* became a government employee with a fixed salary and a set schedule of eight hours per day, although reading time remained approximately two and a half hours.

Since reading aloud was instituted, *lectores* have played an important role in the dissemination of culture. They have always been the linchpin of communication between the microcosm of the factory and the cultural, political, and social world outside the workplace. *Lectores* in Cuba today do an extraordinary job as cultural facilitators, because they lead countless activities that take place on the factory platform. Therefore, their responsibilities have increased at the same time that their profession has become indispensable.

There has always been an intimate relationship between cigars and literature. On one hand, the cigar has been venerated by dozens of writers from all over the world in theatrical works, poems, short stories, and novels. On the other hand, great classic works and their authors, as well as a variety of lesser-known writers, have been represented on cigar labels in lithographs that were first used to decorate boxes, packs, and bundles of Havana cigars in the nineteenth century. The names of cigars (and even of factories) are intertexts themselves; that is, they sport the names of characters from literature, titles of works, or simply the names of authors. A few examples include Don Quijote, Romeo y Julieta, Montecristo, Los Tres Mosqueteros, Cervantes, Shakespeare, Byron, Twain, Dante, Socrates, Walter Scott, Dumas, Sancho Panza, Jean Valjean, and Sherlock Holmes. But of everything that has been seen, read, and heard in cigar facilities, why have *Les Misérables* and *The Count of Monte Cristo* been the books that listeners have responded to most passionately?

An unforgettable passage of *Les Misérables* describes the night Jean Valjean, accompanied by little Cosette, is pursued by Javert. Jean and the girl, thanks to Father Fauchelevent, who is willing to give them lodging and hide them so the nuns will not see them and the pursuer will not find them, take refuge in a convent situated in an alley. Jean Valjean and Cosette stay on to live in the convent, and Father Fauchelevent is amply compensated by Jean Valjean: "Old Fauchelevent, unconscious though he remained of his celebrity, was well rewarded for his good deed: in the first place, because it gave him great satisfaction; secondly, because he had much less work to do; and thirdly because he was able to smoke three times as much as in the past, and with a particular relish, since it was Monsieur Madeleine [Jean Valjean] who paid for the tobacco."[2]

What is most surprising is that life in the convent represents one of the opportunities Jean Valjean has to transform himself into an upstanding man or, rather, a better man. To Jean, jail and the convent are very similar; both are places of captivity. He recalls that the other convicts were able to live anonymously, since "they lived without names, were known only by numbers and to some extent turned into numbers themselves, eyes and voices lowered, hair cropped, subject to the lash and to constant humiliation."[3]

Still, it is in jail where he learns "to read, write, and calculate."[4] He thinks thus of jail and the convent: "On one side the whispered avowal of crimes committed; on the other side, the open confession of faults—such faults!— and such crimes!"[5] These reflections are what cause him to change: "In the first, only chains of metal, in the second the chains of faith. And what came out of these places? From the first a vast malediction, a gnashing of teeth, in hatred, the evil of despair, a rage against all human kind, and a mockery of Heaven; from the second, blessedness and love."[6] And although he is pursued for the rest of his life, Jean Valjean strives only to show love and compassion to others and survives thanks to all he has left: forgiveness, faith, and hope.

In *The Count of Monte Cristo*, Edmond Dantès is unjustly incarcerated for a crime he did not commit. Once in the penitentiary, another prisoner, an *abbé*, shows him where there is a treasure that will make him wealthy so that Dantès can avenge himself on the enemies who have imprisoned him.

His life in the penitentiary transforms him. There he learns to take revenge but also to forgive. In fact, for two years, Dantès learns from his teacher, the *abbé*, who tells him: "Human knowledge is quite limited. When you've learned mathematics, physics, history and the three or four living languages I speak, you'll know everything I do. It won't take more than two years to teach you all that."[7] For two years, Dantès studies with the *abbé*, who instructs him through the spoken word; they have no books. Within six months, Dantès learns to speak Spanish, English, and German.

But the most important aspect is that during those two years of study, neither Dantès nor the *abbé* thinks of escaping from the penitentiary. Studying is transformative, especially for the disciple. This is summarized at the end of the novel when Dantès writes a letter that is read aloud: "The sum of all human wisdom will be contained in these two words: Wait and hope."[8]

But what made these two extremely long novels the cigar makers' favorites at a time when there was so little tradition of reading aloud? Here the listening audience has the last word.

Reading aloud in cigar facilities is a unique cultural practice that has enriched generations of workers while they are busy creating something that is exclusively done by hand. This is precisely why reading aloud has continued to take place, because the action of rolling cigars is a preindustrial job that transports us to times long past, when cigar-making machinery did not exist. Nevertheless, the preservation of the habit of listening among cigar workers has not been easy, especially among young people, who are less accustomed to listening to a text being read aloud. This is currently one of the greatest challenges faced by *lectores*. Thus, the *lector* is an artist who must find interesting material and perfect the manner in which reading aloud is conducted.

In San Juan y Martínez, the small town where I met Santos Segundo Domínguez Mena in 2003, I visited La Caridad Leaf-stripping Plant, the very place in which he first listened to a *lector* as a child. In the workshop were at least eighty women seated in rows of eight workbenches. The platform of the *lector* was a small, modest desk with a tabletop microphone. Ángel Borges, the *lector*, introduced me to his audience and, unexpectedly, asked me to read to them from a book he handed to me. It was *El llano en llamas* [The burning plain and other stories], the highly successful book of short stories written by my Mexican compatriot Juan Rulfo. Since the short story "¡Diles que no me maten!" ["Tell them not to kill me!"] is my favorite, I decided to do a brief introduction about Rulfo and the story. But no one was looking at me. The workers all had their eyes glued to the tobacco leaves.

I could tell by their facial expressions, however, that they were paying attention to what I was saying, and once I started reading, they listened to every word with the devotion of saints. With every word I uttered, they knit their brows, or nodded, or shook their heads, or blinked. Never in my life had I been before such an attentive audience. When I finished reading, they all looked up. I could see in their eyes that they were truly grateful. As for me, naught but my tears could express how rewarded I felt. I was speechless. Then I realized that for a moment, I had become the subject of my study.

A few days later I left Cuba, still intrigued by why *Les Misérables* had been Santos Segundo Domínguez Mena's and his audience's favorite novel. When I got home, I reread that novel. I was surprised by the final lines, which I had completely forgotten. Jean Valjean dies happy, and his remains are interred in a tomb covered with a bare rock. There is no engraved epitaph on it, but years earlier, someone had written in pencil:

> Il dort. Quoique le sort fût pour lui bien étrange,
> Il vivait. Il mourut quand il n'eut plus son ange;
> La chose simplement d'elle-même arriva,
>   Comme la nuit se fait lorsque le jour s'en va.[9]

This has been translated into Spanish:

> Duerme. La suerte persiguióle ruda:
> murió al perder la prenda de su alma.
> Larga la expiación, la pena aguda
> fue; y así obtuvo la celeste palma.[10]

And into English:

> He sleeps. Fate pursued him cruelly:
> He died, his soul's treasure gone.
> Long his atonement, sharp his pain truly
> was; and thereby he earned the sacred palm.[11]

Without giving it much further thought, my intuition told me it was necessary and imperative that I begin to tell the story of Santos Segundo Domínguez Mena and the rest of the *lectores* who were so greatly admired by "an honest man / From where the palm tree grows."

NOTES

———|—■—|———

INTRODUCTION

1. Interview with author, May 31, 2003.
2. Quoted in Frenk, *Entre la voz*, 84–85. The sonnet by Quevedo and the stanza by Sor Juana were translated into English by Patti Firth, as are all subsequent poetry translations in this book unless otherwise noted.
3. Martí, *Obras completas*, 5: 417.
4. See the following works: Bahloul, *Lecturas precarias*; Bourdieu, *Capital cultural*; Chartier, *Cultura escrita*; idem, *El orden de los libros*; *Practiques de la lecture* and *Sociedad y escritura en la edad moderna*. See also Chevalier, *Lectura y lectores*; Coelho, *Problemática da leitura*; Coleman, *Public Reading*; Curran, *Grace before Meals*; Darnton, *The Forbidden Bestsellers*; Fish, *Is There a Text in This Class?*; Fornet, *El libro en Cuba*; González Acosta, *Joyas de papel*; González Sánchez, *Homo viator, homo scribens*; Hoggart, *The Uses of Literacy*; Litvak, *Musa libertaria*; Lyons, *Readers and Society*; Manguel, *A History of Reading*; Martínez Martín, *Lectura y lectores*; McKitterick, *The Uses of Literacy*; Ong, *Oralidad y escritura*; Ortega et al., *Conquista y contraconquista*; Peroni, *Historias de lectura*; Petit, *Lecturas del espacio íntimo*; Poblete, *Literatura chilena*; and Webb, *The British Working Class Reader*.

CHAPTER 1

1. Quoted in Rivero Muñiz and Piedra-Bueno, *Pequeña antología del tabaco*, 63.
2. Nelson, "From 'Listen, Lordings,'" 111.
3. See The Holy Rule of Saint Benedict, http://www.kansasmonks.org/RuleOfStBenedict.html; accessed December 23, 2008.
4. Ibid.
5. Eckenstein, *Women under Monasticism*, 222, 237.
6. Ong, *Oralidad y escritura*, 74, 113.

7. Quoted in Frenk, *Entre la voz*, 11.

8. A number of critics have alluded to the prologue of *Celestina*. See Chevalier, *Lectura y lectores*, 322; Frenk, *Entre la voz*, 26; and Gilman, *La España de Fernando de Rojas*, 322.

9. Quoted in Frenk, *Entre la voz*, 26; original emphasis.

10. Cervantes, *Don Quixote*, 290.

11. Based on a study by Michel Moner, Margit Frenk posits this idea; see Frenk, *Entre la voz*, 22.

12. Chartier, "Reading Matter and 'Popular' Reading," 275.

13. Chartier, *Sociedad y escritura*, 140.

14. Nelson, "From 'Listen, Lordings,'" 113–114.

15. Ibid., 116

16. *Diccionario de la lengua española*, 21st ed.

17. Foucault, *Discipline and Punish*, 121–122.

18. Rivero Muñiz, "La lectura," 195.

19. *Diccionario de la lengua española*, 21st ed.

20. Foucault, *Discipline and Punish*, 149.

21. Bermúdez, "Las leyes," 146.

22. Martínez, *Lectura y lectores*, 186.

23. Lyons, "New Readers in the Nineteenth Century," 313.

24. String literature (*literatura de cordel*) "refers to the way booklets were often suspended from lines (*cordel* means 'cord' or 'string') stretched between two posts" (Slater, *Stories on a String*, xiv). "The Iberian chapbook flowered in the sixteenth century when the ties between Spain and Portugal were particularly close. . . . Those printed compositions—known as *pliegos sueltos* in Spain, *folhas volantes* in Portugal—were originally a catchall for traditional and new ballads by known authors (*romances vulgares*) as well as other forms such as *bailes*, *xácaras*, and *villancicos*. Many of the first booklets to appear in the streets of Madrid and Lisbon dealt with historical subjects. Toward the beginning of the seventeenth century, however, the number of nontraditional themes increases. Some stories are pirated editions of ballads by well-known poets and playwrights such as Góngora or the Portuguese Gil Vicente. Others are clearly imitative 'Moorish' stories, exotic adventure ballads, or burlesque treatments of assorted rogues and ruffians" (ibid., 8). Also see Chartier, *Sociedad y escritura*; Marco, *Literatura popular en España*; and Neuberg, *Chapbooks*.

25. Lyons, "New Readers in the Nineteenth Century," 335.

26. Hugo, *Les Misérables*, 98.

27. See González Pérez, *Journalism*; González Stephan, *La historiografía literaria*; Poblete, *Literatura chilena*; Ramos, *Desencuentros*; Rotker, *Fundación de una escritura*; Sommer, *Foundational Fictions*.

28. F. Portuondo, *Historia*, 381–382.

29. Hero de Neiva's case was not unique. Other slaves, such as Juan Francisco

Manzano, had been publishing since 1821. However, these were extraordinary cases. See Duque de Estrada, *Explicación de la doctrina cristiana*; U. Martínez Carmenate, *Juan Francisco Manzano*.

30. For a thorough study of the origins and developments of these societies, see Quiroz, "Orígenes de la sociedad civil en Cuba."

31. Rivero Muñiz and Piedra-Bueno, *Pequeña antología del tabaco*, 291.

32. Saturnino Martínez (together with Segundo Álvarez, of similar working-class background) became a high-ranking Mason. Masons at the time advocated education of the individual. See Alexander, *A History*; Aramburu, *La masonería cubana*; and Friera, "Historia de un emigrante." I am grateful to Alfonso Quiroz for having told me about Aramburu's book.

33. Rivero Muñiz, "La lectura en las tabaquerías," 192. Rivero Muñiz's source of information is Fernando Ortiz's *Contrapunteo cubano del tabaco y del azúcar* (127) [Cuban counterpoint: Tobacco and sugar]. See also Ortiz, "Los negros esclavos," 243. It seems, however, that reading aloud took place in the early 1800s. The Havana Society supervised a hospice that included a Casa de Beneficencia [almshouse] for the indigent women and vagabonds and the Casa de Educandas [school for poor and orphaned girls] for the care and education of white, poor, orphan girls. The Casa also had fifty-four slaves by 1805. The Casa de Beneficencia generated a "considerable income from the manufacture of cigars" because the girls rolled the cigars for the royal lottery (Shafer, *The Economic Societies*, 292–294). Reading aloud at the Casa is not mentioned by Shafer; nevertheless, this practice probably took place while the girls either rolled the cigars or while they carried out some other manual activity.

34. Webb, *The British Working Class Reader*, 34.

35. Rivero Muñiz, *Tabaco*, 2: 270–271.

36. Quoted in González, *El bello habano*, 232.

37. Curran, *Grace before Meals*, 12–13.

38. Eckenstein, *Women under Monasticism*, 222, 237.

39. Cabrera Infante, *Holy Smoke*, 54.

40. Moratín's father, Nicolás, was a lawyer and professor of poetry at the Imperial College and had his son, Leandro, apprenticed to a jeweler so he could develop his artistic skills. See Gies, *Nicolás Fernández de Moratín*, 13–17, 23, 29, 46.

41. J. Portuondo, "*La Aurora*," 41.

42. Ibid., 40.

43. Rivero Muñiz, "La lectura en las tabaquerías," 213; the order was published June 8, 1866, in *Gaceta de la Habana*, the official government newspaper.

44. Fornet, *El libro en Cuba*, 190.

45. For the complex issues of separatism, anarchism, reformism, autonomism, associationism, and Masonic lodges before, during, and after the Ten Years' War, see Aramburu, *La masonería cubana*; Casanovas, *Bread, or Bullets!*;

Quiroz, "Loyalist Overkill"; Rivero Muñiz, *Tabaco*; Stubbs, *Tabaco en la periferia*; and Thomas, *Cuba*.

46. F. Portuondo, *Historia*, 434.

47. Maeztu, *Autobiografía*, 59.

48. Ibid., 59-60.

49. Stubbs, *Tabaco en la periferia*, 102.

50. Ibid., 113.

51. Quesada Monge, "Anarquismo y feminismo."

52. Rivero Muñiz, "La lectura en las tabaquerías," 220-221.

CHAPTER 2

1. Emilia Pardo Bazán (1851-1921) was a literary critic, essayist, novelist, and short story writer. She was the founder of several Spanish literary journals and wrote hundreds of articles for Latin American newspapers. Pardo Bazán was also a professor at the Universidad Central (Spain). *La tribuna* is one of her first novels. Faustina Sáez de Melgar also wrote a novel based on a woman cigar maker: *Rosa la cigarrera de Madrid*. A twentieth-century Spanish novel that mentions the institution of the reader was written by Alberto Insúa: *Humo, dolor, placer*.

2. Pardo Bazán, *The Tribune of the People*, 71; original emphasis.

3. Quiroga, *El habano al rojo vivo*, 19.

4. Pérez Vidal, *España en la historia del tabaco*, 251.

5. Mérimée, *Carmen*, 569.

6. Ibid., 571.

7. Ibid., 571-572.

8. Pérez Vidal, *España en la historia del tabaco*, 258. None of the most recent studies of the history and culture of cigar factories in Spain mention reading aloud, with the exception of the study by Pérez Vidal. See Baena Luque, *Las cigarreras sevillanas*; Candela Soto, *Cigarreras madrileñas*.

9. Pardo Bazán, *The Tribune of the People*, 66.

10. Ibid., 69.

11. Ibid., 66.

12. Pérez Vidal, *España en la historia del tabaco*, 284.

13. Work started at the factory in Alicante at the beginning of the nineteenth century in an old building that had been a poorhouse, known as "Casa de Misericordia"; the factory in La Coruña was also started at the beginning of the nineteenth century and functioned with few personnel: 120 workers in the building which had once been the Arsenal de la Palloza, located on the outskirts of the city, and which was known as the Almacén General de Víveres. The factory in Santander was opened temporarily in 1835, in a room in the civilian hospital building, but in 1838, it was moved to an old convent that had belonged to the

Sisters of the Order of St. Clare, and which had also been used as a military barracks. The factory in Gijón has a more interesting story behind it. In 1837, plans
got under way for the Augustinian nuns to move out of the convent as soon
as possible so that the factory could occupy the space. It was not until March
2, 1843, that the last Mass was said in this convent and the factory was opened
with 1,200 women working there. The factory in Bilbao was established in a
place called Santucho, in Begoña, a few kilometers from the capital. This factory
took advantage of a four-story building that had been built as a refuge and that
during the war had been used as military barracks; the factory opened on July
1, 1878. The factory in Logroño was the last to open, but was set up in a building with a long history. In the sixteenth century, it was a monastery occupied
by the Brothers of Mercy; later, it served as a military hospital, a warehouse, an
arsenal, office building, barracks, etc., and was not turned into a factory until
1890 (Pérez Vidal, *España en la historia del tabaco*, 239–246).

14. Pardo Bazán, *The Tribune of the People*, 70.

15. Pérez Vidal, *España en la historia del tabaco*, 259.

16. Pardo Bazán, *The Tribune of the People*, 84.

17. Ibid., 83.

18. Ibid., 84.

19. Ibid., 88.

20. Ibid., 86–87.

21. Ibid., 84.

22. Ibid., 87.

23. Ibid., 88.

24. Ibid., 105.

25. Ibid., 103.

26. Ibid., 104.

27. Ibid., 85.

28. Ibid., 90–91.

29. Epigraph in Pérez Vidal, *España en la historia del tabaco*, 261.

30. Ibid., 257.

31. Mérimée, *Carmen*, 571.

32. Ellis indicates that Mérimée created a stereotype, which Louÿs then utilized to describe the "bad Sevillian *cigarrera*." With this in mind, Ellis made his
visit to the factory in Seville. See *The Soul of Spain*, 88–89. The inside of the factory is also depicted later by Armando Palacio Valdés in *La hermana San Sulpicio*, but here the cigar workers are depicted almost identically to those described
by Mérimée: seductive, dressed in rags, making noise, etc.; see 204–208.

33. Ellis, *The Soul of Spain*, 88–89.

34. In the old factory in Seville (prior to the nineteenth century), when someone was caught stealing tobacco, a security guard who would arrest the cigar maker

was immediately summoned. Once the supervisor learned what had occurred, the detainee's statement was taken, and he was transferred to the jail inside the factory, where he was held incommunicado. While the statement was being taken, the factory guards and one of the most trusted gatekeepers went to search the home of the accused. Once there, they gathered all tobacco he had in his home, if any was found, and seized his belongings in order to pay the costs associated with his stay in jail. During all of this, the factory doors were kept locked in order to prevent anyone from escaping and running to warn those at the home of the accused. If the number of stolen cigars was few, the accused might be freed on the condition that he was never to return to the factory, but if the amount was over two ounces, he could be sentenced to up to five years in prison. There was a jail right inside the factory, and the jailer had the task of cleaning it and tending the prisoners without abusing them (Pérez Vidal, *España en la historia del tabaco*, 249–251).

35. In *The Tribune of the People*, the employee who steals does so out of need: at home, her husband beats her if she does not bring him cigars. Thus, Pardo Bazán portrays domestic violence and, in this case, the injustice suffered by this woman who is forced to obey patriarchal laws at home and government laws in the factory. In the end, the woman is the one who loses everything, as she is dismissed from her job at the factory.

36. Pardo Bazán, *The Tribune of the People*, 127.

37. Ibid., 137.

38. Ibid., 205.

39. Ibid., 104; original emphasis.

40. See Baena Luque, *Las cigarreras sevillanas*; Candela Soto, *Cigarreras madrileñas*.

41. Pérez Vidal, *España en la historia del tabaco*, 285–286.

42. See Ferreiro and Munilla, *Las cigarreras*. The operetta depicts the transformation of manual labor to mechanized workshops, which led to labor struggles within the Spanish cigar industry at the end of the nineteenth century.

CHAPTER 3

1. Campbell and Porter, *The Cigar Industry of Tampa, Florida*, 127.

2. *Tobacco Leaf*, January 17, 1885. In 1860, the population of Key West was 2,832; in 1870, 5,061; and by 1890, 18,080. See Westfall, *Key West*, 16.

3. Castellanos, *Motivos de Cayo Hueso*, 141.

4. The *voluntarios* were organized militias comprising both loyalist Spaniards and Cubans. Their existence led to loyalist excesses and persecution of creole reformists and separatists alike. See Quiroz, "Loyalist Overkill."

5. Westfall, *Key West*, 22; F. Portuondo, *Historia*, 431.

6. Castellanos, *Motivos de Cayo Hueso*, 141.

7. Gálvez, *Tampa*, 167.

8. Castellanos, *Motivos de Cayo Hueso*, 182–183.

9. Hugo, *Oeuvres complètes*, 44: 495–497. I am grateful to Roberto González Echevarría and Giancarlo Paolillo, who helped me translate this letter from the French into Spanish.

10. Martí, *Obras completas*, 4: 300. This quotation from José Martí was translated by Patti Firth, as are all subsequent translations of Martí unless otherwise noted.

11. Ibid., 5: 352.

12. Quoted in ibid., 4: 399.

13. Ibid.

14. Ibid., 4: 398.

15. Ibid., 4: 400.

16. Castellanos, *Motivos de Cayo Hueso*, 157–158, 164.

17. Martí, *Obras completas*, 4: 415.

18. Poyo, *"With All, and for the Good of All,"* 42. I would like to express my gratitude to Prof. Gerald E. Poyo for his kind advice when I was writing the Spanish manuscript.

19. El Grito de Yara was the declaration of war for Cuban independence that took place on October 10, 1868. Carlos Manuel de Céspedes, the leader of the movement, proclaimed Cuba's independence from Spain, freed his slaves, and included them in his armed forces.

20. Poyo, *"With All, and for the Good of All,"* 56.

21. Martí, *Obras completas*, 4: 301–302.

22. Poyo, *"With All, and for the Good of All,"* 81.

23. Martí, *Obras completas*, 5: 54.

24. Poyo, *"With All, and for the Good of All,"* 87.

25. Ibid., 92.

26. Ibid.

27. Martí, *Our America by José Martí*, 249.

28. Martí, *Obras completas*, 4: 267; Rivero Muñiz, *The Ybor City Story*, 54.

29. Rivero Muñiz, *The Ybor City Story*, 51.

30. Martí, *Our America by José Martí*, 262.

31. In Rivero Muñiz, *The Ybor City Story*, 52.

32. In Castellanos, *Motivos de Cayo Hueso*, 253–254.

33. Ibid., 263.

34. Ibid., 163.

35. Martí, *Obras completas*, 5: 43.

36. Castellanos, *Motivos de Cayo Hueso*, 268–271.

37. Martí, *Obras completas*, 3: 191.

38. See letter dated October 27, 1894, in ibid., 3: 310.

39. Martí, *Obras completas*, 5: 69.

40. Pierre Bourdieu suggests interpreting the social world in such a way that

human beings are seen as "agents" who construct social space. The social world is not forever static, because the agents of which it is composed are not forever static. The "occupation" of human beings is what constructs the social world: some are "apprentices," others are "teachers," and still others are "apprentice-teachers." The occupation is "capital," which results from the combination of a variety of types of capital and grants to individuals entrance into the social world. See *Capital cultural*, 30–33.

41. Martí, *Obras completas*, 5: 449–450.

42. In Alpízar Leal, *Documentos inéditos*, 51.

43. Martí, *Obras completas*, 4: 293.

44. Ibid.

45. One of the few accounts of the *lectores* in Key West in the early twentieth century can be found in Kathryn Hall Proby's *Mario Sánchez*, 23–25. Sánchez's father, Pedro, was a *lector* and is depicted in Mario's carving *The Reader and the Cigar Makers* (1963).

46. Martí, *Obras completas*, 5: 66.

47. Ibid., 3: 13.

CHAPTER 4

1. It is quite possible that this is the novel *La bête humaine*. I can find no translation into Spanish of a novel by Zola with the name *La canalla* and the correct context. I gratefully acknowledge the assistance of Noël Valis and Bettina Lerner, who suggested it was possibly a translation into Spanish of *La bête humaine*.

2. *Tampa Morning Tribune*, December 19, 22, 1903 ; *La Revista*, no. 19 (1903), 121–123.

3. García Márquez, *Chronicle of a Death Foretold*, 50.

4. Mormino and Pozzetta, *The Immigrant World of Ybor City*, 50.

5. In Rivero Muñiz, *The Ybor City Story*, 12–13. Unless otherwise specified, information about Tampa comes from this exceptional study.

6. Ibid., 25.

7. Gálvez, *Tampa*, 159.

8. Mormino and Pozzetta, *The Immigrant World of Ybor City*, 50.

9. Pino City later changed its name to West Tampa.

10. Mormino and Pozzetta, *The Immigrant World of Ybor City*, 81–82.

11. Epigraph from Rivero Muñiz and Piedra-Bueno, *Pequeña antología del tabaco*, 70. For more detailed information regarding Martí's presence in Tampa, see Mañach, *Martí*, 269–277.

12. Gerald E. Poyo points out that, starting in the 1880s, Martí called on his compatriots in the exile community to speak of the marked social divisions that existed among them. See *"With All, and for the Good of All,"* 81.

13. In Rivero Muñiz, *The Ybor City Story*, 51.

14. Martí, *Our America by José Martí*, 249–250.

15. This was an observance of the twentieth anniversary of the killing of eight medical students who were executed by the Spaniards in Cuba.

16. In Medina, "The Tampa Cubans," 636.

17. Martí, *Obras completas*, 4: 297.

18. Rivero Muñiz, *The Ybor City Story*, 88, 97.

19. Ibid., 95.

20. Ronning, *José Martí*, 19–51.

21. Gálvez, *Tampa*, 139.

22. Ibid., 140.

23. *Tampa Tribune*, February 10, 1890.

24. Roberto González Echevarría traces the steps of Gálvez y Delmonte as a historian and baseball player in the highly interesting book *The Pride of Havana*.

25. Gálvez, *Tampa*, 134–138, 165.

26. I gratefully acknowledge the valuable assistance of Maggie Doherty of the University of South Florida with my research of the Tampa press. I also would like to express my deepest gratitude to Paul Eugen Camp, of the University of South Florida's Special Collections, for his enormous assistance in regard to Florida bibliography.

27. Gálvez, *Tampa*, 139.

28. Ibid., 94.

29. Ibid.

30. "Memoria del Centro Español," 1896.

31. Gálvez, *Tampa*, 170.

32. Ibid., 159.

33. Mormino and Pozzetta, *The Immigrant World of Ybor City*, 177–196.

34. "Memoria del Centro Español," 1893. The Board of Directors discussed one of the projects undertaken by the Education Division: "With the goal of establishing a small library, we wrote a memorandum to all our esteemed members, encouraging them to help with such a commendable enterprise, to which many of them responded by donating several works of a variety of types, some of significant worth, and in harmony with our literary needs" (6).

35. Gálvez, *Tampa*, 169–177.

36. Ibid., 179.

37. Ibid., 174.

38. Ibid., 168–169.

39. Ibid., 169.

40. Ibid., 140.

41. *Tampa Morning Tribune*, February 10, 1890.

42. Gálvez, *Tampa*, 186–187.

43. Martí, *Obras completas,* 4: 413.

44. Mormino and Pozzetta, "The Reader Lights the Candle," 16.

45. *Tampa Morning Tribune,* November 4, 1902.

46. *Tampa Tribune,* November 4, 1902.

47. Méndez, *Ciudad de Cigars,* 94.

48. *Tampa Morning Tribune,* November 8, 1902.

49. Ibid.

50. Mormino and Pozzetta, "The Reader Lights the Candle," 16.

51. Ibid.

52. I would like to thank Rolena Adorno for acquainting me with this term. According to this concept, someone publishes erroneous information (voluntarily or involuntarily), and that same information is repeated by others who think the information is correct.

53. *Tampa Morning Tribune,* April 1, 1903.

54. Ibid.

55. Ibid., November 6, 1902.

56. On September 6, 1907, an emotional letter written by Milián to the editor of the *Tampa Tribune* was published. In it, he addresses the issue of the burial of an indigent man. He explains how concerned he is, because he believes that the poor deserve to be buried in a proper place. And he adds: "I am a poor man, who has a large family to support, and have nothing in the world but my personal work to support six children. I challenge anyone, be he American, Spaniard, Cuban, Italian, negro or white, who has called at the door of my home or office for help during the six terms I have served as mayor of this city and who would say that I have not assisted or helped him with medicines, doctor bills, cash, merchandise or in any other way; hereby I call upon the citizens of West Tampa to answer in the columns of your paper when have I denied them help?"

57. *Tampa Tribune,* November 13, 1902.

58. *Tampa Morning Tribune,* November 14, 1902.

59. Ibid., March 3, 1901.

60. Ibid.

61. *Tampa Tribune,* March 3, 1901.

62. *Tampa Morning Tribune,* April 2, 1901.

63. Mormino and Pozzetta, *The Immigrant World of Ybor City,* 107.

64. Mormino and Pozzetta, "The Reader Lights the Candle," 15.

65. *Tampa Tribune,* February 10, 1904.

66. Ibid.

67. Ibid., September 25, 1904.

68. Social-Ethnic Study of Ybor City, Tampa, Florida, 66–67. Photocopy of a typescript prepared by the Tampa Office of the Federal Writers' Project of the Works Progress Administration, Archives of Oral History of Florida, University of South Florida. The material was gathered in 1935.

69. Taken from an article published by Octavio J. Monteressi in *La Traducción*, November 17, 1922. I am grateful to Bettie Pérez, granddaughter of Ramón Valdespino, for her great hospitality in Tampa, the copy of this article, that of the de la Campa article in note 71 that I quote, as well as for important information about the life of her grandfather.

70. Bryan, "A Study of the Latin Press in Ybor City."

71. *El Heraldo Dominical*, November 19, 1922, following the death of Ramón Valdespino. This part of my study, unless otherwise specified, is attributed to that article.

72. Ibid.

73. Ibid.

74. Bryan, "A Study of the Latin Press in Ybor City."

75. Printed on page 1, next to the name of the newspaper, in the April 6, 1929, edition.

76. *Heraldo Dominical*, November 19, 1922.

77. The poem appeared in *Tampa Ilustrado* on October 19, 1912. It was translated from Spanish to Italian by Eulalia Valdespino:

Of art the inspiration most sublime
roamed free, not knowing its destination,
attribute of the soul with light divine,
without finding its place in the Creation.

Rome arises in a haze of glory
Its legions bringing science through the sword,
And under its bright banners is the word
which starts the pages of our History.

Full tired of power and of conquests now,
at truce with desire and anxiety,
it sees the crown upon its artists' brow,
immortal diadem of Artistry!

Oh Italy! Supreme Art shines its light
upon your ideas and on your greatness!
Before you the world bows, as is your right,
and constantly exclaims: "May you be blessed!"

78. The poem is found in the Valdespino family archives. Bettie Pérez generously gave me a copy.

79. Mormino and Pozzetta, *The Immigrant World of Ybor City*, 50, 109.

80. *Diario de Tampa*, September 25, 1908.

81. Ibid., December 5, 1908; original emphasis.

82. Ibid., September 25, 1908.

83. Ibid.

84. *Tampa Morning Tribune*, May 5, 1903.

85. *Tampa Tribune*, June 27, 1905. Part of the speech given by Sandalio Romaella was published in *La Revista: Semanario Hispano Cubano* (no. 27, year III) and edited by *lector* Eliseo Pérez. In his speech, Romaella said: "I am a Spaniard, but I have always advocated for Cuban independence, as I have for the independence of all the peoples in the world. For that reason, I have always been the target of the diatribes of my fellow countrymen, but I have never been able to stop feeling this revolutionary spirit, which controls my every action and guides me along the path of civilization and progress" (209).

86. *Tampa Tribune*, May 21, 1904.

87. Ibid., May 14 and May 21, 1904.

88. Ibid., June 3, 1904.

89. Ibid., February 10, 1906.

90. Ibid., November 17, 1906.

91. Ibid., February 5, 1907.

92. Ibid.

93. Ibid., August 5 and August 6, 1908.

94. *Diario de Tampa*, July 7, 1909.

95. Gálvez, *Tampa*, 190.

96. *Diario de Tampa*, February 6, 1911.

97. It was common for players of *la bolita* to bet on numbers based on their dreams. This was done using a numerological dream interpretation system called *la charada china*, which associated animals, persons, or objects with specific numbers. For example, if someone dreamed about or saw a monkey riding in a street car, the dream or sighting was converted to numbers; the person would bet on 34 for monkey and 45 for streetcar in *la bolita*. *El bolitero* carried a *charada* book with him at all times to help potential customers. The book was small enough to fit in his shirt pocket and contained numbers 1 to 100 and their respective meanings (Eddie Contreras, interview with author, December, 7, 2007). I would also like to thank Jorge Pérez López for having explained to me about *la bolita*.

98. *La Revista: Semanario Hispano Cubano*, no. 42 (December 16, 1904): 339–340.

99. *La Revista: Semanario de Literatura, Ciencias, Artes y Sport*, no. 8 (October 4, 1903): 43–44.

100. Ibid., no. 1 (August 16, 1903): 1.

101. Ibid., no. 22 (May 27, 1905): 171.

102. Ibid., no. 36 (September 9, 1904): 290.

103. Ibid., no. 7 (February 7, 1904). This issue says that "anyone wishing to

purchase single issues of *La Revista* may contact Mr. J. M. Leal in West Tampa; Mr. Luis García in Ellinger; and the newspaper's print shop in Ybor" (51). Luis García worked in the editing department.

104. In his memoirs, written toward the end of his life, Arthur D. Massolo notes the following: "Ybor-City was in those days [ca. 1907] completely separated from Tampa. It was almost a different city, where no English was spoken and Spanish was the official language. . . . One thing that pleased me immensely was the fact that all cigarmakers were well organized in a labor union which took due and honest care of their relations with the manufacturers who were also of latin extraction. In each and every factory, day after day for three long hours, from a platform raised high in the center of the *galea* [*sic*] working room, a reader provided with powerful lungs and a vibrant voice, for amplifiers were not known, gave the workers, in correct Castilian, the news of the day and read what many writers had written on social problems. No wonder then that I was confronted by workers that had very little to learn and were well informed on everything that was going on in the world. My Italian friends were not second to anyone. They knew what they were talking about and when I got together with them I found out that I was facing people who were willing at all times to improve their knowledge. With the kind of schooling they were getting in the factory for a small weekly contribution, they could stand before any so-called intellectual and put him in the right spot" ("Father and Son," 79–80). I am grateful to Laurie Deredita for making this unpublished memoir available to me.

105. *El Diario de Tampa*, July 3, 1908.

106. Ibid.

107. Cuaderno índice, El Centro Asturiano, which is part of the Tony Pizzo Collection at the University of South Florida. The library was donated to the same university by El Centro Asturiano. I gratefully acknowledge the assistance of Willie García, who put me in touch with so many institutions and people in Tampa and who allowed me to conduct research at El Centro Asturiano during the summer of 2004. During the same trip, I greatly benefited from the advice I received from Eddie Contreras and Judge E. J. Salcines, both Tampa residents.

108. *El Cubano* (1915), 14.

109. The library at El Círculo Cubano no longer exists, nor is there a catalogue of the same. The books I have listed are those I found on the shelves during my research visit at El Círculo on August 12, 2004.

110. See the *Tampa Morning Tribune*, March 9, 1916, for a review of the opening of the Cuesta Library, thus named because of the sponsorship of the Cuesta Factory. The *Tampa Daily Times*, January 1, 1914, includes a review of the opening of the Carnegie Library in West Tampa. El Círculo Italiano also had a library. See Mormino and Pozzetta's bibliography in "The Reader Lights the Candle," 26.

111. Social-Ethnic Study of Ybor City, Tampa, Florida, 402.

112. Mormino and Pozzetta, "The Reader Lights the Candle," 19.

113. *Tobacco Leaf*, November 14, 1900.

114. See Ramos, *Amor y anarquía*, 16.

115. Mormino and Pozzetta, "The Reader Lights the Candle," 18.

116. Between 1921 and 1926, when reading aloud resumed, the following were published: in 1922, *El Bombín* magazine; in 1923, *Revista Latina* in 1923, *Tampa Social* in 1925, *Alfa: Revista Literaria del Hogar*.

117. Ingalls and Pérez, *Tampa Cigar Workers*, 138.

118. Ibid., 137.

119. Ibid.

120. *Tobacco Leaf*, October 14, 1922.

121. For example, between 1923 and 1925, the following novels were published in installments: *El idilio en el Cauca*, by G. Núñez Prado; *La atalaya del diablo o La barba azul*, by Eugenio Sue, translated by Joaquín Delgado; *Las tres duquesas*, by Henri Demesse, translated by Andrea León; *La mujer de hielo*, by Adolfo Belot, translated by Gerardo Blanco; *Tierra levantina*, by B. Morales San Martín; and *La casa de la Troya*, by Alejandro Pérez Lugín. Starting in July 1925, *La mujer de hielo* and *La casa de la Troya* were published simultaneously.

122. Mormino and Pozzetta, "The Reader Lights the Candle," 20.

123. *El Bombín* magazine, August 17, 1922.

124. Cruz, *Anna in the Tropics*, 29.

125. Manea and Navalón, "Juventud y permanencia del Quijote," 53.

126. Levin, *The Gates of Horn*, 46–47, 246–252.

127. See Gaultier, *Bovarysm*, with regard to this concept.

128. The *Diccionario de la Real Academia Española* defines a "chaperone" [*escucha*] as 1. "Action of listening. 2. In nunneries and girls' schools, the one who is charged with the task of being in the parlor to accompany those who receive visitors in order to hear what is said. 3. Maid who slept near her mistress' bedroom in order to be able to hear if she was called. 4. Small window installed in the large rooms of palaces where counsels and high tribunals were convened, so that the king, whenever he wished, could listen to what was being voted on in the counsels without being seen . . . 6. Sentinel who advances at night near the location of the enemy in order to observe their movements" (882).

129. For an excellent study of this chapter and the history of Spanish libraries in the context of *Don Quixote*, see Dopico Black, "Canons Afire."

130. Cruz, *Anna in the Tropics*, 26.

131. *La Gaceta*, October 1930–October 1931.

132. Campbell and Porter, "The Cigar Industry of Tampa, Florida," 23.

133. Tolstoy, *Anna Karenina*, 692.

134. Mormino and Pozzetta, "The Reader Lights the Candle," 20.

135. *La Gaceta*, November 25, 1931.

136. *Tampa Daily Times*, November 27, 1931.

137. *La Gaceta*, November 27, 1931.

138. *Tampa Daily Times*, December 7, 1931.

139. Ibid., November 29, 1931.

140. *La Gaceta*, November 27, 1931.

141. Ibid.

142. Ibid.

143. Ingalls and Pérez, *Tampa Cigar Workers*, 183.

144. Ibid.

145. Gloria M. de la Llana Deese, interview with author, August 16, 2004.

146. Mormino and Pozzetta, *The Immigrant World of Ybor City*, 182–183.

147. *Tampa Daily Times*, March 27, 1934.

148. Mary Fontanills, interview with Gary Mormino, July 26, 1983.

149. Domenico Giunta, interview with Gary Mormino, May 18, 1984.

150. *La Gaceta*, August 26, 1941.

151. *Tampa Morning Tribune*, October 8, 1949.

152. *St. Petersburg Times*, May 14, 1999.

153. *Tampa Daily Tribune*, April 23, 1946.

154. Ibid.

155. Wilfredo Rodríguez, interview with Gary Mormino, May 23, 1984.

156. *Tampa Times*, May 22, 1981.

157. Ibid.

158. Ibid.

159. Ibid.

160. Yglesias, *A Wake in Ybor City*, 26. Other novels that focus on the culture and history of tobacco but not particularly on *lectores* are *Los dedos de la mano* (written in 1951), by Enrique A. Laguerre, and *Parrish* (1958), by Mildred Savage. In addition, a play by Steven Knight, *The President of an Empty Room* (2005), is set in the Partagás factory in Havana.

161. Archives, Hillsborough County Public Library, Tampa, Florida.

162. Ibid. The musical was publicized in the *Tampa Times* on April 18, 1976.

CHAPTER 5

1. Epigraph from Vega, *Memorias de Bernardo Vega*, 93.

2. The first biography of Luisa Capetillo was written by Norma Valle Ferrer, *Luisa Capetillo: Historia de una mujer proscrita*. This information is attributed to this source, 85.

3. Ramos, *Amor y anarquía*, 33.

4. Ibid., 14.

5. Valle Ferrer, *Luisa Capetillo: Historia*, 131.

6. Ramos, *Amor y anarquía*, 74. All citations from the texts written by Luisa Capetillo come from this book unless otherwise specified.

7. Ibid.

8. Valle Ferrer provides this information (*Luisa Capetillo: Historia*, 67), based on the study by Igualdad Iglesias de Pagán: *El obrerismo en Puerto Rico*, 295.

9. Ramos, *Amor y anarquía*, 74–75.

10. A more complete volume of Capetillo's writings was published by Norma Ferrer. See *Luisa Capetillo: Obra completa*.

11. Ramos, *Amor y anarquía*, 89.

12. Ibid., 106.

13. Ibid., 106–107.

14. Ibid., 108.

15. Ibid., 109.

16. Ibid., 104.

17. Ibid., 84.

18. See Hewitt, *Southern Discomfort*, 1–7, 215.

19. Ramos, *Amor y anarquía*,74.

20. Ibid., 166.

21. Ibid., 16.

22. Ibid., 173.

23. See Glasser, *My Music Is My Flag*, 34–37, about Puerto Rican cigar workers who were also musicians.

24. Vega, *Memorias de Bernardo Vega*, 134.

25. Valle Ferrer, *Luisa Capetillo: Historia*, 83.

26. I gratefully acknowledge William Luis for having told me about Bernardo Vega's worthy book. For a more in-depth study of the life and culture of Bernardo Vega, see Luis, *Dance between Two Cultures*.

27. Gompers wrote: "In the shop there was also reading. It was the custom of the cigarmakers to chip in to create a fund for purchasing papers, magazines, and books. Then while the rest worked, one of our members would read to us perhaps for an hour at a time, sometimes longer. In order that the reader might not be the loser financially, each one of the other men in the shop gave him a definite number of cigars" (*Seventy Years of Life and Labour*, 1: 80–81). Regarding his own experience as a reader, he stated: "I had a habit of saving any interesting magazine or newspaper articles to read to my shopmates. Others did the same. As my voice was strong and the men could hear me easily whenever I read, they always asked me to read more than my period" (ibid., 81). His favorite newspaper was the *New York Sun* because, among other things, it published book reviews. However, he, like his coworkers, enjoyed reading *Irish World* and *Workingmen's Advocate* (ibid., 80–81). At the David Hirsch & Company Factory, the workers read in English and communicated in both English and German, since most employees were from Germany. Gompers met Martí, who introduced him to Charles A. Dana, editor of the *New York Sun* (ibid., 2: 63); he also

met some Cuban cigar workers in other factories (ibid., 64). He does not mention anything about reading in cigar factories in England (his father was a cigar worker, so he knew the trade). In fact, Gompers was outraged about the fact that, in England, workers were not allowed to smoke in the factory. In addition, taking tobacco home, unlike in the United States or Cuba, was forbidden (ibid., 1: 18). German workers in Chicago had a very dynamic culture at the end of the nineteenth century. They had cultural institutions such as the Chicago Workers' Association, the Labor Press, and book clubs and lending libraries. However, reading aloud did not take place in these factories. See Keil and Jentz, *German Workers in Chicago*, chaps. 2 and 5.

28. My discussion of reading aloud in New York's cigar factories is a summary of the information set forth by Bernardo Vega in *Memorias de Bernardo Vega*.

29. See Hewitt, *Southern Discomfort*, 214.

30. Vega, *Memorias de Bernardo Vega*, 40–41.

31. Ibid., 40.

32. Ibid., 55.

33. Ibid., 41.

34. Martí, *Obras completas*, 3: 225.

35. Vega, *Memorias de Bernardo Vega*, 44.

36. Ibid., 129–130.

37. Ibid., 135.

38. Valle Ferrer, *Luisa Capetillo: Historia*, 94.

39. Vega, *Memorias de Bernardo Vega*, 260.

40. Ibid., 261.

CHAPTER 6

1. Gálvez, *Tampa*, 191.

2. Information on reading in 1905 is based on Collins, "Literature and Cigar Making."

3. Ibid., 468.

4. Ibid.

5. Gálvez, *Tampa*, 191.

6. García Galló, *Biografía*, 175.

7. Gálvez, *Tampa*, 192–193; original emphasis.

8. In the wake of Ortiz's essay, *Cuban Counterpoint: Tobacco and Sugar*, a large number of very important studies about tobacco were published. Nevertheless, no study has focused exclusively on cigar factory *lectores*. Still, all those studies have great value, and as is made evident by way of sources I have cited or quoted, they have contributed a great deal to this study. See *Biografía del tabaco habano*, by Gaspar Jorge García Galló, and *Biografía íntima del tabaco*, by

Reynaldo González. For labor studies, see *Tabaco en la periferia*, by Jean Stubbs. With regard to literary and cultural studies, see *Holy Smoke*, by Guillermo Cabrera Infante; *Fernando Ortiz: Contrapunteo y transculturación*, by Enrico Mario Santí; *Sugar's Secrets: Race and the Erotics of Cuban Nationalism*, by Vera Kutzinski; and *Dance between Two Cultures*, by William Luis.

9. I am grateful to Dr. Alfonso J. García Osuna for having told me about the film and for having been so generous as to lend it to me. A *lector* also appears in *Die Another Day* (2002), in which James Bond (Agent 007) embarks on a mission in a minefield in the demilitarized zone separating North and South Korea. His operation takes him from there to Hong Kong then to Cuba and London. In Havana, he goes into a cigar factory to meet someone. As he walks through the *galera*, a *lector* is reading a newspaper. The *lector* appears for only two seconds. He is sitting among the cigar rollers and does not have a proper platform, as most *lectores* do in Havana's factories. Another *lector* appears briefly in the film *Cuba* (1979), directed by Richard Lester. An interesting novel about a woman who places an ad in the newspaper as a "professional reader" and is hired as such is *La lectrice*, by Raymond Jean (1986). A film with the same title was released in 1988, directed by Michel Deville and based on both of Jean's novels, *La lectrice* and *Un fantasme de Bella B* (1983).

10. See Pérez Firmat, *The Cuban Condition*, for a thorough analysis of Carlos Loveira's novel, *Juan Criollo*, in which the institution of the reader is mentioned. Colombian writer Juan Manuel Roca published a poem titled "Lector de tabaquería" in *Ciudadano de la noche*, 49.

11. García, *The Agüero Sisters*, 12.

12. Ibid., 60.

13. González Echevarría states that "Latin American history, as in *Cien años de soledad*, appears as being made up of a series of high points common to the whole continent and reducible to a single, shared story. . . . Archival fictions are also mythic because, ultimately, they invest the figure of the Archive with an arcane power that is clearly originary and impossible to express, a secret that is lodged in the very expression of the Archive, not separate from it, and thus impossible to render wholly discursive. . . . The Archive cannot coalesce as a national or cultural myth, though its make-up still reveals a longing, for the creation of such grandiose politico-cultural metastory" (*Myth and Archive*, 175). In Cristina García's novel, we see the very same "desire" to return to the past and begin a "political-cultural metafiction" from the Archive.

14. García, *The Agüero Sisters*, 30.

15. Ibid., 149.

16. Ibid.

17. Ibid., 31.

18. Ibid., 37.

19. Ibid., 32.

20. Ibid., 61.

21. García Galló, *Biografía*, 180.

22. *United States Tobacco Journal*, January 25, 1930.

23. Ibid.

24. Ibid.

25. *Bohemia*, July 1951, 39.

26. García, *The Agüero Sisters*, 31.

27. The term "throne" is used in *United States Tobacco Journal*, January 25, 1930.

28. García Galló, *Biografía*, 180. See also Guillén, *Prosa de prisa*, 243–245, for more biographical information.

29. Gaspar Jorge García Galló published his *Biografía del tabaco habano* in 1959, although he started to write it at the end of the 1930s. García Galló is one of Fernando Ortiz's main sources for *Cuban Counterpoint*, in which he refers to reading aloud in cigar factories. The 1950s magazine *Bohemia* published a few articles about the *lectores*, but, as opposed to contributing to the history of the *lectores*, the articles criticize their work and make reference to errors made by them while reading aloud. The July 1951 issue of *Bohemia* cites the names and nicknames of the following *lectores*, including one woman: Pancho Santo Domingo, Nicolás Rojas, Bernardo Lobo, Luz Hernández, Juan Quezada, Juan Buttari, Ambrosio Borges, "Chetuki," "El Trichuelo," Venancio Lladó, "Quribú," Juan Díaz Muro, "Pancho" Asensio, "Panchito" Montoto, José la Paz, Leopoldo Noriega, and Rodolfo González Urra. The article mentions only the last name of a *lector* (Córdova) who read in the Gener Factory for forty years (102–103). The March 1950 issue of *Bohemia* mentions two *lectores*: "El Chino Eduardo" and "Cachivache," 8.

30. García Galló, *Biografía*, 172–173.

31. In "Studied for Action: How Gabriel Harvey Read His Livy," Anthony Grafton and Lisa Jardine use the terms "professional reader" and "facilitator" to describe the profession practiced by Gabriel Harvey in the sixteenth century (48). Although Harvey read both aloud and to himself, historians refer to him as a "facilitator" because he was also a political advisor. I have taken the term from this article.

32. Leal, *Breve historia*, 123.

CHAPTER 7

1. Interview with author, May 31, 2003.

2. Interview with author, August 16, 2001.

3. Interview with author, May 24, 2003.

4. Interview with author, June 2, 2003.

5. Interview with author, August 7, 2001.

6. Interview with author, May 29, 2003.

7. Interview with author, August 8, 2001.

8. Interview with author, May 23, 2003.

9. Interview with author, August 14, 2001.

10. These surveys were conducted in 2000 and 2001 by *lector* Francisco Águila Medina at the LV-9 Factory, Santa Clara.

11. I am grateful to Sonia Navarro Fragoso, director of the San Juan y Martínez Library, for having provided me with this information. In my interview with her (May 31, 2003), she stated the following: "Since we were in need of a building, we assigned ourselves the task of ferreting out traditions: ten-line stanzas, *punto guajiro, los guateques*, among other things. The technical team researched tastes, preferences, and needs, and that's how we started to bring them the bibliography [out into the field], and we even gave them recommendations of texts. They [those in the field] were familiar with, for example, the poetry of El Indio Naborí [Jesús Orta Ruiz], but we started to introduce them to Benedetti, Vallejo, and Neruda, and we made them happy by bringing them what they asked us for, but at the same time we inserted classics that we wanted them to become aware of, and they liked that. They asked us for novels and short stories, but sometimes there weren't any, because the lending library—it wasn't that we didn't have any in our collection—but, rather, so that the lending library wouldn't be too depleted—we circulated it. For example, we put together fifteen minilibraries that housed small collections of varied genres. There were places in which, due to security and demand, these minilibraries were left for up to a month, and the cigar facility was one such place. There are minilibraries at the Municipal Committee headquarters, at the fire department, at the senior center, and at the Revolutionary Defense Committee headquarters."

12. Interview with the author, May 29, 2003.

13. Interview with author, May 20, 2003.

14. Interview with author, May 31, 2003.

15. Interview with author, August 7, 2001.

16. I interviewed Francisco Águila in 2001 and in 2003. He had started to keep a record in 2000.

17. Interview with author, May 20, 2003.

18. Interview with author, May 27, 2003.

19. Interview with author, May 15, 2003.

20. Interview with author, May 16, 2003.

21. I am grateful to *lector* Francisco Águila for having provided me with these records.

22. Interview with author, May 31, 2003.

23. Interview with author, May 22, 2003.

24. Interview with author, May 28, 2003.

25. I was unable to locate this book, although it may be *Utopia selvagem*, by Darcy Ribeiro.

26. I am grateful to Zoé Nocedo Primo, senior specialist at the Museo de Tabaco, for sharing information about this program. I am very grateful to Nancy Stout for having provided me with valuable information regarding the location of this museum and some key factories in Havana.

27. Correspondence from Francisco Águila, August 15, 2005.

28. Since I began my research in Cuba in 2001, not only have training classes been held, but in July 2003, monthly salaries were increased from 148 pesos to 231 pesos. This represents the first salary increase since 1960 (I am grateful to *lectora* Zuraida González for having written to me to bring me up to date in this regard). And, surprisingly, in 2006, the salary was increased again to 305 pesos. Additionally, I have been asked to serve on the National Technical Advisory Council of *Lectores* and *Lectoras*. My advice has been requested via letters about curriculum for *lectores*, and I have been invited to teach literature courses on several occasions.

CHAPTER 8

1. I would like to thank Alejandro Aura and Carmen Boullosa for having provided me with guidance regarding the area of Banderilla, Veracruz.

2. Interview with author, April 27, 2005.

3. Interview with author, April 27, 2005.

4. Jorge Saldaña, one of Mexico's most distinguished radio and television announcers, was from time to time a *lector* at La Perla in the early 1940s (Erick Fernández Saldaña, interview with author, September 6, 2007).

5. Trujillo Bolio, *Operarios fabriles*, 303. The article appeared in the newspaper *El Socialista* on July 14, 1872.

6. Ibid.

7. Ibid., 311.

8. Interview with author, April 26, 2005.

9. Other activities also take place in factories. For example, large factories have soccer teams, and the trophies they win are displayed in the workshops. The teams practice twice a week. Thus, employees can spend time together outside the workplace. There are also other sports-related activities sponsored by towns, such as running or walking races. October 1, the Day of the Cigar Worker in Mexico, is a day off for the workers. On that day, factory owners give parties in a banquet hall and pay half the cost of the party; the cigar workers pay the other half. Everyone brings their families to the banquet hall, where there is usually a band playing, and they eat special dishes prepared for the occasion. On Christmas, the employees work half a day, and cider and champagne are brought into the cigar factory. Workers drink toasts and have hors d'oeuvres. *Posadas* (nine celebrations that take place from December 16 to December 24 and include religious observances and Christmas parties with piñatas) were held after work in the past, although that practice has been discontinued.

CHAPTER 9

1. Interview with author, July 24, 2004.
2. Interview with author, July 21, 2004.
3. I would like to thank Ángel Estévez for having provided me with information regarding La Aurora.
4. Interview with author, July 22, 2004.
5. Félix B. Caignet wrote *El derecho de nacer* and *La madre* originally as radio soap operas.
6. Martí, *Cartas a María Mantilla*, 42.
7. Since that time, I have been sending books (mainly classics of world literature) to the cigar factory.

EPILOGUE

1. Bourdieu, *Capital cultural*, 32.
2. Hugo, *Les Misérables* (1982), 486–487.
3. Ibid., 488.
4. Ibid., 98.
5. Ibid., 489.
6. Ibid.
7. Dumas, *The Count of Monte Cristo*, 49.
8. Ibid., 441.
9. Hugo, *Les Misérables* (1951), 1510.
10. Hugo, *Los miserables*, 1036.
11. Translated by Patti Firth.

BIBLIOGRAPHY

BOOKS, ARTICLES, AND MANUSCRIPTS

Álbum de la fábrica de cigarros "La Belleza." Havana: Guerra Hermanos y Cía., 1892.

Alexander, Robert J. *A History of Organized Labor in Cuba.* Westport, Conn.: Praeger, 2002.

Alpízar Leal, Luis, ed. *Documentos inéditos de José Martí a José D. Poyo.* Havana: Editorial Ciencias Sociales, 1994.

Amtower, Laurel. *Engaging Words: The Culture of Reading in the Later Middle Ages.* New York: Palgrave, 2000.

Aramburu, Joaquín Nicolás. *La masonería cubana.* Havana: A. Miranda y Cía., 1893.

Baena Luque, Eloísa. *Las cigarreras sevillanas: Un mito en declive (1887–1923).* Málaga, Spain: University of Málaga, 1993.

Bahloul, Joelle. *Lecturas precarias: Estudio sociológico sobre los "poco lectores."* Trans. Alberto Cue. Mexico City: Fondo de Cultura Económica, 2002.

Balboa Navarro, Imilcy. *Los brazos necesarios: Inmigración, colonialización y trabajo libre en Cuba, 1878–1898.* Valencia, Spain: Centro Francisco Tomás y Valiente, Universidad Nacional de Educación a Distancia, 2000.

Bermúdez, María Teresa. "Las leyes, los libros de texto y la lectura, 1857–1876." In Seminario de Historia de la Educación en México, *Historia de la lectura en México.* Mexico City: El Colegio de México, 2000, 127–152.

The Book of True Love. Trans. Saralyn R. Daly, ed. Anthony N. Zahareas. University Park: Penn State University Press, 1978.

Bourdieu, Pierre. *Capital cultural y espacio social.* Trans. Isabel Jiménez. Mexico City: Siglo Veintiuno, 2002.

Brothers, Betty. *Wreckers and Workers of Old Key West.* Litoky, Fla.: J. F. Brooks, 1972.

Bryan, Lindsay M. "A Study of the Latin Press in Ybor City, Tampa, Florida." Typed transcription. Library archives of the University of South Florida, Tampa, dated April 7, 1939.

Bueno, Salvador, ed. *Costumbristas cubanos del siglo XIX*. Caracas: Ayacucho, 1985.

——, ed. *José Martí y su periódico Patria*. Barcelona: Pablo de la Torriente, 1997.

Cabrera Infante, Guillermo. *Holy Smoke*. New York: Harper & Row, 1985.

Caignet, Félix B. *El derecho de nacer*. Havana: Radioguía, no. 167 (August 1948).

Campbell, Archer Stuart, and W. Porter McLendon. *The Cigar Industry of Tampa, Florida*. Gainesville: University of Florida Press, 1939.

Candela Soto, Paloma. *Cigarreras madrileñas: Trabajo y vida (1888–1927)*. Madrid: Editorial Tecnos, 1997.

Cárdenas, Francisco. *Estado de la población y del trabajo en las islas de Cuba y Puerto Rico*. Madrid: Tipografía Gutemberg, 1884.

Casanovas Codina, Joan. *Bread, or Bullets! Urban Labor and Spanish Colonialism in Cuba, 1850–1898*. Pittsburgh, Penn.: University of Pittsburgh Press, 1998.

Casasús, Juan. *La emigración cubana y la independencia de la patria*. Havana: Editorial Lex, 1953.

Castellanos, Gerardo. *Motivos de Cayo Hueso*. Havana: Ucar García y Cía., 1935.

Castilla y del Busto, Alberto. "A Cuba." In Andrés de Piedra-Bueno and José Rivero Muñiz, eds., *Pequeña antología del tabaco*. Havana: Editorial Revista Tabaco, 1946, 63.

Cervantes, Miguel de. *Don Quixote*. Trans. John Rutherford. New York: Penguin, 2000.

——. *Exemplary Novels IV. Lady Cornelia. The Deceitful Marriage. The Dialogue of the Dogs*. Trans. John Jones and John Macklin. Warminster, Eng.: Aris & Phillips, 1992.

Chartier, Roger. *Cultura escrita, literatura e historia*. Mexico City: Fondo de Cultura Económica, 1999.

——. *El orden de los libros: Lectores, autores, bibliotecas en Europa entre los siglos XIV y XVIII*. Trans. Viviana Ackerman. Barcelona: Gedisa, 2000.

——. *Pratiques de la lecture*. Marseilles: Rivages, 1985.

——. "Reading Matter and 'Popular' Reading: From the Renaissance to the Seventeenth Century." In Guglielmo Cavallo and Roger Chartier, eds., *A History of Reading in the West*, trans. Lydia G. Cochrane. Oxford: Polity Press, 1999, 270–290.

——. *Sociedad y escritura en la edad moderna: La cultura como apropiación*. Trans. Paloma Villegas and Ana García Bergua. Mexico City: Instituto Mora, 1995.

Chevalier, Maxime. *Lectura y lectores en la España del siglo XVI y XVII*. Madrid: Turner, 1976.

Coelho, Jacinto do Prado, et al. *Problemática da leitura: Aspectos sociológicos e pedagógicos*. Lisbon: Instituto Nacional de Investigação Científica, 1980.

Coleman, Joyce. *Public Reading and the Reading Public in Late Medieval England and France*. Cambridge: Cambridge University Press, 1996.

Collins, H. James. "Literature and Cigar Making." *Bookman* 21 (July, 1905): 467–471.

Cooper, Patricia A. *Once a Cigar Maker: Men, Women, and Work Culture in American Cigar Factories, 1900–1919*. Urbana: University of Illinois Press, 1992.

Craik, Edward Lillie. *The Pursuit of Knowledge under Difficulties*. London: Knight & Co., 1845.

Cruz, Nilo. *Anna in the Tropics*. New York: Theatre Communications Group, 2003.

Curran, Patricia. *Grace before Meals: Food Ritual and Body Discipline in Convent Culture*. Urbana: University of Illinois Press, 1989.

Darío, Rubén. *Selected Writings*. Trans. Andrew Hurley, Greg Simon, and Steven F. White; intro. Ilan Stavans. New York: Penguin Books, 2005.

Darnton, Robert. *The Forbidden Bestsellers of Pre-Revolutionary France*. New York: W. W. Norton, 1995.

Dopico Black, Georgina. "Canons Afire: Libraries, Books, and Bodies in Don Quixote's Spain." In Roberto González Echevarría, ed., *Cervantes' Don Quixote: A Casebook*. London: Oxford University Press, 2005, 95–123.

Dumas, Alexandre. *The Count of Monte Cristo*. Trans. Lowell Bair. New York: Bantam Books, 1956.

Duque de Estrada, Nicolás. *Explicación de la doctrina cristiana acomodada a la capacidad de los negros bozales*. Havana: Biblioteca Nacional José Martí, 2006.

Eckenstein, Lina. *Women under Monasticism: Chapters on Saint-Lore and Convent Life between A.D. 500 and A.D. 1500*. New York: Russell & Russell, 1963.

Ellis, Havelock. *The Soul of Spain*. Boston: Houghton, Mifflin, 1909, 1926.

Ferreiro, Luis, and Ángel Munilla. *Las cigarreras*. Madrid: R. Velasco, 1897.

Fish, Stanley. *Is There a Text in This Class? The Authority of Interpretive Communities*. Cambridge, Mass.: Harvard University Press, 1980.

Flaubert, Gustave. *Madame Bovary*. Trans. Geoffrey Wall. London: Penguin Books, 1992.

Fornet, Ambrosio. *El libro en Cuba: Siglos XVIII y XIX*. Havana: Editorial Letras Cubanas, 1994.

Foucault, Michel. *Discipline and Punish: The Birth of the Prison*. Trans. Alan Sheridan. New York: Random House, (1978) 1995.

Frenk, Margit. *Entre la voz y el silencio*. Alcalá de Henares, Spain: Centro de Estudios Cervantinos, 1997.

Friera, Florencio. "Historia de un emigrante a Cuba: Saturnino Martínez (1837–1905): Los orígenes del movimiento obrero y el fin del dominio español en Cuba." *Boletín del Instituto de Estudios Asturianos* 43, no. 129 (January–March 1989): 191–237.

Gálvez y Delmonte, Wenceslao (Gálvez, Wen). *Tampa: Impresiones de emigrado*. Ybor City, Fla.: Establecimiento Tipográfico Cuba, 1897.

García, Cristina. *The Agüero Sisters*. New York: One World Books, 1997.

García Galló, Gaspar Jorge. *Biografía del tabaco habano*. Santa Clara, Cuba: Universidad Central de las Villas, 1959.

García Márquez, Gabriel. *Chronicle of a Death Foretold*. Trans. Gregory Rabassa. London: Harper & Row, 1983.

Gaultier, Jules de. *Bovaryism*. Trans. Gerald M. Spring. New York: Philosophical Library, 1970.

Gelabert, Francisco de Paula. *Tipos y costumbres de la Isla de Cuba*. Havana: El Avisador Comercial, 1881.

Gies, David Thatcher. *Nicolás Fernández de Moratín*. Boston: Twayne, 1979.

Gilman, Stephen. *La España de Fernando de Rojas*. Madrid: Taurus, 1978.

Glasser, Ruth. *My Music Is My Flag: Puerto Rican Musicians and Their New York Communities, 1917–1940*. Berkeley & Los Angeles: University of California Press, 1995.

Gompers, Samuel. *Seventy Years of Life and Labour: An Autobiography*. 2 vols. New York: Augustus M. Kelley, 1967.

González, Reynaldo. *El bello habano: Biografía íntima del tabaco*. Vitoria-Gasteiz, Spain: Ikusager Ediciones, 1998.

González Acosta, Alejandro. *Joyas de papel*. Havana: Universidad de la Habana, 1983.

González Echevarría, Roberto. *Myth and Archive: A Theory of Latin American Narrative*. Cambridge: Cambridge University Press, 1990.

———. *The Pride of Havana: A History of Cuban Baseball*. New York: Oxford University Press, 1999.

González Pérez, Aníbal. *Journalism and the Development of Spanish American Narrative*. Cambridge: Cambridge University Press, 1993.

González Sánchez, Carlos Alberto. *Homo viator, homo scribens: Cultura gráfica, información y gobierno en la expansión atlántica (siglos XV–XVII)*. Madrid: Marcial Pons, 2007.

González Stephan, Beatriz. *La historiografía literaria del liberalismo hispanoamericano del siglo XIX*. Havana: Casa de las Américas, 1987.

Grafton, Anthony, and Lisa Jardine. "Studied for Action: How Gabriel Harvey Read His Livy." *Past and Present*, no. 129 (November 1990): 30–78.

Guillén, Nicolás. *Prosa de prisa, 1929–1972*. Havana: Editorial Arte y Literatura, 1975.

Hewitt, Nancy A. *Southern Discomfort: Women's Activism in Tampa, Florida, 1880s–1920s*. Urbana: University of Illinois Press, 2001.

Hoggart, Richard. *The Uses of Literacy: Aspects of Working Class Life with Special Reference to Publications and Entertainments*. Harmondsworth, U.K.: Penguin, 1958.

Hugo, Victor. *Les Misérables*. Ed. Maurice Allemand. Paris: Gallimard, 1951.

———. *Les Misérables*. Trans. Norman Denny. London: Penguin Books, 1982.

———. *Los miserables*. Mexico City: Porrúa, 2004.

———. *Oeuvres complètes de Victor Hugo*. 48 vols. Paris: Hetzel, 1880–1892.

Ingalls, Robert, and Louis A. Pérez, Jr. *Tampa Cigar Workers: A Pictorial History.* Gainesville: University Press of Florida, 2003.

Insúa, Alberto. *Humo, dolor, placer.* Madrid: Castalia, 1999.

Jean, Raymond. *Un fantasme de Bella B. et autres récits.* Le Paradou: Actes Sud, 1983.

———. *La lectrice: roman.* Arles: Actes Sud, 1986.

Jover Zamora, José María. *Política, diplomacia y humanismo popular: Estudios sobre la vida española en el siglo XIX.* Madrid: Turner, 1976.

Keil, Hartmut, and John B. Jentz, eds. *German Workers in Chicago: A Documentary History of Working-class Culture from 1850 to World War I.* Urbana: University of Illinois Press, 1988.

Knight, Steven. *The President of an Empty Room: A Story of Voodoo, Heroin, and Tobacco.* London: Nick Hern Books, 2005.

Kutzinski, Vera M. *Sugar's Secrets: Race and the Erotics of Cuban Nationalism.* Charlottesville: University Press of Virginia, 1993.

Laguerre, Enrique A. *Los dedos de la mano.* Río Piedras, P.R.: Editorial Cultural, 1978.

Leal, Rine. *Breve historia del teatro cubano.* Havana: Editorial Letras Cubanas, 1980.

Levin, Harry. *The Gates of Horn: A Study of Five French Realist Novelists.* New York: Oxford University Press, 1963.

Litvak, Lily. *Musa libertaria: Arte, literatura y vida cultural del anarquismo español (1880–1913).* Barcelona: Antoni Bosch, 1981.

López Isla, Mario Luis. *La aventura del tabaco: Los canarios en Cuba.* Gran Canaria, Spain: Centro de la Cultura Popular Canaria, 1998.

López Segrera, Francisco. *Cuba: Cultura y sociedad (1510–1985).* Havana: Editorial Letras Cubanas, 1989.

Loveira, Carlos. *Juan Criollo.* Havana: Consejo Nacional de Cultura, 1962.

Luis, William. *Dance between Two Cultures: Latino Caribbean Literature Written in the United States.* Nashville, Tenn.: Vanderbilt University Press, 1997.

Lyons, Martin. "New Readers in the Nineteenth Century: Women, Children, Workers." In Guglielmo Cavallo and Roger Chartier, eds., *A History of Reading in the West,* trans. Lydia G. Cochrane. Oxford: Polity Press, 1999, 313–344.

———. *Readers and Society in Nineteenth-century France: Workers, Women, Peasants.* New York: Palgrave, 2001.

Maeztu, Ramiro de. *Autobiografía.* Madrid: Editora Nacional, 1962.

Mañach, Jorge. *Martí: Apostle of Freedom.* Trans. Coley Taylor. New York: Devin-Adair, 1950.

Manea, Norman, and Antonio Navalón. "Juventud y permanencia del Quijote." *Letras Libres* (August 2005): 53–56.

Manguel, Alberto. *A History of Reading.* New York: HarperCollins, 1996.

Manzano, Juan Francisco. *Autobiografía del esclavo poeta y otros escritos / Juan Francisco Manzano.* Ed. William Luis. Madrid: Iberoamericana, 2007.

Marco, Joaquín. *Literatura popular en España en los siglos XVIII y XIX: Una aproximación a los pliegos de cordel.* Madrid: Taurus, 1977.

Martí, José. *Cartas a María Mantilla.* Havana: Editorial Gente Nueva, 2001.

———. *Documentos inéditos de José Martí a José D. Poyo.* Comp. Luis Alpízar Leal. Havana: Editorial Ciencias Sociales, 1994.

———. *Obras completas.* 26 vols. Havana: Editora Nacional de Cuba, 1963–1973.

———. *Our America by José Martí: Writings on Latin America and the Struggle for Cuban Independence.* Trans. Elinor Randall, Juan de Onís, and Roslyn Held Foner; ed. Philip S. Foner. New York: Monthly Review Press, 1977.

———. *Selected Writings.* Trans. Esther Allen. New York: Penguin, 2002.

Martínez Carmenate, Urbano. *Domingo del Monte y su tiempo.* Havana: Ediciones Unión, 1997.

Martínez Martín, Jesús A. *Lectura y lectores en el Madrid del siglo XIX.* Madrid: Consejo Superior de Investigaciones Científicas, 1991.

Massolo, Arthur D. "Father and Son: His Life and Mine." Unpublished memoir. Port Washington, N.Y.: February 7, 1963.

McKitterick, Rosamond. *The Uses of Literacy in Early Mediaeval Europe.* Cambridge: Cambridge University Press, 1990.

Medina, Pablo. *The Cigar Roller.* New York: Grove Press, 2005.

———. "The Tampa Cubans and the Culture of Exile." *Antioch Review* 62, no. 4 (Fall, 2004): 635–643.

"Memoria del Centro Español." Pamphlet, Tony Pizzo Collection, University of South Florida, Tampa.

Méndez, Armando. *Ciudad de Cigars: West Tampa.* Tampa: Florida Historical Society, 1994.

Mérimée, Prosper. *Carmen.* Trans. Anonymous. In Barrett H. Clark, ed., *Great Short Novels of the World.* New York: Robert M. McBride, 1927, 556–592.

Mormino, Gary R., and George E. Pozzetta. *The Immigrant World of Ybor City: Italians and Their Latin Neighbors in Tampa, 1885–1985.* Urbana: University of Illinois Press, 1987.

———. "The Reader Lights the Candle: Cuban and Florida Cigar Workers' Oral Tradition." *Labor's Heritage* (Spring, 1993): 4–27.

Nelson, William. "From 'Listen, Lordings' to 'Dear Reader.'" *University of Toronto Quarterly* 46, no. 2 (Winter, 1976/1977): 110–124.

Neuberg, Victor E. *Chapbooks: A Guide to Reference Material on English, Scottish, and American Chapbook Literature of the 18th and 19th Centuries.* London: Woburn Press, 1972.

Ong, Walter J. *Oralidad y escritura: Tecnologías de la palabra.* Trans. Angélica Scherp. Mexico City: Fondo de Cultura Económica, 2002.

Ortega, Julio, et al. *Conquista y contraconquista: La escritura del Nuevo Mundo: Actas del XXVIII Congreso del Instituto Internacional de Literatura Iberoamericana.* Mexico City: Colegio de México, 1994.

Ortiz, Fernando. *Cuban Counterpoint: Tobacco and Sugar.* Trans. Harriet de Onís. New York: Knopf, 1947.

―――. "Los negros esclavos: Estudio sociológico y de derecho público." *Revista Bimestre Cubana* (1916).

Palacio Valdés, Armando. *La hermana San Sulpicio*. Madrid: Librería de Victoriano Suárez, 1928.

Pardo Bazán, Emilia. *The Tribune of the People*. Trans. Walter Borenstein. Cranbury, N.J.: Associated University Presses, 1999.

Pérez Firmat, Gustavo. *The Cuban Condition: Translation and Identity in Modern Cuban Literature*. Cambridge: Cambridge University Press, 1989.

Pérez, Louis A., Jr. *Cuba: Between Reform and Revolution*. Oxford: Oxford University Press, 1988.

Pérez Vidal, José. *España en la historia del tabaco*. Madrid: Centro de Estudios de Etnología Peninsular, 1959.

Peroni, Michel. *Historias de lectura: Trayectorias de vida y de lectura*. Mexico City: Fondo de Cultura Económica, 2003.

Petit, Michele. *Lecturas del espacio íntimo al espacio público*. Mexico City: Fondo de Cultura Económica, 2001.

Poblete, Juan. *Literatura chilena del siglo XIX: Entre públicos lectores y figuras autoriales*. Santiago: Editorial Cuarto Propio, 2003.

Portuondo, Fernando. *Historia de Cuba hasta 1898*. Havana: Editora Universitaria, 1965.

Portuondo, José Antonio. *"La Aurora" y los comienzos de la prensa y de la organización obrera en Cuba*. Havana: Imprenta Nacional de Cuba, 1961.

Poumier, María. *Apuntes sobre la vida cotidiana en Cuba en 1898*. Havana: Editorial Ciencias Sociales, 1975.

Poyo, Gerald E. *"With All, and for the Good of All": The Emergence of Popular Nationalism in the Cuban Communities of the United States, 1848–1898*. Durham, N.C.: Duke University Press, 1989.

Primer censo de obreros de la industria tabacalera. Havana: Imprenta El Siglo XX, 1947.

Proby, Kathryn Hall. *Mario Sánchez: Painter of Key West Memories*. Key West, Fla.: Southernmost Press, 1981.

Quesada Monge, Rodrigo. "Anarquismo y feminismo: Las mujeres en el debate anti-imperialista (1892–1902)." *Escáner Cultural*, no. 21 (September–October 2000).

Quintero Rivera, A. G. *Lucha obrera: Antología de grandes documentos en la historia obrera puertorriqueña*. San Juan, P.R.: Centro de Estudios de la Realidad Puertorriqueña, 1972.

Quiroga, Orlando. *El habano al rojo vivo*. Havana: Centro Nacional de Derecho de Autor, Unión Nacional de Escritores y Artistas Cubanos, 2002.

Quiroz, Alfonso W. "Loyalist Overkill: The Socioeconomic Costs of 'Repressing' the Separatist Insurrection in Cuba, 1868–1878." *Hispanic American Historical Review* 78 (1998): 261–305.

―――. "Orígenes de la sociedad civil en Cuba: La Habana y Puerto Príncipe (Camagüey) en el Siglo XIX." *Ibero-Americana Pragensia* 18 (2006): 89–112.

Ramos, Julio. *Amor y anarquía: Los escritos de Luisa Capetillo.* Río Piedras, P.R.: Ediciones Huracán, 1992.

——. *Desencuentros de la modernidad en América Latina: Literatura y política en el siglo XIX.* Mexico City: Fondo de Cultura Económica, 1989.

Rivero Muñiz, José. "La lectura en las tabaquerías." *Revista de la Biblioteca Nacional* (October–December, 1951): 190–272.

——. *Tabaco: Su historia en Cuba.* 2 vols. Havana: Instituto de Historia, Comisión Nacional de la Academia de Ciencias de la República de Cuba, 1965.

——. *The Ybor City Story (1885–1954) [Los cubanos en Tampa].* Trans. Eustasio Fernández and Henry Beltrán. Tampa, Fla., 1976.

——, and Andrés de Piedra-Bueno. *Pequeña antología del tabaco.* Havana: Editorial "Revista Tabaco," 1946.

Roca, Juan Manuel. *Ciudadano de la noche.* Bogotá: Fundación Simón y Lola Guberek, 1989.

Rodríguez Solís, E. *Majas, manolas y chulas: Historia, tipos y costumbres de antaño y ogaño.* Madrid: Imprenta de Fernando Cao y Domingo de Val, 1886.

Rojas, Fernando de. *La Celestina.* Ed. Joaquín Benito de Lucas. Madrid: Plaza & Jones, 1984.

——. *Celestine, or the Tragic-Comedie of Calisto and Melibea.* Trans. James Mabbe, ed. Guadalupe Martínez Lacalle. London: Tamesis Books, 1972.

Ronning, Neale. *José Martí and the Emigré Colony in Key West.* New York: Praeger, 1990.

Rose, Jonathan. "Rereading the English Common Reader: A Preface to the History of Audiences." *Journal of the History of Ideas* 53, no. 1 (1992): 47–70.

Rotker, Susana. *Fundación de una escritura: Las crónicas de José Martí.* Havana: Casa de las Américas, 1991.

Rulfo, Juan. *The Burning Plain and Other Stories.* Trans., intro. George D. Schade. Austin: University of Texas Press, 1971.

Sáez de Melgar, Faustina. *Rosa la cigarrera de Madrid.* 2 vols. Barcelona: Est. Tipográfico–Editorial de Juan Pons, 1878.

Santí Mario, Enrico. *Fernando Ortiz: Contrapunteo y transculturación.* Madrid: Colibrí, 2002.

Savage, Mildred. *Parrish.* New York: Simon & Schuster, 1958.

Seminario de Historia de la Educación en México. *Historia de la lectura en México.* Mexico City: El Colegio de México, 2000.

Shafer, Robert Jones. *The Economic Societies in the Spanish World (1763–1821).* Syracuse, N.Y.: Syracuse University Press, 1958.

Slater, Candace. *Stories on a String: The Brazilian Literatura de Cordel.* Berkeley & Los Angeles: University of California Press, 1982.

Sommer, Doris. *Foundational Fictions: The National Romances in Latin America.* Berkeley & Los Angeles: University of California Press, 1991.

Stubbs, Jean. *Tabaco en la periferia: El complejo agro-industrial cubano y su movimiento obrero, 1860–1959.* Havana: Editorial Ciencias Sociales, 1989.

Thomas, Hugh. *Cuba, or The Pursuit of Freedom*. New York: Da Capo Press, 1998.

Tolstoy, Leo. *Anna Karenina*. Trans. Constance Garnett. Garden City, N.Y.: Nelson Doubleday, 1944.

Torres Sánchez, Concha. *La clausura femenina en la Salamanca del siglo XVII: Dominicas y Carmelitas Descalzas*. Salamanca, Spain: Ediciones Universidad de Salamanca, 1991.

Traugott, Mark, ed. *The French Worker: Autobiographies from Early Industrial Era*. Berkeley & Los Angeles: University of California Press, 1993.

Trujillo Bolio, Mario. *Operarios fabriles en el Valle de México, 1864–1884*. Mexico City: El Colegio de México, 1997.

Truquin, Norbert. *Mémoires et aventures d'un prolétaire à travers la révolution: L'Algérie, la République Argentine et le Paraguay*. Paris: F. Maspéro, (1888) 1977.

Valdés, Zoé. *Yocandra in the Paradise of Nada*. Trans. Sabina Cienfuegos. New York: Arcade Publishing, 1995.

Valle Ferrer, Norma. *Luisa Capetillo: Historia de una mujer proscrita*. Río Piedras, P.R.: Editorial Cultural, 1990.

———. *Luisa Capetillo: Obra completa: "Mi patria es la libertad."* San Juan, P.R.: Departamento del Trabajo y Recursos Humanos, 2008.

Vega, Bernardo. *Memorias de Bernardo Vega: Contribución a la historia de la comunidad puertorriqueña en Nueva York*. Ed. César Andreu Iglesias. Santa Rita, P.R.: Ediciones Huracán, 1977.

Villaronda, Guillermo. "Elogio al tabaco habano." In Andrés de Piedra-Bueno and José Rivero Muñiz, eds., *Pequeña antología del tabaco*. Havana: Editorial Revista Tabaco, 1946.

Vincent, David. *Bread, Knowledge and Freedom: A Study of 19th Century Working Class Autobiography*. London: Europa, 1981.

Webb, R. K. *The British Working Class Reader, 1790–1848: Literacy and Social Tension*. London: George Allen & Unwin, 1955.

Westfall, L. Glenn. *Key West, Cigar City, USA*. Key West, Fla.: Cigar City Trilogy, 1997.

Yglesias, José. *A Wake in Ybor City*. Houston, Tex.: Arte Público Press, 1998.

NEWSPAPERS, MAGAZINES, JOURNALS, AND WEB SITES

Abadía de San Benito, 1997–2003. Buenos Aires, Argentina. July 15, 2002. http://www.sbenito.org./regla/rb.htm; accessed December 23, 2008.

Alerta—Diario Independiente, Havana

El Audaz, Tampa

La Aurora, Havana

Bohemia, Havana

Bohemia, Tampa

El Bombín magazine, Tampa

El Cubano, Tampa

Diario de la Marina, Havana

Diario de Tampa, Tampa
Diario Trabajadores, Havana
La Gaceta, Havana
La Gaceta, Tampa
Granma, Havana
Habano, Havana
El Heraldo Dominical, Tampa
The Holy Rule of Saint Benedict. http://www.kansasmonks.org/RuleOfStBenedict.html; accessed December 23, 2008.
La Raza, Tampa
La Revista: Semanario de Literatura, Ciencias, Artes y Sport (became *La Revista: Semanario Hispano Cubano*), Tampa
Revista Tabaco, Havana
Revista Tampa Latina, Tampa
St. Petersburg Times, St. Petersburg
El Siglo, Havana
El Tabaco, Havana
Tampa Daily News, Tampa
Tampa Daily Times, Tampa
Tampa Daily Tribune, Tampa
Tampa Ilustrado, Tampa
Tampa Morning Tribune, Tampa
Tampa Tribune, Tampa
Tobacco Leaf, New York
Trabajadores, Havana
Traducción Valdespino (became *La Traducción*), Tampa
United States Tobacco Journal, New York

INTERVIEWS

Águila Medina, Francisco. Interview with author, May 14, 2003; August 14, 2001, Santa Clara, Cuba.
Baxin Fiscal, Santiago. Interview with author, April 26, 2005, San Andrés Tuxtla, Mexico.
Borges Somonte, Ángel. Interview with author, May 31, 2003, San Juan y Martínez, Cuba.
Campos Iglesias, Bernardo. Interview with author, May 29, 2003, El Corojo, Pinar del Río, Cuba.
Cantero Marín, Lázara. Interview with author, May 20, 2003, Trinidad, Cuba.
Carbonell Farina, Jorge. Interview with author, July 22, 2004, Palmar Abajo, Dominican Republic.
Castillo Rodríguez, Petronila. Interview with author, May 20, 2003, Trinidad, Cuba.

Chavollera, Nicolás. Interview with author, May 16, 2003, Santa Clara, Cuba.

Collado Polanco, José. Interview with author, July 24, 2004, Tamboril, Dominican Republic.

Contreras, Eddie. Interview with author, December 7, 2007, Tampa, Florida.

Contreras, María de Lourdes. Interview with author, April 27, 2005, Banderilla, Veracruz, Mexico.

De la Llana Deese, Gloria. Interview with author, August 16, 2004, Tampa, Florida.

Domínguez Mena, Santos Segundo. Interview with author, May 31, 2003, San Juan y Martínez, Cuba.

Fernández Saldaña, Erick. Interview with author, September 6, 2007, Montreal, Canada.

Fontanills, Mary. Interview with Gary Mormino, July 26, 1983, Tampa, Florida. Gary Mormino Archives, University of South Florida, Tampa.

Giunta, Domenico. Interview with Gary Mormino, May 18, 1984, Tampa, Florida. Gary Mormino Archives, University of South Florida, Tampa.

González Artiles, Luis. Interview with author, May 23, 2003, Cabaiguán, Cuba.

González Martínez, María Caridad. Interview with author, May 28, 2003, Pinar del Río, Cuba.

González Muñoz, Cristina. Interview with author, May 21, 2003, Placetas, Las Villas, Cuba.

González Valdivia, Zuraida. Interview with author, May 22, 2003, Cabaiguán, Cuba.

Herdesa Álvarez, Fortunato Heriberto. Interview with author, May 22, 2003, Guayos, Sancti Spíritus, Cuba.

Jaques, Manuel. Interview with author, July 21, 2004, Santiago, Dominican Republic.

Lara Reyes, Odalys. Interview with author, August 16, 2001, Havana, Cuba.

Lombillo Pérez, Grycel Valdés. Interview with author, August 7, 2001, Havana, Cuba.

Miló González, Yuneimis. Interview with author, May 27, 2003, Pinar del Río, Cuba.

Montero Gutiérrez, Maricela. Interview with author, May 21, 2003, Trinidad, Cuba.

Morales Reyes, Irenia. Interview with author, May 15, 2003, Manicaragua, Las Villas, Cuba.

Murrieta Hernández, Mateo. Interview with author, April 27, 2005, Banderilla, Veracruz, Mexico.

Mustelier, Josefa. Interview with author, May 22, 2003, Guayos, Sancti Spíritus, Cuba.

Navarro Fragoso, Sonia. Interview with author, May 31, 2003, San Juan y Martínez, Cuba.

Pereira Caballero, Jesús. Interview with author, August 7, 2001; June 4, 2003, Havana, Cuba.

Pérez, Bettie. Interview with author, August 14, 2004, Tampa, Florida.

Pichardo, William. Interview with author, July 22, 2004, Santiago, Dominican Republic.

Rodríguez, Wilfredo. Interview with Gary Mormino, May 23, 1984, Tampa, Florida. Gary Mormino Archives, University of South Florida, Tampa.

Rodríguez Pérez, Carmen. Interview with author, May 24, 2003, Camagüey, Cuba.

Subiadur, Cibelys. Interview with author, May 13, 2003, Havana, Cuba.

Téllez, Luis. Interview with author, May 15, 2003, Havana, Cuba.

Torres Iglesias, Magalys. Interview with author, May 29, 2003, Vivero, Pinar del Río, Cuba.

Valdés, Zaida. Interview with author, August 8, 2001, Havana, Cuba.

Valdés Pérez, Ariel. Interview with author, May 13, 2003, Havana, Cuba.

Valdivia Cruz, Ana María. Interview with author, May 20, 2003, Sancti Spíritus, Cuba.

Valle Rodríguez, Marta. Interview with author, May 16, 2003, Manicaragua, Cuba.

Véliz Callazo, Olga Lidia. Interview with author, June 2, 2003, Viñales, Pinar del Río, Cuba.

CORRESPONDENCE

Águila Medina, Francisco. Santa Clara, Cuba: August 15, January 1, 2005; September 21, June 15, March 10, March 8, 2004; December 1, September 5, 2003; November 5, May 3, January 18, 2002

Campos Iglesias, Bernardo. San Luis, Pinar del Río, Cuba: July 2, 2003

Cantero, Lázara. Trinidad, Sancti Spíritus, Cuba: July 7, 2003

González Martínez, María Caridad. Pinar del Río, Cuba: May 26, February 19, 2004

González Valdivia, Zuraida. Cabaiguán. Sancti Spíritus, Cuba: August 17, 2004; July 4, 2003

Morales, Irenia. Manicaragua, Las Villas, Cuba: October 6, 2004

Valdivia Cruz, Ana María. Sancti Spíritus, Cuba: July 8, 2003

Véliz, Olga L. Viñales, Cuba: November 3, 2004; July 20, 2003

INDEX

CPSIA information can be obtained at www.ICGtesting.com
Printed in the USA
BVOW04s0509270913

332031BV00001BA/51/P

9 780292 725768